# WOODROW WILSON CENTER SERIES

Michael J. Lacey, editor, *Religion and Twentieth-Century American Intellectual Life*

Michael J. Lacey, editor, *The Truman Presidency*

Joseph Kruzel and Michael H. Haltzel, editors, *Between the Blocs: Problems and Prospects for Europe's Neutral and Nonaligned States*

William C. Brumfield, editor, *Reshaping Russian Architecture: Western Technology, Utopian Dreams*

Mark N. Katz, editor, *The USSR and Marxist Revolutions in the Third World*

Walter Reich, editor, *Origins of Terrorism: Psychologies, Ideologies, Theologies, States of Mind*

Mary O. Furner and Barry Supple, editors, *The State and Economic Knowledge: The American and British Experiences*

Michael J. Lacey and Knud Haakonssen, editors, *A Culture of Rights: The Bill of Rights in Philosophy, Politics and Law—1791 and 1991*

Robert J. Donovan and Ray Scherer, *Unsilent Revolution: Television News and American Public Life, 1948–1991*

William Craft Brumfield and Blair A. Ruble, editors, *Russian Housing in the Modern Age: Design and Social History*

Nelson Lichtenstein and Howell John Harris, editors, *Industrial Democracy in America: The Ambiguous Promise*

Michael J. Lacey and Mary O. Furner, editors, *The State and Social Investigation in Britain and the United States*

Hugh Ragsdale, editor, *Imperial Russian Foreign Policy*

Dermot Keogh and Michael H. Haltzel, editors, *Northern Ireland and the Politics of Reconciliation*

Joseph Klaits and Michael H. Haltzel, editors, *The Global Ramifications of the French Revolution*

René Lemarchand, *Burundi: Ethnic Conflict and Genocide*

James R. Millar and Sharon L. Wolchik, editors, *The Social Legacy of Communism*

James M. Morris, editor, *On Mozart*

Blair A. Ruble, *Money Sings: The Changing Politics of Urban Space in Post-Soviet Yaroslavl*

*Continued on page following index*

## THE WOODROW WILSON INTERNATIONAL CENTER FOR SCHOLARS



## ABOUT THE CENTER

The Center is the living memorial of the United States of America to the nation's twenty-eighth president, Woodrow Wilson. Congress established the Woodrow Wilson Center in 1968 as an international institute for advanced study, "symbolizing and strengthening the fruitful relationship between the world of learning and the world of public affairs." The Center opened in 1970 under its own board of trustees.

In all its activities the Woodrow Wilson Center is a nonprofit, nonpartisan organization, supported financially by annual appropriations from the Congress, and by the contributions of foundations, corporations, and individuals. Conclusions or opinions expressed in Center publications and programs are those of the authors and speakers and do not necessarily reflect the views of the Center staff, fellows, trustees, advisory groups, or any individuals or organizations that provide financial support to the Center.

# *Between the State and Islam*

*Edited by*

CHARLES E. BUTTERWORTH
*University of Maryland*

I. WILLIAM ZARTMAN
*The Johns Hopkins University*
*School of Advanced International Studies*

WOODROW WILSON CENTER PRESS

AND

CAMBRIDGE
UNIVERSITY PRESS

PUBLISHED BY THE PRESS SYNDICATE OF THE UNIVERSITY OF CAMBRIDGE
The Pitt Building, Trumpington Street, Cambridge, United Kingdom

CAMBRIDGE UNIVERSITY PRESS
The Edinburgh Building, Cambridge CB2 2RU, UK
40 West 20th Street, New York, NY 10011-4211, USA
10 Stamford Road, Oakleigh, VIC 3166, Australia
Ruiz de Alarcón 13, 28014 Madrid, Spain
Dock House, The Waterfront, Cape Town 8001, South Africa

http://www.cambridge.org

WOODROW WILSON CENTER
1300 Pennsylvania Avenue, N.W., Washington, DC 20004-3027



First published 2001

Printed in the United States of America

*Typeface* Sabon 10/13 pt. *System* QuarkXPress [BTS]

*A catalog record for this book is available from the British Library.*

*Library of Congress Cataloging in Publication Data*

Between the state and Islam / edited by Charles E. Butterworth, I. William Zartman.
p. cm—(Woodrow Wilson Center series)
Includes bibliographical references and index.
ISBN 0-521-78352-6 (hb)—ISBN 0-521-78972-9 (pb)
1. Islam and state—Islamic countries. 2. Islam and politics—Islamic countries. 3. Islamic countries—Politics and government. I. Butterworth, Charles E. II. Zartman, I.William. III. Series.

BP173.6.B47 2000 322'.1'0917671–dc21 00-034257

ISBN 0 521 78352 6 hardback
ISBN 0 521 78972 9 paperback

# Contents

# Acknowledgments

One of the great joys of bringing a book to life is being able to thank publicly all those who contributed to its coming about. First and foremost, we wish to express our gratitude to the Woodrow Wilson International Center for Scholars (WWICS) under whose auspices and sponsorship the conference that gave rise to this volume was held in February 1994. James Morris, director of the History and Culture Division of WWICS, and Susan Nugent provided invaluable guidance in planning and carrying out the conference. Special thanks are due also to Clark Merrill, Department of Government and Politics at the University of Maryland, for his capable editing of the manuscripts and to Ross Corbett, also of the Department of Government and Politics, for his efforts to bring all the papers together into a single format. To all these individuals and to the institutions they represent, as well as to our very learned co-authors, we are most grateful.

This book is dedicated to Saad Eddin Ibrahim and the others who stand up between the state and Islam and suffer for it.

# Between the State and Islam

# Introduction

CHARLES E. BUTTERWORTH AND
I. WILLIAM ZARTMAN

Much attention, perhaps too much, has been lavished on the way Islam in its current manifestations affects or threatens to affect politics in the Middle East.[1] Equally as much attention has been placed on the durability of the Arab state.[2] In contrast, there is almost total neglect of the forces that struggle against Islamic conformism and state hegemony. Yet by manifold pluralistic and innovative activities, such forces fill the gap between these two competing absolutes. To be sure, civil society has drawn the attention of some scholars. Still, because such scholars have focused their inquiry solely on the contemporary world, they have largely ignored the relation of civil society either to Islam and the state or to its antecedents in earlier eras.[3]

[1] See, for example, Nazih Ayubi, *Political Islam* (London: Routledge, 1991); Edmund Burke III and Ira Lapidus, eds., *Islam, Politics, and Social Movements* (Berkeley: University of California Press, 1988); Charles E. Butterworth and I. William Zartman, eds., *Political Islam* (special issue 522 of *The Annals of the American Academy of Political and Social Science*, 1992); Alexander Cudsi and Ali E. Hillal Dessouki, eds., *Islam and Power* (Baltimore: Johns Hopkins University Press, 1981); Ali E. Hillal Dessouki, ed., *Islamic Resurgence in the Arab World* (New York: Praeger, 1982); Henry Munson, *Islam and Revolution in the Middle East* (New Haven: Yale University Press, 1988); and John Ruedy, ed., *Islam and Secularism in North Africa* (New York: St. Martin's Press, 1994).

[2] See Hazem Beblawi and Giacomo Luciani, eds., *The Rentier State* (London: Croom Helm, 1987); Adeed Dawisha and I. William Zartman, eds., *Beyond Coercion: The Durability of the Arab State* (London: Croom Helm, 1988); Giacomo Luciani, ed., *The Arab State* (Berkeley: University of California Press, 1990); Giacomo Luciani and Ghassan Salamé, eds., *The Politics of Arab Integration* (London: Croom Helm, 1988); and Ghassan Salamé, ed., *The Foundations of the Arab State* (London: Croom Helm, 1987).

[3] See Augustus Richard Norton, ed., *Civil Society in the Middle East* (Leiden: E. J. Brill, 1995), and also Jillian Schwedler, ed., *Toward Civil Society in the Middle East? A Primer* (Boulder: Lynne Rienner, 1995). See also, as exceptions to this judgment, Iliya Harik, "Rethinking Civil Society: Pluralism in the Arab World," *Journal of Democracy* 5/3 (July 1994): 43–56; and Şerif Mardin, "Civil Society and Islam," in John A. Hall, ed., *Civil Society: Theory, History, Comparison* (Cambridge, England: Polity Press, 1995), 278–300.

There is more to political life, even more to communal life, however defined, than what can be revealed by exclusive attention to resurgent or insurgent Islam, to the vagaries of the organized state, or even to contemporary civil society. Much is to be learned about the intricate workings of Arab societies and their development from a consideration of the expression of ideas in all its manifestations—philosophy, literary works, sermons, political tracts, even current events commentary—as well as from a study of periodicals and the press, both as they appear now and as they have changed over time. Yet those willing and able to pursue such an inquiry are all too few, and the counter-balance they provide to the trend noted above is regrettably slight.[4] Beneath a veneer of fantasy and banality, television programs, sermons, and political commentaries frequently contain a deeper analysis of the basic fears and aspirations that circulate in Arab society from East to West. Yet they have rarely been subjected to the type of study that takes them at anything deeper than their surface value. Similarly, even though Naguib Mahfouz has long been appreciated as a thoughtful interpreter of Egyptian and Arab politics and a sometimes acerbic critic of the way religious zealotry harms more than it helps, much the same as his compatriot, Tawfik al-Hakim, few scholars focus on the role either thinker plays in shaping public life.

Similarly, against so much attention to the struggle for orthodoxy within militant Islam, there is little material available about the many attempts at reform, anti-conformism, and interpretive thinking within the same religion. Even while commentators from within the fold persist in generalizations of the type "Muslims have continued to assume that only a 'religious leader' can provide good government for the Muslim community"[5]—as if all Muslims were of one mind on such matters—Islamic thinkers apply the Quran variously to the challenges of modern life, and their efforts are usually lost on analysts trying to portray—pos-

[4] See Rashid Khalidi's survey of ʿAbd al-Ghanī al-ʿUraysī's thought as it was expressed in his daily newspaper *al-Mufīd*, Wadad al-Qadī's excellent analysis of ʿAlī Mubārak's gigantic *ʿAlamuddīn*, and Marwan R. Buheiry's account of Būlus Nujaym and *La Revue Phénicienne* in Marwan R. Buheiry, ed., *Intellectual Life in the Arab East, 1890–1939* (Beirut: American University of Beirut Press, 1981). See also Paul Khoury, *Une lecture de la pensée arabe actuelle: Trois études* and *Tradition et modernité: Matériaux pour servir à l'étude de la pensée arabe actuelle: I. Instruments d'enquête* (Münster: Paul Khoury, 1981).

[5] See Jamal al-Suwaidi, "Arab and Western Conceptions of Democracy," in David Garnham and Mark Tessler, eds., *Democracy, War, and Peace in the Middle East* (Bloomington: Indiana University Press, 1995), 87, in what is an otherwise insightful chapter.

itively or negatively—the current of the mainstream.[6] On the other side, the attention devoted to presenting the *mukhābarāt* (state security) monolith of a regime and its single party ministry of mobilization has completely overshadowed any attempt to explain the important contributions, beleaguered existence, and real problems of independent thinkers and opposition parties.[7]

Or again, the notion that modernism means pluralism[8] suggests a necessary societal force pushing against any conformities, notably those of belief and politics; it implies that only technological innovation and social differentiation can erode and crack monoliths. The interdisciplinary leap from the study of new technologies and new social forces to the analysis of their impact on political and belief systems has been made too infrequently, so that politics and religion are examined and discussed in a vacuum. The work of Émile Durkheim and Daniel Lerner has been left by the wayside as attention shifts away from the paradigms of development and modernization.

This collective volume seeks to limit these excesses and remedy such shortcomings by showing how debate and study about the Middle East might be refocused. Between the two polar absolutes of the restrictively hegemonic state and oppressively conformist religion anchored on conflicting bases of authority surge forces of skepticism, liberty, and creativity. As they have in the past, these forces find expression in thought and action that remain staunchly independent of all efforts at control. To be sure, these expressions are themselves often flawed, vulnerable, and confused, if not outright contradictory. Nonetheless, they exist vigorous, independent, innovative, and ever persistent. Not yet able to topple the monoliths, these forces still manage to hold their own. Indeed, in one respect they may even be said to have the favored position: for them, not losing is the beginning of winning, whereas for state and religion, not winning is the beginning of losing. These efforts are not new: they existed in the nineteenth century, perhaps even earlier, and they

[6] See Ali E. Hillal Dessouki, ed., *Islam and Politics*; François Burgat, *L'Islamisme au Maghreb* (Paris: Karthala, 1988); John Esposito, ed., *Voices of Resurgent Islam* (New York: Oxford University Press, 1983); Abdel Salam Sidahmed and Anoushiravan Ehteshami, eds., *Islamic Fundamentalism* (Boulder: Westview, 1996). But see the fine chapters on Islamic reformists in Nazih Ayubi, *Political Islam*.

[7] Michael Hudson, *Arab Politics* (New Haven: Yale University Press, 1977). But see Susan Waltz, *Human Rights and Reform: Changing the Face of North African Politics* (Berkeley: University of California Press, 1995); and I. William Zartman, "The Challenge of Democratic Pluralism," in John Ruedy, ed., *Islamism and Secularism in North Africa*.

[8] See S. N. Eisenstadt, *Modernization: Protest and Change* (Englewood Cliffs: Prentice Hall, 1966), 2–3.

come and go, much like the sea, ebbing and flowing in their efforts to push back authority and conformism. In sum, however influential religion appears in word and deed, however evident the trappings of state authority, people do come into being, thrive, marry, raise families, think, laugh, and cry without regard to—indeed, sometimes in utter defiance of—the strictures of religious or state authority.

Of most immediate interest as a counter to current scholarly endeavors are the ways defiance is expressed, the ways people struggle to preserve room for freedom of thought and action as well as of inventiveness and innovation with respect to politics, religion, and life in general. These expressions take place in the midst of an ongoing dialectic that pervades the Middle East. The nineteenth century opened the Islamic Arab world to a permanent conflict between two antagonistic ways of thought. Into a world of ancient, but authentic and unquestioned, mores came antithetical ways and thoughts typical of modern enterprise and its desire to spread learning and wealth. The old was forced to give way to the new, however genuinely rooted in self-identity was the old and however artificial the new. So, too, did the alien usurp the place of the familiar.

A crude version of the conflict is played out daily before Arab eyes via television and the cinema. Tales of marital infidelity, scenes of opulence, suggestive—even explicit—flirtations and seductions, and myriad instances of successful challenges to traditional authority float across the Mediterranean, enticingly accessible yet frustratingly unattainable. The morning after, many of the beguiled recoil in horror from what that world seems to prize. More promising are the attempts by reformers to challenge traditional authority in the name of rightly reasoned interpretation and to overcome economic stagnation or out-moded patterns of governance by calling for technological innovations and pluralistic competition. Vestiges of such attempts at challenge and change hang even in the closets of leaders of opposition parties and organizers of professional groups.

But the image of confrontation and nothing but confrontation is incomplete. The confrontation gives rise to a dialectic in which the extremes are finally bridged and a synthesis produced. Therein lies the significance of the thoughts and activities presented here. For the television and cinema audiences whose impressions lack precision and cohesion, the extremes have been bridged so partially that the resulting synthesis is as inchoate as it is incomplete. Even so, its confused dissonance prepares a context of both receptivity and resistance for the writings and actions of the other groups. The very task of journalists and professors writing for a wider public represents synthesis after analysis; as they seek to mold and inform that emerging view, they increase the receptivity of their own followers to some aspects of the synthesis while strengthening their resistance to others. Similarly, reform-minded religious scholars seek an authentically modern political system of debate and choice along with a contemporaneous interpretation of belief and practice so as to move Islam from the fifteenth or sixteenth century to the twenty-first. At the same time, political activists and professional organizers strive for progressive strategies and programs that reflect the interests of the people.

Yet a dialectic—any dialectic, but especially this one of commentary, exchange, analysis, and attempt at criticism as well as reform—moves on, until its own internal logic of confrontation leading to synthesis and synthesis giving way to new confrontation is broken. By drawing attention to the dialectical character of the confrontation, we wish to focus on the manifold ways individuals and groups thrive without undue concern about the demands of the state and religious hegemonies. Remember, Muslim experience today is not that of the painful awakening of the nineteenth century—neither that called for by Jamāl al-Dīn al-Afghānī and Muḥammad ʿAbduh, nor that of the al-ʿAlawī's. Moments of synthesis have occurred in the meantime, moments later to be opposed by a new antithesis that decries the preceding synthesis as a sell-out to another group (most often to foreign modernists). In this sense, the Islamist revival or resurgence of today may well be yet another antithesis, returning the subject to its recurrent confrontation.

The struggle during the nineteenth century between reformers and their critics provides the context within which, in the first part of this work, are presented themes, voices, and actors focused on reform, harmony, or synthesis, as well as their opposites. So, too, does the conflict between their twentieth-century counterparts frame the analyses set forth in the second part. Yet the two parts are not completely congruent. Although external information and sources of independent thought and action disseminated by multiple types of media have penetrated the Middle East and North Africa since Napoleon's invasion of Egypt, the latest and most dramatic vehicle is the satellite dish that captures foreign television. Along with other intrusive communications technology, it sets the twentieth century apart from the nineteenth. Ineffectively banned in Algeria and Iran by militants both of the state and of Islam, the satellite dish receives images that cannot be censored in the same manner as books and newspapers. Potentially, an even greater threat is posed by the growing use of cyberspace around the world. Yet another external source of information and thought is found in international cooperation, as is manifested by the growing trends toward professionalization, privatization, democratization, and globalization.

As did the Napoleonic invasion and those other intrusive phenomena, these, too, flow like flood waters under the door no matter how tightly it is closed or even sealed. They gain pressure through the backing they receive from transnational institutions such as universities, multinational corporations, private voluntary organizations, and financial institutions. And they are reinforced by other events in distant places, such as the collapse of the Communist Party in the Soviet Union. At the same time, there is a need for some kind of fallow, fertile ground waiting to be tilled. Otherwise, the external influences would have far less impact. Difficult as it is to pinpoint these internal sources of change and challenge, they appear to arise more from the simple playing-out of human nature than anything else. Dissatisfaction and restiveness under the insufficiencies and constraints of religious and political authority, natural tendencies to strike out independently from the controls of unity and consensus, and separate interests derived from the specialization and differentiation accompanying modernization are sources of creativity and questioning, that is, of confrontation and subsequent compromise or synthesis.

It is on this kind of struggle and these phenomena that the chapters here focus, first from the experience of the nineteenth century and then from that of the twentieth.

# Part I

## Nineteenth Century

# Preface

CHARLES E. BUTTERWORTH

Television programs, the World Wide Web, electronic mail, faxes, and long distance telephone hook-ups via satellite are now as commonplace as air travel. They are usual means for citizens in one part of the globe to learn about events in other parts or to keep in touch with far-flung friends and colleagues. Such ready means of communication and even the easy awareness of one another resulting from them are relatively new phenomena. Though air travel and telephone communication have been with us for a long while, the others and especially the ready resort to them are the consequences of technological advances made in the mid-1980s and 1990s.

Yet the world, especially that part of it under scrutiny here with respect to the two monoliths of state and religion, has not therefore changed dramatically. A moment's reflection suffices for discerning that to speak of resistance to, or circumvention of, these two has not become possible only now. Indeed, the chapters that follow illustrate the numerous ways in which individuals and groups successfully eluded the long tentacles of the state as well as the apparent omnipresence of religion even as they sought to reform or drastically alter one or the other. To be sure, one attempts to escape, improve, or transform only what is there to be acted upon; no one in the nineteenth century would ever have denied the need to be constantly aware of the sovereign and his subalterns or of the designated representatives of religion and their enthusiastic votaries, official or not.

Still, the plaintive cry of Jamāl al-Dīn al-Afghānī, picked up and rendered even more poignant by Muḥammad Iqbāl, was addressed neither to rulers per se nor to religious authorities, but to fellow Muslims generally. Where, they wanted to know, had the Muslim people gone wrong? What had they done to bring about so thorough a reversal of fortune that they were now deemed backward and held subject by those they had formerly contemned? The same question, albeit somewhat transformed, is now posed in the West in terms of "Why are they not like us?" or "Why did the technological revolution occur only in the West?" But these can be formulated in a more neutral manner so as to probe what is truly at issue: "What are they like?" or "How does their cultural, economic, and political life differ—if, indeed, it does—from ours?" and, even more to the point, "How does cultural, economic, and political life assist or impede technological development?"

In his discussion of the impact technology change had and did not have on the Arab world of the nineteenth century, Zahlan focuses on technology and technology change rather than on science. Indeed, he denies that science was sought or nurtured by Arab countries or institutions during the nineteenth century. He sees technology, especially technological change, as playing an important role in the political, social, and economic evolution—if one can speak of evolution rather than stagnation—of the Arab world. Differently put, the social, political, and cultural context of the area hampered both scientific and technological activity. Nothing changed, not technologically, socially, politically, economically, or culturally.

To be sure, technological advances made their way to the Arab world. But they did so as part of a colonial enterprise. The English and French brought new modes and machines, but little to nothing was done to develop indigenous cadres capable of taking over these new technologies once the colonialists departed. As Zahlan's exposition unfolds, we see that the rulers of the Arab world were as much to blame for not developing local receptivity as the colonialists. Not religion, not unquestioning adherence to old ways, but lack of far-sightedness seems to have been the culprit. To be sure, they were politically naive, even imprudent, in not discerning how important it would eventually be to have a well-developed country. Simple greed prevented these sovereigns and their representatives from considering the more distant horizon and prompted them to pursue immediate personal gain rather than to assume the onerous task of developing their countries. Chance, at least as it became manifest in the terrible murrain epidemic of 1842–3, also played an important role. This single event set back several projects to turn Egypt into a nation that manufactured its own large machines.

Zahlan compares, but only in passing, Japan with Egypt on the issue of developing indigenous technology. Japan succeeded where Egypt failed. Why? Though Zahlan does not dwell on it, the reason seems to be that Japan kept to itself and used foreigners rather than allowing itself to be used by foreigners. Egypt could not bring about such a policy because too many entrepreneurs were anxious to do business on their own account, and those responsible for granting permission saw all too readily that their immediate advantage lay in allowing the process.

Zahlan tells no tale of religious traditionalists trying to keep things as they once were, mythically or not. Rather, he speaks of rulers who did not understand how to achieve local development—but also, at least indirectly, of colonial and imperial powers who did nothing to further local development either. New technologies were imported into the region, promising students were sent off to England and France to study the disciplines behind these inventions, but the populace was never taught to master them. In some important respect, no one wanted new—as opposed to traditional—knowledge to become too widespread. Even the otherwise well-intentioned who sought to promote learning refused to allow certain kinds of inquiry and discussion. Thus in 1882 an English faculty member was dismissed from the Syrian Protestant College in Beirut for making favorable references to the scientific achievements of Darwin and Lyell in a commencement address. The openness to science that one would not dare stifle at home was to be silenced in the Middle East. The interesting question is not what the board of the college feared, but what vacuum of power in Beirut allowed this to occur. It becomes all the more pertinent when due note is accorded Zahlan's emphasis on the way Egypt's limited political culture—that is, the general educational level of the populace—kept it from making advances in the technological domain.

Mardin takes us away from the Arab heartland in order to focus on the dual relationship between citizen and state, religion and rulership, as manifested in Islamic regimes and experienced by Muslims in non-Islamic regimes. While no one can deny the strength of the image of constant interplay between those learned in Islamic subjects (the *ʿulamāʾ*) and the rulers or those in power (the *ruasāʾ*)—especially of the principle that rulers resolve disputes about matters having to do with the citizens by calling for and then following a pronouncement by a religious scholar or scholars—it is not always so evident in practice. But it is not therefore nonexistent. Through a detailed analysis of the life and activities of Abdurreshid Ibrahim and Ahmet Zeki Velidi Togan, who flourished in late-nineteenth- and early-twentieth-century Russian Asia, Mardin illustrates the intricacies of this relationship.

Eschewing the conventional explanation that Christianity differs from Islam in that it insists on keeping Caesar distinct from God whereas Islam not only renders unto Caesar his due but actually embraces him as too superficial, Mardin draws attention to the way Western capitalism allows the market to take over the state. He infers that whereas judgments thus become subordinated to market demands in the West, moral imperatives are constantly invoked to guide statecraft within Islam. This, as Alaoui also notes, gives rise to repeated attempts at political and religious reform. The changes that occurred to a somewhat obscure Sufi organization, the Nakshbandi order, in the far reaches of the Ottoman Empire and the way they affected the lives of Ibrahim—a bonafide *ʿālim*, even a Qadi, as well as a political agitator—and Togan—a modern intellectual and sometime ruler (indeed, he was president of the Bashkurt Republic between 1918 and 1920)—vividly illustrate the complexities of this interaction.

Ibrahim fought for his people and cause by becoming more deeply rooted in Islam and its traditions. Consequently, he became a fierce opponent of Russia and its embrace of Enlightenment philosophy. For him, such opposition was but an example of railing against the injustice of pharaoh. Togan, much more committed to the world of ideas and to the freedom of intellectual pursuit, wavered between falling back on his Turkishness and the ethical as well as the political core of his Islamic upbringing, but finally moved more to the Islamic side than to the Turkish. Though he accepted the principles of Enlightenment philosophy, he rejected the historicism to which it seemed to have succumbed. He found himself most authentically or fully defined not as a Turk, but as a Muslim. In this sense, he resuscitated the Muslim moral imperative. Yet, as Mardin's careful portrait of their highly eventful lives shows, neither of these colorful figures fits the paradigm all too often evoked when reference is made to the way political activists or reformers allow themselves to be guided by reference to Islam.

With Alaoui, we return to the Arab world—the Mashriq as well as the Maghrib. Focusing on the history of Islamic political thought, he depicts it as falling into two categories—both of which are linked to Islam. The first is guided by a desire to implement Islam in daily life and thus finds itself contesting or criticizing what goes on in the political realm. The second is more accepting of what is and seeks ways to improve it without scolding. Alaoui links Ibn Taymiyya and al-Afghānī as representatives of the first, while contenting himself with al-Ghazālī and Ibn Khaldūn as representative of the second.

In keeping with his desire to speak about how thought effects political change, Alaoui examines those thinkers who represent the first group—that is, the contesting, criticizing, or opposing group. In his eyes, reform is always opposition. Aware that such an interpretation is not without problems, he pursues it nonetheless and presents as so many instances of opposition those calls for reform that are based on trying to bring the backward Arabic/Islamic world closer to that of the modern West. Such calls are necessarily cast in religious tones, and the authors he examines—al-Ṭahṭawī, al-Afghānī, ʿAbduh, and al-Kawākibī—demonstrate that religion is the cry used to rally the Muslim peoples.

It is in the name of Islam, not human decency or the rights of man, that calls for reform are made. Justice is Islamic justice, not some idea that floats in the air. Justice has a Quranic underpinning and thus does not depend on what is right by nature. Still, those making these pronouncements do so in order to effect political change, change that strikes as much at the official representatives of religion as at political rulers. Were it feasible to voice such criticism in general or even universal terms, that might have been done. But the recent memories of the French revolution and the declaration of the rights of man notwithstanding, these reformers found it more politic to keep their sights fixed on the particular—on the Islamic, even on the Arab, rather than on the simply human.

# 1

# On What Is Between, Even Beyond, the Paradigms of the State and Islam

CHARLES E. BUTTERWORTH

## INTRODUCTION

The study of Islam, Islamic or Muslim society and polity, and the Arabic, Iranian, and Turkish Middle East has a history. It is, after all, no different from any other intellectual pursuit except, perhaps, in its relative newness. Leaving the fanciful disquisitions of Chardin aside, not to mention the *Persian Letters* spoof of Montesquieu, learned individuals began to focus on this area only in the early part of the nineteenth century. Some decades later, from the later nineteenth century on through the early twentieth century, scholars concentrated on identifying the whole, defining what made Islam and things Islamic unique and thus different from what was not Islam or Islamic. They approached the subject by textual analysis.

The book that defines Islam as a faith, even a practiced faith, was ready to hand insofar as copies of the Quran were abundant. So, too, were copies of treatises about the strictures of the Quran—books explaining the way different legal schools interpreted this book as well as the sayings and deeds of the prophet, others defending the beliefs set forth by the book and the prophet, and yet others chronicling the early days and years of Islam and its political ventures. Other works, however, had first to be recovered—sometimes even discovered. These texts—writings in philosophy, collections of poems, epistles on the art of ruling, even literary tales and essays—provided a broader vision of what constituted this older culture and its tradition.

The study of these works (often carried out by individuals born and schooled in the Middle East whose native tongue was Arabic, Persian, or Turkish) first resulted in generalizations about Islam and the peoples within the Islamic world. Directed to those who knew little to nothing about the area and most often transmitted in English, French, German, Italian, and Spanish—that is, in the tongues of peoples distant from the area—the goal of such study was less to recognize similarity than to seize upon difference. Yet both indigenous and foreign scholars had a common link of long residence in particular countries of the area and intimate familiarity with the language or languages used by the people of these countries. Their generalizations were based, then, on deep, first-hand knowledge of the subject in its many aspects and details.

This period of scholarship gave way to one that sought to delve more deeply into particular areas, practices, traditions, and peoples. The large-scale generalizations of the earlier period were reconsidered and modified, often as a result of new textual work, especially archival research, but also as a result of more self-conscious ethnography. Assumptions of uniformity gave way to ones of variety, smooth surfaces were seen to be rippled if not cataclysmic, and simple transitions of power came to be understood as complex and fraught with violence. In short, study rooted in the methods of the social sciences replaced the old humanism and its textual concentration.

Notable exceptions notwithstanding, scholars within this new wave were more often of foreign origin. Less familiar with the languages of the area than their predecessors, they also remained on site for shorter periods of time. Two trends developed: for the most part, these new scholars shied away from the broad picture painted by their predecessors and toiled at answering more particular questions; at the same time, they paid greater attention to surface events and to the common people. Some of the new scholarship thereby came to resemble sophisticated journalism, especially in its focus on the immediate and the popular. Yet, ever conscious that they had not fully succeeded in explaining the polities of the Middle East and their workings nor in distinguishing them from—or comparing them to—polities in the West, these scholars continued to apply new concepts and forge new theories in their quest of understanding: studies of one-party rule gave way to those of ruling elites, just as investigations of centers of power and influence were replaced by those of relationships between center and periphery, and emphasis on the lives of particular rulers bowed to concentration on disenfranchised and marginal groups.

These reflections should indicate that while scholarship can be spoken of in terms of patterns and trends that are sometimes mistaken, it is no more monolithic and uniform than the phenomena it studies. That much can be admitted, as can the fact that some of the earliest individuals to study Islam and the Islamic Middle East did so less out of disinterested curiosity than out of a desire to gain control—spiritual, economic, or political—over its peoples and social groupings. And it is important to acknowledge that in tandem with each different stage of scholarly endeavor to understand the area, its culture, and its peoples are to be found just as many instances of vulgarization as well as of imaginative attempts to reach general conclusions from particular incidents. Precise examples are Gustave Flaubert's *Bouvard et Pécuchet*, Gérard de Nerval's *Voyage en Orient*, Edward W. Lane's *Manners and Customs of the Modern Egyptians*,[1] Tawfiq al-Hakim's *Diary of a Country District Attorney*, Father Habib Ayrout's *Le fellah égyptien*, or, more recently, Richard Critchfield's *Shahhat an Egyptian*, even Kathryn K. Abdul-Baki's *Fields of Fig and Olive: Ameera and Other Stories of the Middle East* and Philip Roth's *Operation Shylock: A Confession*. Moreover, fictional accounts by those living in the area—Évelyne Accad, Driss Chraibi, Émile Habiby, Sahar Khalifeh, Naguib Mahfouz, Amos Oz, and Nawal El Saadawy—as well as journalism and memoirs permit nonscholars access, albeit less accurate access, to these same topics.

So much by way of preface is needed both to appreciate the aspirations and merits of the present volume and to explain why those contributing to it pass over, even reject, some of the current attempts to validate scholarship. To be sure, opinions too readily accepted have occasionally led scholars to emphasize one aspect of the culture at the expense of another or to neglect an awkward fact. But, as noted, these temporary imbalances are readily corrected unless attempts to reestablish equilibrium inadvertently push matters too far in the opposite direction. Today, this push and pull centers upon religion and politics or, more precisely, upon Islam and democracy. Most representative of those who deny a single political role to Islam, indeed, who deny there is such an entity as Islam, are Mohammed Arkoun and Olivier Roy. Opposing them by portraying Islam as four-square behind democracy are John Esposito and John Voll.

[1] As an antidote to Edward Said's intemperate criticism of Lane (*Orientalism* [New York: Pantheon, 1978], 161), see Jason Thompson's excellent study of Lane and his travels to, as well as writings on, Egypt: "Edward William Lane in Egypt," *Journal of the American Research Center in Egypt* 34 (1997): 243–61. The article reveals Lane's deep familiarity with the people, customs, and language of the Egyptians; in footnote references to other articles of his own, Thompson shows that he has an enviable grasp of Lane's writings, published as well as unpublished, and of the relevant contemporary literature.

## THE TRADITION MISAPPREHENDED

Taking a cue from Michel Foucault, if not his erstwhile publicist Edward Said, Arkoun and Roy claim to have seen what their predecessors missed: the multiple expressions of Islam, the shortcomings of overly circumscribed social scientific study, and the tendency of scholarship to distort reality so as to subjugate it.[2] They speak as though they are the first to discern that, given so many Muslims, it is difficult to speak of one Islam. At the same time, they overlook the extent to which many Muslims think they have something in common with other Muslims—the extent to which this commonality is what makes them Muslims and what scholars seek to identify and define. They also give the impression, as though Thomas Kuhn were unknown to them, that they consider themselves the first to have identified the shortcomings of social science.

Arkoun, for example, contends that his approach is dynamic rather than static (1), in that he uses a "bundle of methods taught by the social sciences rather than one method privileged over all others" and is comparative rather than ethnographic and specific. So he claims to battle "the great Western experts in Islamology [*sic*]" (2) and to be engaged in "constructing a historical and epistemological critique of the principles, postulates, definitions, conceptual tools, and discursive procedures of logical reasoning used in the Islamic context." He identifies his critique as informed by the work of Clifford Geertz and the postmodern thinking of Michel Foucault. Thus his approach, insofar as it "aims to problematize a domain of knowledge, to think through and reflect upon historical circumstances, to deconstruct cognitive systems and ethico-juridical codes, and to historicize beliefs and nonbeliefs" is superior to one that seeks "to increase the mass of available data, rework interpretations, or extend the exploration of a single domain of reality" (3). Arkoun does not consider the latter completely void of merit. Rather, the exclusiveness of the approach bothers him, even though in following the first he must exclude the second. Most important, however, is his denial of any such thing as objective reason. For him, demands that "arguments be more 'objective,' more 'neutral,' less 'polemical'" are merely part of the Western attempt to extend and enforce its hegemony. Yet he never identifies the insight permitting him to arrive at this judgment.

[2] For what follows, page references within parentheses are first to Mohammed Arkoun, *Rethinking Islam: Common Questions, Uncommon Answers*, trans. and ed. Robert D. Lee (Boulder: Westview Press, 1994), and then to Olivier Roy, *The Failure of Political Islam*, trans. Carol Volk (Cambridge: Harvard University Press, 1994).

In *Rethinking Islam*—a compilation of Arkoun's responses to a series of twenty-four questions that admit of grouping, but show no definite order—Arkoun presents himself as primarily intent on providing a sociology of Islam. He brings back environmental and social determinants much as W. Montgomery Watt first sought to apply them, yet refuses to take seriously the actual phenomena of religion—even to the point of explaining them all away. Thus, in speaking of revelation, he asserts:

Taking into consideration all the experiments generated in the societies of the Book/book, one could say it is a revelation each time that a new vocabulary comes to radically change man's view of his condition, his *being-in-the-world*, his participation in the production of meaning. (34)

Such a "definition of revelation," he boasts, "has the merit of making a place for the teachings of Buddha, Confucius, African elders, and all the great voices that recapitulate the collective experience of a group in order to project it toward new horizons and enrich the human experience of the divine." In other words, like a new Humpty-Dumpty, Arkoun calls things as he sees them and cares little for how they are presented by those who first brought them to our attention. What, one wonders, would he make of the following explanation of revelation, an explanation advanced by one so renowned for his knowledge that he was familiarly called "the second teacher," second, that is, after Aristotle:

Now the craft of the virtuous supreme ruler is kingly and joined with revelation from God. Indeed, he determines the actions and opinions in the virtuous religion by means of revelation. This occurs in one or both of two ways: one is that they are all revealed to him as determined; the second is that he determines them by means of the faculty he acquires from revelation and from the Revealer, may He be exalted, so that the stipulations with which he determines the virtuous opinions and actions are disclosed to him by means of it. Or some come about in the first way and some in the second way. It has already been explained in theoretical science how the revelation of God, may He be exalted, to the human being receiving the revelation comes about and how the faculty acquired from revelation and from the Revealer occurs in a human being.[3]

There is no room in this statement for sundry voices that sum up or recapture a group's "collective experience" so as to move it "toward new

[3] The second teacher is none other than Abū Naṣr al-Fārābī (870–950), and this passage is taken from the opening lines of his *Book of Religion* (Kitāb al-Milla), trans. Charles E. Butterworth, in Alfarabi,*The Political Writings: "Selected Aphorisms" and Other Texts* (Ithaca: Cornell University Press, forthcoming); for the Arabic text, see *Abū Naṣr al-Fārābī, Kitāb al-Milla wa Nuṣūṣ Ukhrā*, ed. Muhsin Mahdi (Beirut: Dār al-Machreq, 1968), 41–66.

horizons" or somehow "enrich the human experience of the divine." No, Alfarabi, unlike Arkoun, articulates what it means to receive revelation and how it affects political life. He points clearly to the implications of speech about revelation and to how they must affect anyone who believes that another has received it. Arkoun's inattention to detail or negligence is also manifested in his failure to analyze the arguments of previous interpreters in detail or by name despite insisting on how mistaken they are; instead, he presents them as dupes of a particular movement—Orientalism—or victims of a historical period.

Persuaded that political Islam has failed, Roy proposes to investigate what it offers as an alternative to Muslim societies (vii). Like Arkoun, he dismisses the idea of there being one Islam—an idea he attributes to the Orientalists (vii and 7)—and criticizes the Enlightenment view of reason, albeit not as adamantly as Arkoun. He finds political Islam to be naive in that it fails to recognize how rooted it is in history (viii–ix) and attributes its failure to errors that are both intellectual (the desire for an Islamic polity to achieve virtue presupposes virtue in its leaders) and historical (no new society has been founded). As Roy sees it, sociological influences explain the Islamist movement: increased educational opportunities but insufficient chances of employment and greater urbanization of society.

Yet Roy falls prey to the very generalizations he deplores: for him, political Islam is monolithic. He can make this claim only insofar as he ignores—and is ignorant of—the details of what occurs in particular countries, and his references betray his limited grasp of Islamic culture: all are secondary, and most are sympathetic to his own position. Moreover, when he speaks about the past or the tradition, he cites no sources; his generalizations gloss over issues, but do so without providing evidence he knows the details that would justify the generalizations.

Although Roy correctly discerns that the Islamists have a weak grasp of politics, he overstates the case by attempting to see a dialectic at work: there is, for example, no necessity for emphasis on political virtue to lead to mysticism, his claims to the contrary notwithstanding. Similarly, his assertion that society "defined in modern terms" is "one in which the distinction among social, political, and economic authorities is recognized" (37) ignores that it has never not been so recognized, while his contention that coining terms is a sign of trying to bring religion into the language overlooks the more obvious possibility that it is an attempt to bring an older language into step with modern Western terminology (39–49).

In sum, Roy's book is based on a superficial reading of secondary sources, many of them journalistic accounts of what has happened in particular countries and why. He has tried to weave a sociological explanation to account for the different transformations of society, but the limitations in his Arabic vocabulary—like those in his attempts to use the tradition—undermine his tentative explanations. Thus, he intimates familiarity with an issue or a text by citing key words only to take one out of context and use it as though it alone meant what the phrase or expression means.[4] Similarly, because his reading is limited to modern secondary accounts and translations of recent thinkers, he makes sweeping and erroneous generalizations about the tradition or incorrectly credits contemporary activists with innovations to which they never laid claim.[5]

Clearly, then, these books by Arkoun and Roy fail on at least two counts. First, by condemning traditional scholars for giving a monolithic view of Islam without ever citing whom they have in mind, they oblige their readers to accept on faith an accusation to the effect that all prior scholars—especially those who focus on the tradition—have misunderstood what they studied. Yet in trying to label Bertrand Badie an Orientalist, a charge he cannot even lay at the feet of his source (see p. 14, n. 12), Roy reveals confusion about what Orientalist scholarship might

[4] Errors in the handling of Arabic terms abound:

(a) *ʿulamāʾ*, the plural of *ʿālim*, is given an "s" to make it plural as in "ulamas" while the singular for school, *madrasa* (pl. *madāris*), is treated as a plural (28); similarly, the singular for legal opinion, *fatwā* (pl. *fatāwin* or *fatāwā*), is treated like a plural (29);

(b) *amīr* is rendered as "leader," but nothing is said of *amīr al-muʾminīn*, and *shūra* is termed "advisory council" (42); later, it is correctly referred to as "consultative council" (which in Arabic would be *majlis al-shūra*), yet rendered *majlis-i-shuraʾ*, as in Persian, and attributed to the Arabic-speaking Hasan al-Turabi (45, n. 35);

(c) the Arabic for "those who have the power to bind and unbind" is said to be *ahl al-hall wal-aqd*, but the English clause calls for *ahl al-ʿaqd wa al-ḥall*; when the terms are reversed, as occurs so often in Arabic, this should be reflected in the translation.

Roy, unlike Arkoun, is no Arabist; in fact, his experience has been more in Afghanistan than the Arab world. Since his argument in no way depends on recourse to Arabic terminology, one wonders what prompted him to weaken it by such obvious errors.

[5] For example:

(a) the concept of *wilāyat al-faqīh* is traced to Khomeini (30), despite Khomeini's own refusal to make such a claim in his *Islamic Government*;

(b) the listing of qualifications for the leader is attributed to Maududi (43), in flagrant neglect of the whole medieval tradition;

(c) the claim that Maududi was the first to criticize contemporary society by using the term *jahiliyya* (41 and n. 25) ignores Alfarabi and the whole medieval tradition;

(d) the account of al-Afghani relies on Kedourie (33 and n. 5);

(e) the discussion of the Muslim Brotherhood draws on nothing more recent than Richard Mitchell's book of 1969 (35 and n. 1).

be.[6] Worse, his awareness of what constitutes the tradition of Islam is woefully inadequate. In other writings, but not in the volume under review, Arkoun has studied the tradition. Were it not for his penchant in those other works to mistake the ephemeral and the peripheral for the core, one might think he did understand the tradition.

Second, in claiming that there are many Muslims but no Islam, both authors betray a curious lack of common sense. On the one hand, it is obvious that manifold difficulties await anyone temerarious enough to attempt a description or definition of Islam as a single phenomenon. But on the other, we must ask what practicing Muslims think of as they invoke the word. Surely, we must strive for a working idea of a single Islam, all the while being aware that it is only a working idea or working definition. To do so is not to engage in a self-defeating Orientalism or to prolong a meaningless and romantic notion of religion as monolithic. It is, rather, to start with the phenomena and to take them as they first appear, that is, to gain a full appreciation of the surface before attempting to delve beneath it.

Only by a firm grasp of what Islam represents in its multitudinous manifestations as well as in its historical development can anyone hope to address intelligently the questions Mohammed Arkoun's interlocutors put to him. The attack upon reason as a Western imposition, attractive as it is for its boldness, reveals itself as foolhardy when reconsidered. What might a scholar, or any normally intelligent person, propose as a substitute for reason—sentiment? Is it not ironic and ever so detrimental to Arkoun's position that the only serious case for sentiment (but sentiment as the good natural conscience of a being not corrupted by society or fellow humans) as a guide is set forth in Rousseau's paradoxical *First Discourse*, written in response to the question posed by the Academy of Dijon "Whether the Re-establishment of the Sciences and the Arts has contributed to Purifying Morals," and later in the treatise that brought him so many troubles, *Émile or On Education*? By the same token, it is no more sufficient to point to the intellectual shortcomings of those promoting political Islam to declare it a failure than it is to invoke a vague notion of this movement being swept away by a coming historical cycle. The facts, especially in Algeria, but even in Roy's own bailiwick of Afghanistan, are all too clearly against such wishful thinking.

[6] For a different view of Badie, see below, Jean Leca, Meriem Vergès, and Mounia Bennani-Chraibi, "Daniel Lerner Revisited, The Audio-Visual Media and its Reception: Two North African Cases," n. 1.

## TOWARD A MORE CATHOLIC VIEW OF ISLAM

Arkoun and Roy err in a more fundamental way, but one common to most contemporary students of the Middle East, in that they seek to explain politics, culture, social relationships, in short, everything, by recourse to Islam. Great as the temptation to do so may be, one must never forget that people live, marry, procreate, and die within the nations of this region—many of which formally proclaim themselves Islamic—yet remain, for the most part, outside observers unmoved by the wonders promised to faithful Muslims. Patterns of speech, social customs, even forms of dress are no more unambiguous indicators of what individuals think and believe than other modes of conformity to the larger milieu. Sociological analysis must look below or behind the surface and in doing so be ever alert to the way intelligent thinkers and actors manipulate symbols. What is more, however impressive the numerical and financial superiority of Muslims in the Arab countries of North Africa, as well as in Egypt and Sudan, it pales when compared to the political power and civil rights enjoyed by Christians and other minorities in the Levant.

Two excellent examples of how Islam is both more and less or, alternatively, of how difficult it is to explain phenomena in terms either of our usual understanding of Islam or of that put forth by those hewing to the visions of Foucault are the Arab revolt and the rise of the West. More than a quarter of a century ago, C. Ernest Dawn published his path-breaking studies that, even then, dated back one and two decades and represented the first attempts to subject the available evidence on the Arab revolt to a judicious examination. In *From Ottomanism to Arabism*,[7] Dawn tries to explain how Arab nationalism arose, especially as concerns the Arab revolt of the Sharīf of Mecca, al-Ḥusayn Ibn ʿAlī and his sons. A historian of ideas, yet one ever sensitive to the principle that the explanations people offer for their actions are not to be unquestioningly accepted, Dawn re-examined the basic documents and came up with an explanation at odds with, and more nuanced than, those prevailing.

According to Dawn, Ḥusayn and his sons would not have revolted had they not come to believe that the Turks—especially the Young Turks

[7] See C. Ernest Dawn, *From Ottomanism to Arabism: Essays on the Origins of Arab Nationalism* (Urbana: University of Illinois Press, 1973), especially Chapter 5, "From Ottomanism to Arabism: The Origin of an Ideology," 122–47. In what follows, page references within parentheses are to this book.

of the Committee of Union and Progress—were no longer willing to respect the special status of the Hijaz and of the Arabs. For Ḥusayn as well as his second eldest son ʿAbd Allāh, and here Dawn can point to their writings and public speeches, the soul of Islam was its Arabness. Consequently, they insisted that the Arabs and the Arab language must have a special place in any state daring to call itself Muslim.

Dawn concedes that Ḥusayn's own desire for gaining greater independence and that of the Turks for bringing the Hijaz more completely into the Turkish system had to lead sooner or later to a break (54–5). But the question is why it happened when it did. There are many answers: heavy-handedness by the Young Turks, the weakness into which Turkey had fallen as a result of siding with the Germans in World War I, British wooing of ʿAbd Allāh, and the ideas of revolt put forth by Muḥammad Rashīd Riḍā and ʿAbd al-Raḥmān al-Kawākibī.[8] These thinkers were moved to call for resistance, even revolt, by what they saw as the abandonment of both the caliphate and the *sharīʿa* by the Turks. It was not merely that the Young Turks called for embracing Western constitutional ideas, but that they sought, in addition, to replace the caliphate itself with these ideas and to alter the traditional role of Islam with respect to personal matters—especially as concerned women (69–74 and 82–85). For Muslims to identify with one another across national boundaries, there had to be a caliphate; nothing else would do. Finally, the revolt fits into the larger attempt to regain political, military, and religious pride by patriots gradually recognizing to what extent they were ruled by Westerners not of their choosing.

A recent study by Mahmoud Haddad focused on Muḥammad Rashīd Riḍā[9] corroborates Dawn's earlier analysis. Haddad seeks above all to put Riḍā's writings and the thoughts he expressed therein into historical context, this in order to show that what has heretofore been called Riḍā's wavering or inconsistency about whether the caliphate should be purely spiritual—that is, have a role similar to that of the Roman Catholic papacy—or temporal was a response to the politics of the day. Upon examination, Haddad concludes that though Muḥammad Rashīd Riḍā did indeed express different opinions at different times, he did so always in the service of a single ideal, namely, keeping Islam politically independent.

8 For a more complete analysis of al-Kawākibī's thought, see Chapter 4, below: Said Bensaid Alaoui, "Muslim Opposition Thinkers in the Nineteenth Century."

9 See Mahmoud Haddad, "Arab Religious Nationalism in the Colonial Era: Rereading Rashīd Riḍā's Ideas on the Caliphate," *Journal of the American Oriental Society* 117/2 (April–June, 1997): 253–77.

From this perspective, the attachment of Riḍā, al-Kawākibī, Ḥusayn and ʿAbd Allāh to Islam was an attachment to a larger cultural and above all, political tradition and not merely to a fixed religion. To be sure, there is no reason to suppose that Ḥusayn and ʿAbd Allāh had any more aversion to their activities resulting in greater political power for themselves than did Riḍā and al-Kawākibī with respect to the fame brought upon them by the positions they took. But with all due respect to Machiavelli, Hobbes, and even Lasswell, desire for glory and self aggrandizement can no more be set down as the determining factor for the actions of these four than can a pious conviction that Islam had somehow to be vindicated. The language and symbols of religiou reform—even resurrection—were ready to hand, and so they were used But the language and symbols of returning Islam to its triumphant role are also common to the goal of escaping foreign domination and were first used to this latter end. The thoughts and actions of Riḍā, al Kawākibī, Ḥusayn, and ʿAbd Allāh mesh perfectly with the earlie ones of Jamāl al-Dīn al-Afghānī and Muḥammad ʿAbduh.[10] That the gave way to calls centered primarily upon religious reform with the advent of Muḥammad Iqbāl, Ḥasan al-Bannā, Abū al-Aʿlā al-Mawdūdī and eventually Sayyid Quṭb cannot be denied, but is to be explained as the development of a strategy and not as something essential to th movement.[11]

So, too, with the question about why industrialization and mercantile capitalism succeeded so well and so early in the West. The literature about this issue is abundant and reaches back to at least the time whe Ernest Dawn was first re-examining the question of the Arab revolt.[1

[10] See Muhsin Mahdi, "Modernity and Islam," in *Modern Trends in World Religions*, ec Joseph Kitagawa (La Salle, Ill.: Open Court, 1959), 1–30; and *Die geistigen und soziale Wandlungen im Nahen Osten* (Freiburg I. Br: Romback, 1961).

[11] In addition to the Alaoui article, below, see Charles E. Butterworth, "Prudence vs. Legiti macy: The Persistent Theme in Islamic Political Thought," in *Islamic Resurgence in th Arab World*, ed. Ali E. Hillal Dessouki (New York: Praeger, 1982), 84–114; and "Politi cal Islam: The Origins," in *Political Islam*, ed. Charles E. Butterworth and I. Williar Zartman, a special issue of *The Annals of the American Academy of Political and Socia Science*, 524 (November, 1992): 26–37.

[12] See, for example, K. N. Chaudhuri, "Capital and Trade in the Indian Ocean: Th Problem of Scale, Merchants, Money, and Production," in *Trade and Civilisation in th Indian Ocean: An Economic History of the Rise of Islam to 1750* (Cambridge: Cam bridge University Press, 1985), 203–20; Randall Collins, *Weberian Sociological Theor* (Cambridge: Cambridge University Press, 1986); Mark Elvin, "China as a Counterfac tual," in *Europe and the Rise of Capitalism*, ed. Jean Baechler, John A. Hall, and Michae Mann (Oxford: Basil Blackwell, 1988), 101–12; Edward W. Fox, "The Range of Com munications and the Shape of Social Organization," *Communication* 5 (1980): 275–87 E. L. Jones, "Environmental and Social Conjectures," in *The European Miracle: Env*

Yet common to almost every study about the issue is general ignorance about the Middle East plus a tendency to pass over or ignore it.

That is all the more curious given that none of the factors different scholars identify as contributing to the rise of capitalism in the West is absent from the Middle East. Technology was present, though it certainly came later and remained largely in the hands of the colonialists. Travel by both sea and land—that is, a form of mobility—was as widespread in the Middle East as in the West. To counter the notion that a prolonged feudalism held back the Middle East, one need only reflect on Reischauer's contention that Japan's feudal system is the precise spur for its development. Property rights were as widely recognized in the Middle East as in the West, and sovereignty was as parceled in the one as in the other.

Still, the point is that capitalism and industrialization did not occur in the Middle East until long after they occurred in the West. Why not? And why was there not the same revolution in thinking in the Middle East as occurred in the West? Or, differently stated, is it because there was a revolution in thinking in the West, a break with older ways, that the West became capitalist and industrialized?

For those who do focus on the Middle East with respect to this and similar questions, the tendency today is to explain the differences between what happens there and what happens in the West in terms of religion, that is, in terms of the way Islam differs from either Judaism or Christianity. Here, too, a moment's reflection should give pause. Judaism and Islam have many features in common, from the prominence of the divine law to the refusal to accord the prophet divine status. Is it possible, then, that the explanation for the material success of the West must be cast in terms of Western peoples' nonadherence to the given faith, to a secularist mentality? However hardy such a conjecture is when it comes to speaking about individual religious commitment, it certainly finds grounding when the history of modern Western thought is considered.

*ronments, Economies, and Geopolitics in the History of Europe and Asia*, 2d ed. (Cambridge: Cambridge University Press, 1987), 3–21; Charles P. Kindleberger, "Commercial Expansion and the Industrial Revolution," in *Economic Response: Comparative Studies in Trade, Finance, and Growth* (Cambridge, Mass.: Harvard University Press, 1978), 135–66; Edwin O. Reischauer, "Japanese Feudalism," in *Feudalism in History*, ed. Rushton Colbourn (Princeton: Princeton University Press, 1956), 26–48; Nathan Rosenberg and L. E. Birdzell, Jr., "The Growth of Trade to 1750," in *How the West Grew Rich: The Economic Transformation of the Industrial World* (New York: Basic Books, 1986), 71–96; Jane Schneider, "Was There a Pre-capitalist World-System?" *Peasant Studies* 6 (1977): 20–7; and Robert G. Wesson, "The Western Creativity" and "The Nation-State System: Interaction and Development," in *State Systems: International Pluralism, Politics, and Culture* (New York: Free Press, 1978), 153–211.

Consequently, the analysis or explanation must focus on the peculiar revolution in thinking that occurred in the West, and only in the West, from the end of the fifteenth century until the late eighteenth century.[13]

Such a conclusion is in no way intended to confirm Arkoun's desire to repudiate Western thinking as hegemonic, but merely to point to the way ideas influence action. The reason for pausing to consider these two phenomena—the Arab revolt and the rise of capitalism in the West—is, in the first place, to show that explanations other than those proffered by a Foucault-based historicism have to be entertained, that what has taken place in the Middle East and is occurring even now is both very complex and quite straightforward. Dawn and Haddad demonstrate not only deep familiarity with the basic facts surrounding the controversies they seek to explain, but also an unusual willingness to consider and then reconsider the language people use and why they use some forms of speech rather than others. Differently stated, language—the words used to propose and defend precise courses of action—can be as indicative of personal style while serving to hide one's person as clothing. That a speaker has recourse to religious terminology tells us nothing about his personal convictions in and of itself.

The second reason for such a pause follows from the first. To the extent that the careful scholarship of a Dawn or a Haddad shows how ever so nuanced explanations of past events must be while remaining open to continuous re-examination, the error of blithely rejecting such scholarship on external, a priori grounds is patently revealed. In addition to all else, such a posture risks undoing all the fruits of careful scholarship, of bringing back something like Ernest Renan's narrow-minded positivist judgments of almost a century and a half ago:

> I am the first to acknowledge that we have nothing or almost nothing to learn from Averroes, the Arabs, or the Middle Ages . . . the merit of the history of philosophy resides less perhaps in the positive teachings to be drawn from it than in the picture it provides of the successive evolution of the human mind. The feature characteristic of the nineteenth century is to have substituted the historical method for the dogmatic method in all branches of study relative to the human mind.[14]

[13] For a fuller development of this idea, see Charles E. Butterworth, "Philosophy, Stories, and the Study of Elites," in *Elites in the Middle East*, ed. I. William Zartman (New York: Praeger, 1980), 10–48.

[14] See Ernest Renan, *Averroès et l'Averroïsme: Essai historique* in *Oeuvres complètes de Ernest Renan*, ed. Henriette Psichari (Paris: Calmann-Lévy, 1949), 15. This passage is from the Preface to the first edition of the work published in 1852.

Even the shortcomings of the studies focused on "the rise of the West" are instructive in this respect. Clearly, to date there is no adequate explanation that accounts for what happened in the West and not elsewhere.

## SETTING THE RECORD STRAIGHT

A similar series of questions arises today with respect to democratization. Still, once careful attention is paid to the facts, to what is going on in polities that are either proudly self-identified as Islamic or that must be so considered because the vast majority of the citizens are Muslim, one cannot help but note the presence of democratization or, at the very least, vestiges of nascent democratization. Political Islam, wherever one looks—Tunisia, Egypt, Sudan, Jordan, Saudi Arabia, Pakistan, Malaysia, and Indonesia—is anything but a failure. It is also somewhat democratic, or so it appears from the reports of scholars like John Esposito and John Voll, a judgment with which Glenn E. Robinson concurs.[15] Yet others—Jean-François Bayart, Abdelbaki Hermassi, Aziz al-Azmeh, Ghassan Salamé, and John Waterbury come most readily to mind—trace the difficulty democracy has taking root in such polities to factors having more to do with history, economics, and politics than with Islam.[16]

Starting from an observation similar to the one that guides this book—namely, that "even in medieval Islamic civilization, in the era of the great Muslim empires of the Umayyads and the Abbasids, nonstate structures with important functions in the life of religious faith and action developed" (4)[17]—Esposito and Voll seek to explain that Islam is not antithetical to democracy. Casting the reformers of the nineteenth and early twentieth centuries as modernists rather than reactionaries, they urge

15 See John L. Esposito and John O. Voll, *Islam and Democracy* (New York: Oxford University Press, 1996), and Glenn E. Robinson, "Can Islamists be Democrats? The Case of Jordan," in *The Middle East Journal* 51/3 (Summer 1997): 373–87.

16 See Ghassan Salamé, ed., *Democracy without Democrats? The Renewal of Politics in the Muslim World* (London: I. B. Tauris Publishers, 1994). The articles of Salamé ("Small is Pluralistic: Democracy as an Instrument of Civil Peace"), al-Azmeh ("Populism Contra Democracy: Recent Democratist Discourse in the Arab World"), and Waterbury ("Democracy without Democrats? The Potential for Political Liberalization in the Middle East") are presented as broad essays about the general topic, while those of Bayart ("Republican Trajectories in Iran and Turkey: A Tocquevillian Reading") and Hermassi ("Socio-economic Change and Political Implications: The Maghreb") are case studies.

17 Here and in what follows, references within parentheses are to Esposito and Voll, *Islam and Democracy*.

that these activists were looking for structures that would not jeopardize Islam and thus were not desirous of turning back the clock (5–6). They arrive at such an understanding of Islamic reform, even the reform of recent times, because they look at the particular political phenomenon in a global context while paying especial attention to the particular opinions of the Islamic peoples they seek to explain.

With an eye to the fundamental precepts of Islamic teaching, Esposito and Voll attempt to account for the way recent Muslim reformers have argued for there being basic agreement between the principles of Islamic government and those of democracy. They pay special attention to Abū al-Aʿlā al-Mawdūdī and his account of how sovereignty within Islam is rooted in the principle of divine unity or *tawḥīd*. This, coupled with the idea that each individual human being is on earth as a vicegerent—that is, a khilāfa—of God and thus obliged to carry out His prescriptions to the extent possible, distinguish Islamic political thinking from Western notions of popular sovereignty and untrammeled freedom (21–4). That is clearly a basic difference.

Yet even the most dedicated proponents of the people's will admit some limits to that will. Here, then, at a setting down of the fundamental conditions for living together in community, is where the comparison between the two systems must begin. Though Esposito and Voll do not address this issue, they turn to yet other Pakistani thinkers—Muhammad Iqbal, Fazlur Rahman, and Khurshid Ahmad—to show how the principles of consultation (*shūra*), consensus (*ijmāʿ*), and interpretative judgment (*ijtihād*) embody many of the precepts of democratic practice and theory (25–30). That these principles are rooted in Islamic jurisprudence means that nothing in Islam forbids democracy.

Indeed, there are many features of Islamic doctrine and practice that are perfectly consonant with democratic rule. While opposition that arises as a threat to rulership (*fitna*) is no more tolerated in Islamic government than in any other kind of polity, opposition as difference of opinion (*ikhtilāf*) about particular policies is perfectly acceptable (33–46). Evidence of toleration, a principle that was the cornerstone of civil religion according to Rousseau,[18] is to be found in the freedom Islam has traditionally accorded Jews and Christians, that is, "the people of the Book" (46–8).

Broad, even somewhat elastic, these concepts can at best provide only the foundations for democratization. One must still wonder what actual

[18] See Jean-Jacques Rousseau, *On the Social Contract*, Bk. 4, Chapter 8, end.

evidence of democratic Islamic polities or Islamic movements tending toward democracy can be mustered. To answer such a query, Esposito and Voll offer six case studies. Two—Algeria and Egypt—are instances where Islamic movements or groups have been declared illegal and now function as militant opposition forces. With two others—Malaysia and Pakistan—the Islamic movements or groups function as representatives of the loyal opposition and are fully incorporated into a flourishing parliamentary system. The final two case studies center on Iran and Sudan, instances in which Islamic movements have come to full power.

The cases are well chosen and such that our authors are obliged to draw mixed conclusions. Though democracy is not to be found everywhere in the world of Islam—indeed, out and out opponents of it are sometimes to be found, as in Saudi Arabia—there are instances of it flourishing. What is more, the cases of Pakistan and Malaysia show that the secular character of democracy can be tempered, that democracy need not be opposed to religion. That raises the question of why successive regimes in Tunisia have chosen to act so anti-democratically in order to suppress Islamic political movements that claim to be democratic. The final chapter wrestles with the question with somewhat different results.

## CONCLUSION

In sum, the state and Islam are always with us, just as are the poor. But we need pay no more attention to the state and Islam than we do the poor. Nor does any one of them—the state, Islam, or the poor—constantly play an important role, despite being always present. The emphasis on Islam in academic studies and media commentary is due to the widespread resurgence of Islam as well as to the ample opportunities its claims and pretensions have provided for observing differences between "our" ways and "theirs." Yet, as has always happened during times of political upheaval, other forms of civic life go on. And to understand Middle Eastern society fully, we need to know more about this aspect of communal life.

It would not be amiss to insist that attention also be paid to the influence the media have today on academic trends. Or, more in keeping with the principles of dispassionate academic discourse, it might be appropriate to query why academic attention is focused on a particular problem today and probe for the way this particular problem fits into the larger picture.

The Islamic movements that attract our attention so at the moment came to the foreground and grew stronger as one or another existing political regime was unable to meet the popular expectations it had either created (however inadvertently) or actually promised to meet. Popular associations did not fill the void. In fact, it is perhaps not to be expected that they should have. After all, they first came into being to meet more limited needs—or did they? That is where the study of what is between Islam and the state must begin, namely, at identifying the goals of these private organizations, analyzing how they came into being, and how they function.

# 2

## The Impact of Technology Change on the Nineteenth-Century Arab World

ANTOINE B. ZAHLAN

Technological change has played a decisive role in the political, social, and economic evolution of the Arab world. In what follows, I propose to investigate how the social and political context affected technological development in this region. It is my contention that the politico-cultural environment of the region was the major constraint on scientific and technological activity.

Here, I concentrate exclusively on technology rather than on science. Science was neither sought nor nurtured in any of the countries or institutions of the Arab world during the nineteenth century, although some European scientists undertook research of various kinds in the region.[1] In all cases, however, such research was an extension of European scientific work and had little effect on Arab society. European scientific and technological research did inform European powers about the region's resources and conditions, and this scientific knowledge was eventually utilized in the deployment of European technological capabilities.

The acquisition of technology depends on a small number of interdependent measures. These consist of the transfer of knowledge through national educational institutions established with the assistance of foreign labor, the pursuit of education abroad, the establishment of industrial and technical facilities with the assistance of foreign firms and foreign labor, the creation of national engineering capabilities to plan, design, construct, and manage technical programs, and the institutionalization of extensive research activities in science and technology. All these measures initially depend on a small number (in the hundreds) of individuals. However, if government and society provide a receptive environment, these small beginnings multiply at a high rate.

[1] See Appendix for details.

In this chapter, I shall describe some of the efforts deployed, mostly in Egypt, to acquire technology. I will attempt to explain how and why fairly extensive and promising beginnings failed to bear fruit.

Scientific work refers generally to research of a basic and applied nature, while technology refers to the application of scientific knowledge. A number of ancillary activities, such as education and the translation and preparation of teaching materials, are often included in the description of science and technology in developing countries. One must distinguish between strictly training and educational programs for the transfer of skills and original scientific work. A brief account of some salient features of educational practices will be given merely to emphasize the feasibility of providing education under difficult conditions and to highlight the major political and institutional obstacles to the development of indigenous science and technology.

During the nineteenth century, the Arab region witnessed large-scale and dramatic applications of various technologies. Some of the projects in agriculture, transportation, industry, and engineering will be briefly reviewed to indicate what was attempted and to define the indigenous level of participation. The construction of the Suez Canal, the second largest civil works project in the nineteenth century, had no impact on Egyptian technological capabilities, because the Canal was built under a *produit-en-main* type of contract, an arrangement that continues to be popular in the Arab world today. The subsequent management of the Canal was also in foreign hands.

## BEGINNINGS

Napoleon's invasion of Egypt in 1798–1801 exhibited in a dramatic fashion the weaknesses of the Ottoman Empire and the extent of its technology gap with Europe. Nevertheless, despite European advances in science and technology, the Ottoman-Arab world remained politically intact at the turn of the nineteenth century, and its leadership was conscious of the dangers of technological weakness.

It was during the nineteenth century that every region of the Arab world felt the weight of Western science and technology. Of all the rulers and governors of the Ottoman Empire, it was Muhammad Ali, viceroy of Egypt, and his successors who were the most zealous in their pursuit of Western technological services. But all other leaders of the Ottoman and Arab world were also committed to this quest. For example, after a long struggle, Algeria fell to French imperial designs, but the Algerian leader Amīr ʿAbd al-Qādir lent his name and effort in his Syrian exile to the promotion of this quest. Egypt stands out among the regions of the Ottoman Empire for the scale, duration, complexity, and scope of its efforts extending over the period 1805 to 1882. Activities on a much smaller scale also took place in Syria and Iraq.

Napoleon's invasion of Egypt marked a turning point in the history of the region, for it created conditions that permitted Muhammad Ali, an Albanian officer of the Ottoman army, to seize power from the warring Mamelukes and to set the tone for a new style of government. Muhammad Ali was soon called upon by his suzerain in Istanbul to provide military support to suppress the Wahhabi and Greek national movements. Muhammad Ali's military operations in Arabia from 1811 to 1819, the conquest of the Sudan from 1820 to 1822, and the Greek war from 1822 to 1826 led to continued and heavy emphasis on the development of his armed forces.

Egypt possessed considerable natural resources and economic assets vital to financing Muhammad Ali's military programs. Transportation, trade, and agriculture were the three major economic activities. Much of the transport and trade of the Red Sea and African countries originated or terminated in Egypt. Half of the profitable coffee exports of Yemen went through Egypt. Despite the Cape route, the overland route through Egypt was used extensively for commerce and communications between Europe and India.

In 1800 the population of Egypt was around 2.5 million, and the country had unexploited agricultural potential. In addition to these happy circumstances of plentiful land, water, and a low population, Egypt enjoyed the blessings of having a politically unified country and unique exposure to European science and technology. The French expedition to Egypt had bequeathed the country high-quality artistic, scientific, and technological surveys. Napoleon had been accompanied by some 130 learned Frenchmen who constituted the Commission des Sciences et des Arts. Napoleon appointed distinguished members of the Commission to the Institut d'Égypte. Despite the fact that the French occupation lasted only three years, the team produced a careful, imaginative, and voluminous report.[2]

The old idea of a canal at the isthmus of Suez was revived by the *Description*, and extensive surveys of the region were undertaken. French

2 This report was published as the *Description de l'Égypte ou receuil des observations et des recherches qui ont été faites en Égypte pendant l'expédition de l'armée française, publié par les ordres de Sa Majesté l'Empereur Napoléon le Grand.*

engineers were later responsible for much of the extension of the irrigation canals as well as for a barrage at the apex of the Nile Delta. The *Description de l'Égypte* provided valuable information and inspired thousands of European scholars, engineers, and technicians whose careers would bring them to work in Egypt.

A second unexpected by-product of Napoleon's fleeting association with Egypt was the large number of French scientists, engineers, and army officers who were trained in Egyptian affairs. Muhammad Ali was consequently able to recruit considerable numbers of French professionals to serve in his armed forces and civil administration. Thus, Muhammad Ali started his rule with a relatively rich information base and a large supply of European physicians, technicians, officers, and engineers willing and ready to move permanently to Egypt. Moreover, a considerable European business community was ready to engage in trade with Egypt.

## THE EDUCATIONAL CHANNEL

Persistent European military pressures on the Ottoman and Arab world, as well as rebellion in various regions of the Ottoman Empire, placed a high priority on the development of military might. Many of the schools Muhammad Ali established from 1816 onward were created to train officers. These military schools were open to Turks, Circassians, Greeks, Armenians, and Kurds, but not to Egyptians. Muhammad Ali "purchased" Mamelukes to populate the schools in order to train cadres for his armies.[3]

While most of the troops were Egyptians, the officers were foreigners. The staff and students of the military schools were also European and other non-Egyptians. The level of education of these schools was fairly poor.[4] In view of the ethnic policies and poor quality of the military schools, it is doubtful whether their graduates contributed much toward the technological development of Egypt. These poorly trained officers were later to join the public sector and were responsible for creating difficulties both in the execution of engineering projects and in sponsoring technically deficient or irrational schemes.[5]

3 J. Heyworth-Dunne, *An Introduction to the History of Education in Modern Egypt* (London: Frank Cass, 1968), 117–8.

4 Ibid., 118–21.

5 In *Mémoires sur les principaux travaux d'utilité publique exécutés en Égypte* (Paris: Bertrand, 1872–3), Linant de Bellefonds describes several instances in which army officers were involved by Muhammad Ali in civil engineering projects. In all such cases the officers, according to Bellefonds, displayed technical incompetence.

The armed forces also needed medical care, so in 1826 Muhammad Ali established a hospital and a medical school under the direction of Bartholomew Clot (later known as Clot Bey). The students were recruited from al-Azhar University. They knew no foreign languages and had no scientific preparation. The foreign teachers knew no Arabic. Translators were employed, but they knew no medicine. Many students were given medical assignments after completing only part of this program. Some graduates were sent to Europe, usually France, to receive further medical education. According to Maḥmūd al-Manāwī, the School of Medicine had graduated eight hundred doctors by 1848, and the faculty had translated fifty-five European texts (ninety-two volumes) into Arabic.[6]

When Muhammad Ali's grandson, Abbas, came to power in 1848, Clot resigned as director. Apparently the school became involved in British-French rivalries, and a succession of directors had a difficult time in managing its affairs. Two French directors, Durignéan and Perron, were unable to manage the school. Abbas then turned to Germany, attracting Wilhelm Griesinger in 1850 to serve as director, followed in 1856 by Theodor Bilharz. Despite the difficulties they faced in managing the school, both medical men made important contributions.[7] Bilharz discovered *schistosoma haematobium*, the cause of the blood fluke disease that has plagued Egypt since ancient times.

By 1863, the entire medical staff of 14, together with the director of the school, were Egyptians. Between 1863 and 1899, the school continued under Egyptian management. But after the occupation of Egypt in 1882, the British administration attempted to control all activities in the country. Yet al-Manāwī describes the situation as having continually improved and claims that the Egyptian staff introduced new techniques and standards.[8] The British were not impressed by the school. As late as 1885, it had no physiological, pathological, or anatomical collections, and students learned by rote. Rudolf Virchow visited the school at this time and reported:

> The final results became known to them only at a late period in a most summary form. I have known many and can speak highly of their amiability, but have found not one who could be counted on to contribute in a useful manner to the program of the science and art of medicine.[9]

[6] Maḥmūd al-Manāwī, *Qaṣr al-ʿAinī* (Cairo: Egyptian Medical Union, 1979), 34 and 36–9.
[7] Heyworth-Dunne, *Introduction*, 300.
[8] See al-Manāwī, *Qaṣr al-ʿAinī*, 34 and 36–9.
[9] Cited in R. L. Tignor, *Modernization and British Colonial Rule in Egypt, 1882–1914* (Princeton: Princeton University Press, 1966), 332.

When Naguib Mahfouz entered the School of Medicine as a student in 1898, he found that "the advent of anesthesia and the use of antiseptics in surgery, which had already been in practice elsewhere, were unknown" to many of the teachers.[10] That year the language of instruction was changed from Arabic to English, and the entire teaching staff was removed and replaced by British and German professors.

The quality and relevance of the medical education may also be assessed by the contribution of the medical corps to the quality of health. Here observers of nineteenth-century Egypt appear uniformly critical of the condition of public health throughout the country. Yet, by 1846, the ratio of population to Egyptian doctors was already 5,000 to 1.[11] This, of course, is not a very satisfactory ratio, but at this level one could have expected a more effective control of epidemics and more widespread concern for sanitation and clean water. In 1867, Fox claimed that as simple a matter as smallpox vaccinations were not being properly performed but that the situation began to improve the same year.[12]

Epidemics of cholera, plague, smallpox, and typhus appeared frequently in Egypt with devastating intensity (e.g., 150,000 deaths in 1831). They were often brought to Egypt by pilgrims returning from Mecca who had contracted diseases there from Indian pilgrims. The Indian origin of most of these epidemics appears to have been well established before 1865.[13] British responsibility for this state of affairs was apparently not taken seriously, even though these epidemics occasionally spread to Europe. Despite quarantine and widespread recognition of the severity of such epidemics, they were not effectively controlled until the twentieth century.[14] And even as belated as 1883, a cholera epidemic that killed 100,000 Egyptians indicated persisting defects in the country's health-care system.[15]

Elsewhere in the region, foreigners also dominated the transfer of medical technology. American and French missionary activity in Syria led to the establishment of two schools offering medical training: the

[10] Naguib Mahfouz, *The Life of an Egyptian Doctor* (London: E. & S. Livingstone Ltd., 1966), 22–30. Since the Nobel laureate was not born until 1911, this Naguib Mahfouz is a different person.

[11] The population of Egypt in 1846 is estimated to have been 4.5 million, and the School of Medicine had graduated 800 doctors by then. Abdel R. Omran, "The Population of Egypt, Past and Present," in *Egypt: Population Problems and Prospects*, ed. Abdel R. Omran (Chapel Hill, N.C.: Carolina Population Center, 1973), 13.

[12] T. Fox, "Notes on the Dermatology of Egypt," *Medical Times and Gazette*, 2 February 1867, 111–13 and 165–6.

[13] T. Fox, "The Cholera in Egypt," *British Medical Journal* (1865): 667–70.

[14] See Abdel R. Omran, "The Mortality Profile," in *Egypt: Population*, 39–72.

[15] Tignor, *Modernization*, 349.

Syrian Protestant College, founded in 1866, and the Université St. Joseph, founded in 1870, both in Beirut.

Social policies, not the number or quality of physicians, determine the application of known public health technologies and the quality of diet. Throughout the nineteenth century, Egypt's social policies led to low labor productivity and chronic epidemics. At the same time, Egypt suffered from manpower shortages.

A similar situation prevailed in engineering and agriculture. A school of engineering had existed in Cairo since 1820. Very little is known of its activities, however, until the early 1830s, when it was reorganized under the influence of the Saint Simonians. Heyworth-Dunne states:

> The project of encouraging engineering studies in Egypt, while providing employment for a number of Frenchmen and giving a good opening for the growth of French culture, certainly seemed sincere, and, although it bore fruit in the long run, yet the tradition of the Egyptian engineering service has never been sufficiently strong to remain independent of European experts. In fact, it has really become a part of the traditional system in technical branches of the Egyptian service that serious enterprises are always undertaken by Europeans.[16]

A veterinary school was founded under P. N. Hamont in 1827. Much of its duties concerned military horses. This school, however, appears to have had very little effect on the recurrence or intensity of livestock epidemics. Egypt suffered repeated epidemics of foot and mouth disease that decimated the water buffalo population on which much of its agricultural economy depended.[17] A school of agriculture of dubious quality was also opened in 1835.[18] Muhammad Ali sent for an entire French staff, but as a result of poor planning and management the head of the French mission resigned and the school rapidly deteriorated into a farm.

These educational institutions were the scenes of intense personal rivalries between foreign instructors, whether of the same nationality (e.g., the Frenchmen Clot and Hamont) or different ones (particularly British and French), as well as among professionals recruited from the Middle East—Egyptians, Turks, Armenians. Egypt could not build an educational system that transcended these difficulties, since the government itself was ethnically foreign and ethnic distinctions were central to its policies. Furthermore, educational quality was poor and out of tune with economic needs. The acquisition of technology under these circumstances only intensified and perpetuated dependence.

[16] Heyworth-Dunne, *Introduction*, 300. [17] Ibid., 132.
[18] Ibid., 151–2.

Parallel with the establishment of schools, Egypt dispatched a number of students for study abroad—a total of 349 between 1809 and 1849—many of them for specialized training in industry, engineering, mining, and agriculture. Educational missions to Europe continued throughout the century. Egyptians also went privately to study abroad. In 1869, the Egyptian School in Paris enrolled 140 students: 40 studying civilian subjects, 100 pursuing military studies. In 1870, one finds 15 students enrolled at the Institut International at Turin and 3 more in Britain studying engineering. Between 1863 and 1879, 172 students were sent to be educated in Europe.[19]

We do not yet possess a sound and systematic basis for the comparative study of the effectiveness of labor and educational policies in different societies. Egypt initiated extensive contacts with Europe more than fifty years before Japan, at a time when its rulers were essentially sovereign and politically independent. Yet, the government of Egypt was not as successful as that of Japan in extricating its country from technological backwardness.

A comparison of the educational efforts of both countries may shed light on their different outcomes. On the quantitative side, we find that twenty-nine Japanese students went abroad in the 1860s during the Tokugawa period and a further 187 during the following thirty years of the early Meiji period.[20]

In other words, Muhammad Ali had dispatched a greater number of students by 1849 than Japan had by 1900. Japan, however, undertook these educational measures within the framework of a deliberate and comprehensive policy to build a strong, prosperous, enlightened nation. Between 1861 and 1867, the government of Japan dispatched five missions to the West to discover the causes of Western power and advancement.[21] Also, unlike Egypt, Japan was governed by a regime that did not discriminate against the bulk of its population on the basis of ethnic origin.

Japan, like Egypt, recruited large numbers of European and American teachers, engineers, clerks, and artisans; but, within a short period,

19 Ibid., 393–5.

20 Tasuku Hori, "The Brain Gain in the Modernization of Japan." Paper presented at the UN Economic Commission for Western Asia Seminar on the Arab Brain Drain, Beirut, 4–8 February 1980.

21 The size and date of the five missions were as follows: ninety persons to Europe and America (1861); thirty-six persons to Europe (1862); thirty-four persons to France (1863); and a similar group to Russia (1865); twenty-one persons to France (1867); see Umetawi Noburu, *The Role of Foreign Employees in the Meiji Era in Japan* (Tokyo: Institute of Development Economics, 1971).

Japan established its own institutions to train and educate Japanese workers. Japan's use of foreign expertise is estimated to have totalled 19,000 man-years from 1872 to 1898, an average of 731 persons per year over 26 years. We do not know the numbers of foreign workers employed in Egypt during any period of the nineteenth century, though they were undoubtedly much higher than in Japan. It can be estimated that the number of Europeans employed in the military and civilian sectors in Egypt exceeded 1,000 in the late 1820s, grew to between 8,000 and 10,000 by 1838, and increased further to 90,000 by 1881.[22]

## THE AGRICULTURAL, LABOR, AND INDUSTRIAL CHANNELS

Under Muhammad Ali and his successors, there were widespread efforts to develop agriculture and establish new industries. Civil engineering was heavily relied on for the extension of the irrigation system. All these activities depended on European technical knowledge and labor for project planning and execution.

The distribution, storage, and management of water are central to Egyptian agriculture. The upkeep and expansion of agricultural activity depended on removing silt, extending the canal system, and erecting barrages and dams. Throughout the nineteenth century, all the major civil works, beginning with the Maḥmūdiyya Canal to bring Nile water to the city of Alexandria, were planned and executed by foreigners.

The history of the Khayriyya barrage project (*al-Qanāṭir al-Khairiyya*) illustrates the technological practices of civil engineering in nineteenth-century Egypt. In 1833, Muhammad Ali attempted to block the Rosetta branch of the Nile at the apex of the Delta to increase water flow in the Damietta branch. When Bellefonds was consulted by Muhammad Ali, he demonstrated that the procedure adopted was ill-suited to the task, at which point Muhammad Ali instructed him to identify and execute a suitable project.

Bellefonds proposed the construction of regulating barrages on the Nile. Work began under his supervision in 1833 but was interrupted by plague in 1835. After the epidemic subsided, the project was not resumed. Between 1838 and 1842, bureaucratic arguments for and against the project led to further delays. In 1842, Muhammad Ali, to the surprise of Bellefonds, gave direction of the project to Mougel, who

[22] Roger Owen, "Egypt and Europe: From French Expedition to British Occupation," in *Studies in the Theory of Imperialism*, ed. E. R. J. Owen and R. B. Sutcliffe (London: Longman, 1972), 203.

undertook its redesign. Mougel had come to Egypt in 1839 as a replacement for Louis Charles Lefebvre de Cérisy who had established the Alexandria shipyard between 1829 and 1835. In 1835 Cérisy resigned as the result of intrigues initiated by Shakir Effendi, an ex-pilot from Istanbul harbor, concerning the construction of a dry dock in Alexandria.

The barrage project was not resumed until 1848. In 1853, Mougel was discharged, and Mazhar Bey was called on to complete the work. Finally completed in 1861, the barrage could not, however, retain water to its design capacity because its foundations were too weak to sustain the water pressure.

Surprisingly, the government then lost interest in the project, It remained an eyesore on the Nile until after the British occupation. At that point, the project was turned over to William Willcocks who had acquired engineering experience in this type of problem in India. Beginning in 1884, Willcocks undertook a series of remedial measures and was able to place the barrage in full operational condition by 1890.[23]

From this and numerous similar projects, one is led to conclude that during the entire nineteenth century Egypt was totally dependent on foreign engineering expertise. Not only was the government incapable of providing adequate technical management to complete projects economically, Egyptian organizations were not able to acquire technological competence. The procedures adopted by the Egyptian government were arbitrary, erratic, and whimsical, resulting in long delays, substandard work, poorly performing projects, and an inability to correct errors.

Technology also played an important role in labor productivity. Demand for labor in Egypt was high throughout the nineteenth century, and Egypt was a major destination for workers in the region. Only toward the end of the nineteenth century, did Egypt's population satisfy the demand for labor.

Until 1840, agriculture, the military, and the civil bureaucracy competed for the limited national workforce. Of an estimated population of some 2.5 million in the l820s, Muhammad Ali could extract a male labor force of some 625,000. Of these, in 1832, some 100,000 were in the army, 25,000 in the navy, 68,000 in the civil administration, and 40,000

[23] For a full account, see Bellefonds, *Mémoires*, 431–77, and also Major R. H. Brown, *History of the Barrage at the Head of the Delta of Egypt* (Cairo: F. Diemer, 1896), 1–66. For a brief account, see Helen Anne B. Rivlin, *The Agricultural Policy of Muhammad Ali in Egypt* (Cambridge, Mass.: Harvard University Press, 1961), 233–7.

employed in industry. Thus approximately 392,000 workers were available for employment in agriculture during the early part of the nineteenth century.

The agricultural labor force was expected to cultivate the land, supply corvée labor to remove the accumulated silt in irrigation canals, and provide the manpower to execute large-scale works. The Nile silt had to be removed annually from the irrigation canals, water raised by various mechanical devices, fields cultivated, and products transported and stored.

Truly monumental work was undertaken in agriculture: some 937 kilometers of new canals were dug, calling for the removal of 80 to 110 million cubic meters of earth, and some 800,000 cubic meters of masonry were used to construct new barrages, locks, and dikes.[24] All these works extended the utilization of land and water resources and resulted in substantial increases in agricultural output.

A corvée was usually raised when the demands of agriculture subsided, a period that normally covered nine months a year: mid-January to mid-July and August to November. During this period, each peasant was expected to give sixty days (reduced to forty-five days in 1847) for corvée labor. Peasants frequently had to travel long distances to the site of work, and this time was in addition to the number of fixed days of labor. The peasants were expected to supply their own tools; when they had none, they used their hands.[25]

Rivlin gives a vivid description of the construction (1817–20) of the Maḥmūdiyya Canal.[26] Workers were dispatched by Muhammad Ali to the site before the Turkish engineers, who were responsible at this time for civil works in Egypt, knew of the existence of the canal project. There were 300,000 corvée workers on this project, tools were inadequate, and malnutrition was so bad that during one year alone observers estimated the number of casualties between 12,000 and 100,000. Workers were sometimes buried before it had been ascertained they were dead. Given such circumstances, the project was so poorly executed that the canal never performed satisfactorily despite the fact that a French engineer, Pascal Coste, was later placed in charge.

Hamont described the effects of the undernourished population and the disastrous results on both the labor force and military conscription. Fewer than 90 in 1,000 males between 15 and 30 years old

[24] Bellefonds, *Mémoires*, 341–97.
[25] Rivlin, *Agricultural Policy*, 243–5.
[26] Ibid., 221.

were healthy enough to bear arms, and many of these suffered from serious ailments.[27]

Rivlin quotes R. R. Madden, who noted that one European laborer using proper tools could outproduce ten Egyptian peasants.[28] As David Dreiblatt observes, such discrepancies persist even with the generally more humane treatment of our day: reviewing information on the productivity of manual labor, he finds Tunisian labor productivity in earth-moving at roughly 1.2 cubic meters per day as compared with 10 cubic meters per day in Europe. The consumption of a 4,500 calories per day diet by Malabar workers enabled them to have a daily output 1.8 times that of other Indian workers whose diet consisted of 2,888 calories per day.[29]

In the early nineteenth century, enough was known by Egyptians and Europeans in Egypt about tools and the organization of work that the increase of labor productivity was a genuine option. Although Muhammad Ali attracted large numbers of foreign engineers and purchased large quantities of machinery, neither he nor his bureaucrats ever saw fit to take the appropriate measures to raise the output of the labor force. Thus the social policies practiced by Muhammad Ali were in themselves a major obstacle to the acquisition of the most rudimentary technologies associated with agriculture and civil works.

Although Bellefonds introduced planning in the deployment of corvée labor during the 1840s, the use of workers left much to be desired. Muhammad Ali's inhuman and ineffective use of labor is illustrated by his order to replace the water buffaloes that died in the 1842–3 epidemic of murrain with humans as a source of power for the cotton industries.

Dependent on foreign technical expertise for all serious planning and management, on foreign industry for machinery, and on the abuse of its own laborers, the Egyptian system blocked all mechanisms normally responsible for technological advancement. Although there is no doubt that the output of cotton and many other products increased during this period, the increase did not arise from the scientific and technical advancement of the Egyptian labor force but, rather, from the expansion and extension of the irrigation system, the contribution of foreign technical labor, and the increasing size of the workforce.

[27] P. N. Hamont, "Sur l'état hygiénique de l'Égypte," *Annales d'hygiène* VI (1831), 481–5.

[28] Rivlin, *Agricultural Policy*, 245.

[29] David Dreiblatt, *The Economy of Heavy Earthmoving* (New York: Praeger, 1972), 9 and 44–6.

Another of Muhammad Ali's major objectives was to establish textile manufacturing in Egypt. In the early nineteenth century, a textile industry was considered to be one of the great achievements of the industrial revolution. The rapid invention of mechanical devices for spinning and weaving progressively more complex fabrics eliminated manual textile industries throughout Europe.

Muhammad Ali, under the influence of Joseph Bocti, began the process of "industrialization" by monopolizing all textile production in Egypt in 1818. This he accomplished by centralizing all such production and using extreme and harsh measures to interdict cottage industries. Between 1818 and 1823, Muhammad Ali established 30 different factories with an installed capacity of 1,194 carding machines, 1,962 mule jennies, and 1,750 looms. About 30,000 workers were employed in these factories in the 1820s, though the number varied with the needs of the army.

In 1830, yarn production reached 1,316 tons and utilized a quarter of Egypt's cotton production for that year. Yarn output increased to 5,000 tons in 1837. Some of this yarn was used in local textile mills, which produced 160,000 meters of cloth in 1833, and the balance was exported to Italy and Turkey.[30]

Cotton production in Egypt continued to expand after 1837, while manufacturing in Muhammad Ali's factories peaked in the late 1830s and began to decline thereafter. But the quality of Egyptian textiles was not acceptable to the well-to-do of Egypt, and in 1836 cotton textiles accounted for 32 percent of all imports. In 1836, exports to Europe included linen fabrics, but no cotton textiles.

Like all Muhammad Ali's programs, textile factories were centrally managed. Since they were distributed throughout Egypt, where communication was not speedy, it stands to reason that the day-to-day technical operations of the factories left much to be desired. Machinery requires constant care and maintenance; this is especially the case for the equipment utilized in the early cotton factories. In fact, the most important factor determining the location and development of the British cotton industry was ready access to machine-making shops, whose specialized, technical services were vital to repair and adjust machines that broke down. This is why 75 percent of all mills in England were located in Lancashire by 1838.[31]

[30] Mustafa Fahmy, *La Révolution de l'industrie en Égypte et ses conséquences sociales au 19e siècle (1800–1850)* (Leiden: Brill, 1954), 26–7.

[31] Peter Mathias, *The First Industrial Nation* (London: Methuen, 1969), 132–3.

In Egypt, spare parts and repairs had to depend on workshops in the Bulaq district of Cairo. Moreover, production targets were so high and punishments for failure to meet them so severe that factory managers did not stop for necessary repairs. These practices resulted in a high percentage of wastage of raw materials—estimated at 50 percent by J. A. St. John—poor quality of products, and low factory efficiency.[32] Inadequate management and maintenance were important obstacles to the establishment of cotton manufacturing in Egypt.

Another major obstacle was the lack of indigenous technological development of the machinery once acquired. Textile machinery and technical skills were developing so rapidly in Europe that the knowledge of a British engineer away from the centers of engineering works would become obsolete in less than seven years.[33]

Jules Poulain, a French textile industrialist in Pondicherry, visited Egypt in 1843 and studied the conditions of cotton factories extensively. He found the workers diligent, efficient, able, and skillful. Some of those engaged in carding and spinning were, in his opinion, as competent as the very best in Europe.[34] Poulain was convinced that a profitable and competitive industry could be established in Egypt.

Thus, the difficulties had little to do with the ability of the Egyptian labor force to make use of the technologies accessible to them. Poulain ascribed the difficulties of Egyptian spinning and textile industries to one major cause: the factories did not have managers with competent knowledge of the technology. There was no pool of highly skilled engineers, mechanics, or carpenters whom factories could call upon to design, manufacture, operate, and repair every piece of machinery. Foremen failed to introduce innovations; they even failed to appreciate the importance of maintaining all the machines in good working order to secure an acceptable product. Consequently the cotton industry made no progress in Egypt, and the machines themselves soon became aged and broken down.

[32] E. R. J. Owen, *Cotton and the Egyptian Economy 1820–1914* (London: Oxford University Press, 1969), 46. James Augustus St. John is the author of *Egypt and Muhammad Ali* (London: Longman, Rees, Ormes, Brown, Green, and Longman, 1834).

[33] This aspect was repeatedly emphasized in submissions to the "Parliamentary Select Committee appointed to inquire into the state of the law and its consequences respecting the Exportation of Tools and Machinery." See, for example, the submission by Alexander Galloway in *Accounts and Papers, Session 3 February to 6 July 1825*, vol. 5 (1825), 15.

[34] Jules Poulain, "Rapport à son Altesse Mehemet Ali Vice-Roi d'Égypte sur la filature et le tissage du coton." The report was given to Joseph Hekekyan by Artin Bey and is included in the *Hekekyan Papers*, British Library Add. Mss., 37, 466, XIX, pp. 79–94.

Half of Egypt's cotton factories were abandoned between 1837 and 1840; others were leased to private contractors. By the end of the 1840s, only two cotton factories remained under public control. Apparently the old equipment in the hands of the despised textile workers was still in use in the mid 1850s, when Egypt's total textile output reached nine thousand tons, or nearly twice the "installed" capacity of 1837, the peak year for the "public sector" cotton manufacturing.[35]

Egypt failed to acquire a viable cotton manufacturing technology despite impressive advantages. The cotton industry had exhibited grave deficiencies before 1840 when Britain intervened militarily in Syria and Muhammad Ali was forced to terminate his monopolistic practices in Egypt. Thus the failure of the cotton industry was essentially due to the social context of technology, not to British imperial policy.

Up to 1843, Muhammad Ali was still seriously entertaining the idea of re-equipping the cotton factories. He appears to have thought that the acquisition of machinery and the short-term services of foreign technicians were adequate measures. He does not seem to have understood the dynamic nature of technology or that labor was more than a passive component in industry.

Joseph Hekekyan's diaries for the years around 1843 contain a number of references to the views of Muhammad Ali concerning his difficulties in the industrial sector. He appears to have ascribed his difficulties to the quality of machinery he bought, together with the quality of the technicians dispatched by foreign firms, rather than to his own policies regarding technology.

Muhammad Ali also established a number of factories for sugar refining, the extraction of indigo, rice milling, silk weaving, paper making, glass making, and saltpeter and gunpowder production. The methods were the same as with cotton: foreign technicians were imported to establish the facility; there was poor management, no technological development, inadequate maintenance, and, consequently, limited technology acquisition. A silk weaving project failed, an expensive steam-powered rice mill had to be scrapped, the quality of the indigo extraction and purification could not be maintained, the sugar refining was expensive and of poor quality and could not compete with imports from France even though sugar was locally produced.

A few observations on the power source for the cotton factories illustrate some of the difficulties that arose with the introduction of steam

[35] Owen, *Cotton*, 82–5.

power in Egypt. Joseph Hekekyan and others in Egypt had a full understanding of this technology and saw its enormous possibilities for the country. Here again, despite economic potential and technical feasibility, Egypt failed to acquire this vital technology.

The textile plants were powered by a total of 1,200 water buffaloes. The water buffaloes were changed every two hours.[36] Only three textile factories had steam power installations,[37] and many visitors in the 1830s noted that few of Egypt's seven or eight steam engines were operating. When Colin visited the Bulaq factory in 1834, he was surprised to find all the steam engines shut down and water buffaloes harnessed in the most barbaric fashion to operate the looms.[38] Apparently the steam engines constantly broke down, despite the fact that there were numerous English technicians in Egypt and, as we shall discuss later in more detail, steam engines were designed and manufactured in Egypt.

The economic advantage of steam power was much debated. Some blamed the poor quality of the cotton products on the irregular motions of the water buffaloes. Few seemed to have any concept of energy costs in the textile industry. Poulain undertook to compare the cost of power generated by steam and oxen. A unit of power produced by steam was, according to Poulain's estimate, twice as expensive as one produced by water buffaloes. Nevertheless, energy accounted for only 1 percent of the cost of textiles.

The murrain epidemic in 1842–3 decimated Egypt's water buffalo population, and Muhammad Ali again seriously considered introducing steam power. He asked Hekekyan for an estimate of the cost of manufacturing the engines at the Bulaq engineering works. Hekekyan estimated the cost of one unit at 250 pounds sterling, but added that "if several were to be made, their cost would be less than what he could procure them for from England. . . . The Pasha was not satisfied."[39] Hekekyan later noted that Muhammad Ali Pasha graciously sent his horses to replace the workers who had been put in harness in place of the water buffaloes, but that he did so with the understanding

[36] Felix Mengin, *Histoire sommaire de l'Égypte sous le gouvernement de Mohammad Aly* (Paris: Firmin Didot, 1839), 212.
[37] Fahmy, *La Révolution*, 53.
[38] A. Colin, "Lettres sur l'Égypte. Industrie manufacturière," *Revue des Deux Mondes* 14 (15 May 1838): 521. The British consul in Cairo made the same observations in his report on Egyptian manufacturing as Colin; Public Record Office, London, F078/408B, Campbell to Secretary, London, 6 July 1840.
[39] *Hekekyan Papers*, Add. Mss. 37, 449, II, pp. 66–7 and 149.

that he would be repaid for any horses that died in the mills from the murrain.

## METALLURGICAL AND ENGINEERING INDUSTRIES

During the early nineteenth century, metallurgical and engineering industries were the cornerstone of industrial society. Iron ore and coal, when necessary, could be imported, but the manufacturing and use of equipment and machinery depended on metallurgical and engineering technology. The cost of raw materials (iron and coal) was barely 10 percent of the cost of machinery. Labor and skill accounted for the remaining 90 percent.

Engineering industries designed and produced textile manufacturing equipment, steam boats, railways, and steam engines. In terms of capital investment, employment, and trade, British engineering in the early nineteenth century was dwarfed by the textile industry. The textile industries, however, would have been impossible if not for the creativity, high rate of inventiveness, and quality performance of British foundries and machine makers. As we have already noted, the rate of change in machinery was extremely high, and these inventions required continuous servicing.

Muhammad Ali established foundries and engineering works in Bulaq. These installations were established and managed at the beginning by Thomas Galloway, the son of Alexander Galloway who owned an important engineering firm in London and was considered to be one of England's leading engineers. Well before 1824, Alexander Galloway had established an international market for himself by exporting a mint to Algeria, the largest cotton press ever made in England to Egypt, and sundry other items to Russia, Latin America, and elsewhere.[40] The foundry at Bulaq was part of the Egyptian arsenal under the command of General Edhem Bey.

In 1833, the installed capacity of the furnaces was five tons a day. Available information on iron imports to Egypt indicates that in the late 1830s the foundry was processing some five hundred tons of iron a year. In other words, the foundry was operating at 28 percent of installed capacity.

The Bulaq works were capable of manufacturing iron and brass guns,

[40] "Reports from Committees: Artisans and Machinery," in *Accounts and Papers, Session 3 February to 25 June 1824*, vol. 5 (1824), 14–28.

carriages for artillery, pipes, boilers, steam engines, surgical equipment, anchors, and numerous small items. The musket factory near Bulaq produced eight hundred muskets a month. Foundries and forging equipment at Rosetta specialized in anchors and metal accessories for naval construction. Copper sheets for plating naval vessels were produced at Bulaq in batches of 3.5 tons of copper rolled in some 70 plates. The copper works were run by four English foremen and 20 Arab workers.

In 1840, the engineering works were under the general direction of Hekekyan assisted by an English engineer, Taylor, who was responsible for technical operations. By 1841, Hekekyan had trained eighty-four Egyptians in all phases of engineering works from drawing to fitting. These trainees were capable of designing and producing a large variety of tools and machinery.

At the request of Muhammad Ali, Hekekyan presented a plan in January 1843 to expand the works so as to make Egypt "independent of foreign countries" by manufacturing spinning and weaving machinery, steam engines, and "heavy machinery."[41] The cost of the plan was estimated at ten thousand pounds sterling.

Hekekyan was conscious of the increasing technology gap between Europe and Egypt; Europeans were constantly making improvements, and Egypt was continuously required to import them. Hekekyan believed that the only way out was to design and manufacture machinery in Egypt. But the hopes of Muhammad Ali and the plans of Hekekyan were not to be realized. In the wake of the 1842–3 murrain epidemic, Egypt imported steam plows and steam engines rather than manufacturing them locally.

With the accession of Ibrahim Pasha and Abbas, there was a break in the patient efforts initiated by Hekekyan to develop an indigenous tradition of technology. The introduction of the railway in 1851–4 by Abbas was accomplished by importing rails, locomotives, and rolling stock.

The 1863 murrain epidemic hit in the middle of the cotton boom generated by the American Civil War. Increased demand and the loss of animal power led to a rush to utilize more steam power. Engines were imported in large numbers. Under the "open door" policies practiced by Ismail, a group of European bankers and businessmen established the Société Agricole et Industrielle d'Égypte in 1864 with a capital of one million pounds sterling. The purpose was to import agricultural machinery and provide servicing and maintenance. But in no time the company

[41] *Hekekyan Papers*, Add. Mss. 37, 449, II, pp. 13, and 66–89.

was diverted into construction and real estate. As a result of mismanagement, corruption, and incompetence, the company went bankrupt in 1866. By 1870, thanks to foreign political pressure, Ismail was blamed for the company's failure, and Egypt was forced to pay compensation.[42]

These expensive commercial experiments did not favor the development of local engineering industries. Imports of technology products (steam boats, engines, and railway equipment) grew steadily, and the initially successful experiments at Bulaq died without a whimper.

## TRANSPORTATION TECHNOLOGY

The geographical location of the Arab world has made it a strategic center of communication. Two thousand years ago, the Arabs had discovered or acquired the two basic tools for conquering desert and sea: the camel and the dhow. Along with perfecting these technologies to navigate sea and desert, they advanced the naval sciences of navigation, wind, tide, and coastal geography. By 1800, the Arab transportation network was formidable. No city, village, or distant settlement was economically or socially isolated. The physical survival of communities large and small depended on transport. Transport facilities made it possible for communities to specialize according to their local endowments.

Camel-based transport called for skill in breeding, management, desert navigation, and marketing. Unfortunately, we have no statistical information on either the numbers of camels involved or the tonnage transported. However, the fragmentary information available indicates that millions of tons were transported over long inter-urban distances, and far greater quantities were transported locally from field to stores and to regional urban centers.

Arab rulers have always been conscious of the economic importance of transport activities and the associated trade. Through the first quarter of the nineteenth century, transport of goods originating outside the Arab world, in Asia and Europe, was a relatively small share of regional transport capacity. By the second quarter of the nineteenth century, Asian-European transport requirements had grown sufficiently to attract the interest of Muhammad Ali, who took steps to improve the use of the Alexandria-Cairo-Suez land bridge. He introduced Nile steamers, con-

[42] G. Douin, *Histoire du régime du Khédive Ismail* (Cairo: Société Royale de Géographie d'Égypte, 1933), 242–8.

structed resting places, paved part of the Cairo-Suez route, and employed carriages in addition to camels.

In 1834, only four years after the first successful demonstration of the technical feasibility of the railway in Britain, Muhammad Ali contracted with Thomas Galloway to construct an Alexandria-Cairo-Suez railway. The scheme fell through because Muhammad Ali was unable to secure from Britain an adequate rate for the use of the system.

As for sea transport, the Suez Canal project was revived by Napoleon's expedition of 1798 and by the extensive surveys undertaken by Le Père during the French occupation. The Porte and the British were adamantly set against this French project. Although Muhammad Ali appears to have been opposed to the project, he allowed Bellefonds, as director of Public Works, to undertake extensive surveys of the Canal region.

Bellefonds corrected Le Père's erroneous conclusion that there was a difference between the levels of the Red Sea and the Mediterranean and prepared adequate documentation for the Canal project. The fact that the two seas were at the same level simplified the scheme and increased the chances of its execution. Thus during the entire first half of the century, Egyptian rulers were fully aware of two major new technologies: the railway and the canal.

Egypt possessed the technological base for acquiring and developing these transport technologies. Civil engineering technologies were extensively used in agriculture, and the engineering capacity had been pioneered at Bulaq. However, the evolution of the transportation sector in Egypt took place independently of existing domestic capabilities, since the railway projects and the Suez Canal were planned and executed by foreign firms without reference to technology transfer or to indigenous resources.

The first railway system in an Arab state was constructed in 1851 under Abbas, then viceroy of Egypt, who granted a turnkey construction contract to George Stephenson, the son of the inventor of the first successful railway. By 1882, Egypt had installed 1,518 kms of rails, while no rails had yet been installed in any other country of the Arab East or Mashriq.

Algeria, by then under French occupation, got its railway in 1857. Tunisia gave a concession for the construction of a relatively minor line of 38 kms in 1871. Sudan had a short 53 km railway line in 1875, but railways only came effectively to that country with the Anglo-Egyptian campaign of 1896—as a tool to facilitate conquest.

The introduction of railways in the Mashriq was deeply enmeshed in the rivalry of Britain, France, and Germany to secure hegemony over parts of the crumbling Ottoman Empire. In Egypt, the British railway competed with the French Suez Canal project, while elsewhere the Porte sought German assistance to tighten its control over distant provinces (especially the Hijaz) and to develop the economic potential of the vast agricultural regions of Syria and Iraq. Two strategic lines—one linking Istanbul, Baghdad, and Basra; the other extending to the Hijaz—had both these objectives.[43]

Of importance to us here is that foreign firms planned, constructed, and operated the new transport systems, denying the countries of the region the chance to acquire these technologies for themselves. In Egypt, it was generally the public sector that contracted with foreign firms to design and construct these systems. All equipment and supplies—not least coal—were imported. A few private firms secured concessions for railways serving the agricultural sector. The key operators were all foreign.

When railways were introduced in the Ottoman provinces of the Middle East toward the end of the nineteenth century, France, Britain, Belgium, and Germany competed intensely for contracts and concessions. One common procedure was for some notable to secure a legal decree, or *firman*, granting the privilege of constructing a railway line. This was then followed either by the sale of the concessions to a foreign firm or the establishment of a joint venture with a foreign group. The Ottoman government provided financial guarantees and special terms to foreign firms erecting strategic railways.

Joseph Moutran, for example, secured the concession for a Damascus tramway system and a railway linking Hauran to Damascus in 1890, and Hassan Beyhoum secured a concession for the Beirut-Damascus link in 1891. These two concessions were fused into one in 1892, and the Société des Chemins de Fer Ottomans Économiques de Beyrouth-Damas-Hauran en Syrie was created. The board of the company consisted of Moutran, Beyhoum, and Selim Melhame, director-general of the Ottoman Public Debt, along with twelve Europeans who were responsible for all the technical work and management. The company was essentially French with some Belgian interests.[44]

43 An account of the political and strategic objectives for their transport systems is to be found in Rashid Ismail Khalidi, *British Policy towards Syria and Palestine 1906–1914* (London: Ithaca Press, 1980).

44 Noel Verney and George Dambmann, *Les Puissances dans le Levant en Syrie et en Palestine* (Paris: Guillaumin, 1900), 240–2.

In 1889, Joseph Elias, ingénieur-en-chef in Lebanon, secured a concession in partnership with Pilling for a Haifa-Damascus line, and this concession was then sold to a British firm, the Syria Ottoman Railway Company.[45] In 1892, Khadra secured a concession for a Beirut-Saida tramway line that he then sold to a French company.

The strategic importance of Iraq as an alternative route to India gave it a high place in British interests. In 1835–6, Gen. Francis Rawdo Chesney made his famous expedition with two river steamers, but the expedition failed to develop sufficient British interest in the Euphrates river route to India. In 1857, he secured a concession for a railway line from Sueda to Basra via Baghdad but failed to raise the necessary capital for construction.

In 1872–3, Wilhelm Pressel prepared a technical report for the Porte on the feasibility of a railway line to Basra. In 1891, a French company attempted to secure a contract to implement the Pressel project.[46] Construction of this line was finally begun in the twentieth century by a German firm.

The railway devastated indigenous camel-based transportation, entailing the loss of a profitable and dense transportation network, especially along the Alexandria-Cairo-Suez route, without the compensatory creation of a new technology base in the region. But the greatest devastation of the existing regional transportation system followed the opening of the Suez Canal. Upon its completion, the entire pattern of transport and trade was re-oriented away from inland routes toward seaports. The technological impact of the Suez Canal on the design and use of steamers also led rapidly to the domination of steamships on the high seas. As a consequence, Omani sailing ships or dhows, which had dominated trade in the Indian Ocean until the 1860s, lost out to European steamers.[47]

## FOSSIL ENERGY

At the beginning of the nineteenth century human and animal power provided the only source of energy in Egypt. Muhammad Ali was fully aware of the importance of fossil energy, and as early as 1819 he recruited Colonel Sève (later known as Soliman Pasha) to search for coal in Egypt. Sève spent time in 1820 at Jabal al-Zayt in the Gulf of Suez. The search for coal continued, but with disappointing results. During the Egyptian

45 Ibid., 321.

46 Ibid., 293–307.

47 R. G. Lande, *Oman since 1856* (Princeton: Princeton University Press, 1967).

occupation of Syria, the coal mines in Mount Lebanon were exploited. It appears, however, that only foreigners were involved in exploration for new sources of coal. From this effort, which continued until the eve of the British Occupation in 1882, one may deduce that, over a period of some sixty years, there was no serious effort to develop an indigenous capability for mineral extraction.

Scientific research undertaken by Europeans provided the sole basis for the technical decisions of other foreign advisers and prospectors. For example, in 1877 Dr. Schweinfurth argued on the basis of the geological studies of Professor Oscar Fraas that the petroleum resources of the Gulf of Suez region were trivial. Gen. Charles P. Stone supported this view.[48] Ten years later, when the American geologist L. H. Mitchell refuted the views of Oscar Fraas, he found support in the work of Professor Mayer Eymar from the University of Zurich, who had also conducted geological studies of the Sinai.[49]

In 1841 and 1842, Hekekyan experimented with combinations of asphalt and coal to produce a new source of energy.[50] These experiments, however, led nowhere. Egypt failed to develop and exploit its petroleum resources to fire its steam engines.

After the introduction of railways in Egypt, the consumption of coal increased dramatically. Imports from Britain rose from 30,000 tons a year before the railway to 120,000 tons in 1860, 388,000 in 1865, and 408,000 in 1870. By the end of this period, rapid developments in the exploration and exploitation of oil fields were taking place in the United States.

In Syria and Iraq, the existence of asphalt and oil resources had also been known since earliest times. In fact, the Chesney Euphrates expedition of 1835–6 utilized the locally available asphalt to fire the steamboats. Although Kirkuk oil was utilized as a source of energy for the Baghdad-Basra river steamboats in the 1870s, the exploitation was so primitive that it was cheaper to import coal all the way from Britain.[51]

A refinery was erected in 1871 at Baquba in Iraq. The project failed

[4]8 "Séance du 13 Janvier, 1877," *Bulletin de l'Institut Égyptien*, no. 14: 101–4. The Oscar Fraas studies were "Geologisches aus dem Orient: Sinai, Palästina und Egypten," *Jahresh. Ver. Vat. Nat. Württemb.*, 33 (1867): 145–362; and "Geologische Beobachtungen am Nil, auf der Sinai—Halbinsel und in Syrien," *N. Jahrb.* (1868): 493–8.

[4]9 Ehard Bissinger, *U.S. Consular Reports*, no. 74 (February 1887), 423–6.

[5]0 *Hekekyan Papers*, 37, 448, I, pp. 27, 33.

[5]1 Graham Geary, *Through Asiatic Turkey* (London: Sampson, Low, Marston, Searle, and Rivington, 1878), vol. 2, 15–21 and 98–9.

because the kerosene it marketed did not burn well.[52] Thus, despite high demand for fossil energy, the known existence of petroleum resources, and a steady flow of foreign consultants surveying the Gulf of Suez deposits extending over the entire nineteenth century and into the twentieth century, one does not find a policy dedicated to the acquisition of mining and petroleum technology either in Egypt or Ottoman Iraq.

## MIRAGES OF DEVELOPMENT

Momentous changes in the scientific education of individual Arabs occurred between 1798—when al-Jabartī gazed in bewilderment at the chemical experiments performed by the French scientists who accompanied Napoleon—and 1875—when learned physicians studying at European institutions were introduced to the latest advances in science. Still, by the last quarter of the nineteenth century, the scientific communities of Lebanon, Syria, and Egypt had reached only the level of serious amateurs. In this advancement of learning, Lebanese intellectuals provided much of the leadership.

In Beirut, beginning in 1876, Yaqub Sarruf and Faris Nimr established *al-Muqtaṭaf* (The Selections). Presenting regular news items on agriculture, medical sciences, industry, and education, it became an important vehicle for the dissemination of general scientific information. In 1884, the publishers moved to Cairo, where *al-Muqtaṭaf* continued to appear. In 1892, Jurgi Zeidan, another Lebanese in Cairo, began to publish the periodical, *al-Hilāl* (The Crescent), which also presented news on scientific progress. These were followed in 1898 by *al-Mashriq* (The Orient), a publication of the Université St. Joseph in Beirut, and *al-Shams* (The Sun), a periodical published in Damascus by George Matta and George Saman.

Although none of these periodicals published any original scientific work, their reports were avidly read; and some produced lively controversies. Probably the most famous controversy was caused by the publication in *al-Muqtaṭaf* of a series of articles on the theory of evolution. The author of this series was most likely Shibli Shummayyil, who graduated as a medical doctor in 1871 from the Syrian Protestant College (SPC) in Beirut. In 1875, he went to Europe where he spent most of the year acquainting himself with recent scientific discoveries. In 1882

[52] Kathleen M. Langley, *The Industrialization of Iraq* (Cambridge, Mass.: Harvard University Press, 1967), 30.

*al-Muqtaṭaf* published three unsigned articles, one on Charles Darwin and two on the theory of evolution.[53]

These were followed by the SPC commencement address in 1882 given by Edwin Lewis, who spoke of Darwin as well as of the geologist Charles Lyell in favorable terms. The immediate response of the SPC's Protestant missionary leadership was to dismiss Lewis summarily. The medical students, however, expressed their solidarity with Lewis by going on strike. When the local board of the SPC issued an ultimatum for the students to return to classes or face expulsion, most of the Protestant missionary faculty threatened to resign. In the end, most of the medical students and their professors left. Jurgi Zeidan, who later founded *al-Hilāl*, was one of the medical students to leave; Yaqub Sarruf and Faris Nimr, who, in addition to publishing *al-Muqtaṭaf*, were instructors at SPC, left for Cairo.

Shummayyil continued his writings on evolution, and the debate on the subject eventually involved Muslim and Christian theologians throughout the region. In general, however, it was a debate between amateurs and produced neither original scientific research nor technological developments. Despite lively interest and the introduction of new ideas, institutions committed to science that could provide the basis for a self-sustaining scientific community simply were not to be found.

The above mentioned activities, including the writings of Shummayyil, were mirages and had nothing to do with the social, political, and economic realities of the region. The abilities of Shummayyil, Nimr, Zeidan, and others to absorb the information about modern scientific advances were inconsequential to the region's overall development, nor did they have any influence on educational or economic policies. Nevertheless, the activities of these intellectuals have misled many an observer into believing that they were automatically translated into meaningful development.

## CONCLUSION

The Egyptian government of the early nineteenth century had ample access to foreign expertise: it established national schools, embarked on a massive program of development in agriculture and industry, built a medical school, and dispatched students to study abroad. Other Arab

[53] See *al-Muqtaṭaf* 7 (1882): 65–72 and 131–7.

governments sought to acquire technology during the same period, but none approached the scale of Egypt's accomplishments. The considerable difficulties encountered in teaching technical subjects, in erecting factories, and in executing civil works had little to do with the ability, willingness, or readiness of Egyptians to acquire scientific and technological knowledge. The major obstacles were of a systemic and institutional nature.

In what has preceded, I have sought to describe and analyze some of the systemic constraints that blocked Egypt's path to technological advancement. Its inability to accumulate technology is attributable to a variety of intrinsic factors. These may be summarized as follows.

At the top, ethnic policies discriminated against the employment of native Egyptians in senior, decision-making posts while, at the bottom, there was a crass disregard for the importance of labor in economic development. Employment and promotion were not based on merit or performance, but rather on the presumed ethnic origins and loyalty of the individual. There was no mechanism to translate the experience acquired by workers, technicians, and engineers into rational economic development. Thus, Egypt could neither set itself on a self-reliant course nor reduce its knowledge gap with Europe.

Initially, the educational system and its programs were, for the reasons discussed above, of poor quality. The prevalent arrangements in Egyptian institutions made it impossible for educational organizations to go beyond elementary levels in teaching and translating imported information. Scientific and technological activity calls for long-term state support, career structures based on merit, evolving institutional facilities, and social policies which reflect a respect for labor. The adoption of public policies based on quality naturally conflicts with ethnic favoritism. In addition, the acquisition and accumulation of technology require a considerable amount of planning and coordination. The prevailing political economy in nineteenth-century Egypt and the arbitrariness of the Pasha made such complex planning impossible. The erratic and whimsical nature of Muhammad Ali's "planning" made the systematic pursuit of technological capabilities impossible.

The extension of the irrigation system, the establishment of textile factories, the improvement of the transport systems, the construction of railways, the construction of the Suez Canal, the establishment of schools all involved the importation of foreign technology. The absence of institutional, organizational, and technological developments parallel to these imports resulted in the destruction of the traditional economy and the deepening and perpetuation of technological—and hence of economic and political—dependence. Throughout the nineteenth century, Egypt was unable to develop an institutional structure that could mobilize national expertise or effectively integrate the contributions of foreign experts. Thus, despite sending some promising students abroad for foreign study and training others in local technical schools, Egyptians failed to accumulate the engineering and technological know-how vital to national security and socioeconomic development.

This chapter demonstrates that, contrary to popular belief, no serious *external* constraints were imposed on Egypt regarding the transfer of knowledge and the acquisition of technology before its occupation in 1882. The inability to develop relevant and effective technology policies was a result of *internal* constraints that ultimately derived from Egypt's own political culture.

## APPENDIX: EUROPEAN SCIENTIFIC RESEARCH IN THE ARAB WORLD

European scientific research work in the Arab world was motivated both by imperial designs and by scholarly interest. This research was an extension of European science, and the results were rarely (if ever) utilized directly by Arab planners or governments.

As early as 1749, Frederick Hasselquist, a Swede and a student of Charles Linnaeus, had visited the Middle East to collect information on the natural history of the region. The *Description de l'Égypte*, initiated in 1798, was a monumental project. Later French governments undertook similar scientific studies in Algeria.

During the nineteenth century there was considerable research interest in the region. In 1906, C. Davies Sherborn compiled a *Bibliography of Scientific and Technical Literature Relating to Egypt, 1800–1900*[54] that included some three thousand entries, and even this enumeration is incomplete. Still, the bibliography demonstrates the remarkable scale of research on the region.

[54] Compiled for the Survey Department of the Egyptian Ministry of Finance, this bibliography was published in Cairo in 1910 by the National Printing Department.

Even when scientific research was actually conducted in Egypt, one has the impression that there was little interchange with the mainstream of local intellectual and technological activity. For example, the important medical research of W. Griesinger and T. Bilharz, though conducted at the Qaṣr al-ʿAinī Medical School, appear to have had little influence in Egypt during the nineteenth century.

Hekekyan undertook extensive research of an archaeological and astro-geological nature between 1851 and 1863; from 1851 to 1856, the research continued in collaboration with the British Royal Society and under the patronage of the viceroy of Egypt.[55] In 1863, Hekekyan published the results of his research: *Chronology of the Siriadic Monuments, Demonstrating that the Egyptian Dynasties of Manetho are Records of Astrogeological Nile Observations*.[56]

An illustration of how the relationship between European research activity in the region and national institutions functioned is provided by F. J. Jousseaume in a paper he presented in March 1893 to the Institut d'Égypte, promoting the establishment of a scientific research station to study the Gulf of Aden and the Red Sea.[57] He spoke of his five years on the Red Sea investigating flora and fauna. He also referred to the research of Savigny, Ehremberg, and Walter Innes. Not one of these authors was Egyptian or Arab. Jousseaume argued for the establishment of a zoological and geological institute to be financed by Egypt. In return for Egyptian financing and hospitality to "the most distinguished children of the European nations," Egypt would receive "modern aspirations, ideas, and knowledge."

55 Ahmad Abdel-Rahim Mustafa, "The Hekekyan Papers," in *Political and Social Change in Modern Egypt*, ed. P. M. Holt (London: Oxford University Press, 1968), 68–75.

56 Privately printed, London, 1863.

57 F. Jousseaume, "Avantages que présenterait en Égypte l'établissement d'une station scientifique," *Bulletin de l'Institut Égyptien*, Séance du 5 mars, 1893, Annexe No. 3 (part 4), 157–69.

# 3

# An Islamic Political Formula in Transformation: Islam, Identity, and Nationalism in the History of the Volga Tatars

ŞERIF MARDIN

## INTRODUCTION

Any attempt to draw together the disparate elements of a historical process demands preliminary orientation. The following chapter is based on the notion that within cultures there are certain inner driving forces that, while characterizing them, also serve to reproduce them. Max Weber's approach to such paradigmatic elements was to select what he considered to be representations of these underlying core propellants in the religious traditions he studied, a method he called "ideal typical."[1]

A characteristic of the ideal typical method is that while the structuring elements delimited by the ideal type have some permanence, this permanence is established in relation to a wider surrounding social constellation that itself changes with time. Yet the ideal type retains its force as an invariant prime constituent throughout this progression, thus shedding light on situations that, otherwise, would be impossible to project across time for purposes of comparison. In a narrower context, Weber's method can be used to bring out some distinguishing and long-lasting characteristics of the relation between citizen and state in Islamic cultures. This venue allows me to examine and isolate what I consider a dynamic element in Islamic politics. I shall call this the dyadic formula of Islamic politics. This element is dyadic because it relies on two main players in the political process: the doctors of Islamic Law (*ʿulamāʾ*, sing. *ʿālim*) and the political hegemony represented by the sultan as well as the vizier and the military forces, these being the two poles around which the system is structured. These players are fundamental to the system,

[1] For the ideal-typical method see Anthony Giddens, *Capitalism and Modern Social Theory* (Cambridge: Cambridge University Press, 1992), 142ff.

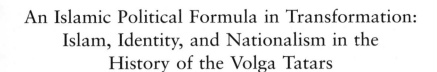

yet their influence varies with changes in the nature of the ambient constellation of social forces in which the ideal typical elements are embedded. For most of Islamic history, the dyadic system has been on the back burner and has functioned more as a dream of just rule. But not always. In this chapter, I attempt to trace its place in Islamic political life, taking as a foil the careers of two political actors in nineteenth-century Russian Asia. Although this is a circumscribed geographical domain, I believe that the interrelations between the ideal-typical core and the shifting social constellation that I try to bring out can illuminate other events in different Islamic contexts. This would include Islamic "fundamentalism" in the present.[2]

It is, of course, true that the dyadic model is only one of at least two main political systems functioning in Islamic societies. The other system, called sultanism, is based on sultanic fiat and tends to deprive the *ʿulamāʾ* of much of their autonomy. This is the system we find most frequently in Islamic history. Still, I am more interested here in the latent element of political contestation in the dyadic system as well as in the ethical discourse it promotes and, finally, in its ability to double as an anchor for individual identity. Anthony Giddens has indicated that under the conditions of modernity the formation of individual self-identity becomes a central concern in an entirely new manner and that this holds for all societies in the "global village" today.[3] Thus, as Islamic society becomes more modern, the dyadic formula becomes increasingly important for our understanding of it. Although sultanism generally prevailed in the history of Islamic societies, the binary system based on the autonomous role of the *ʿulamāʾ* and their support of concerned citizens has always survived as the latent and Islamically fully legitimate system ready to take over wherever the *ʿālim*'s leadership of the community became necessary and possible. The present is such a period when sultanism, which minimizes the individual responsibility of the common citizen, is becoming less relevant.

I shall try to demonstrate three types of situations in which we may follow the workings of the dyadic formula. First, we find the dyadic formula arising out of opposition to the Czar of all the Russias, a situation symbolized as a war waged against the unjust rule of pharaoh. Second, it gains a new focus during the relative "secularization" of the Islamic thrust, due to the appearance of a new type of "free-floating"

[2] For Islamic fundamentalism, see the following articles in *Fundamentalisms Observed*, ed. Martin E. Marty and Scott Appleby (Chicago: University of Chicago Press, 1991): John D. Voll, "Fundamentalism in the Sunni Arab World," 345–402; Abdulaziz A. Sachedina, "Activist Shi'ism in Iran, Iraq, and Lebanon," 403–50; and Mumtaz Ahmad, "Fundamentalism in South Asia: The Jamaat Islami and the Tablighi Jamaat," 457–520.

[3] See below, pp. 87–8 and n. 91.

intellectual.[4] Third, though I do not examine it in detail here, the dyadic formula becomes prominent during the revitalization of Islam in the twentieth century.

Let me now describe the character I impute to the dyadic formula of Islamic politics. I consider the Quranic source of this formula to be the primal ethical foundation of Islam. Much has been said about this element and about the relation of its ontology to the political system of Islam; in my case, I conceive of the ethical foundations of Islamic politics not as a vague omnipresence brooding in the sky, but as anchored in social structure.

We may begin with one of the deepest expressions of Islamic ontology, namely the Quranic command to establish the good and combat evil. This injunction is associated with a view of the good society and the politics used to bring it to life as consisting in the very fulfillment of the ethical Quranic commands. Such a foundation, in turn, sets the role of the *ʿulamāʾ* as primary political actors who assume a position as guardians of the morality and society of Islam and come to embody the role of political contestation. From this foundation follows a theory of political legitimation based on the role of the *ʿulamāʾ*, they being held responsible for the fulfillment of their role. Notice that the binary system, insofar as it is also a system of personal ethics incumbent upon individuals, has in its larger dimension a role in the building of the individual's place in society. The entire system is framed by a conception of time as sacred history. It is reproduced through institutions that carry this message of ethical responsibility as well as by a *habitus* in the sense in which Bourdieu uses this term.[5] Another element of importance for us is the extent to which the *ʿālim* plays a role in the everyday life of the Muslim simply in the way he performs the characteristic mosque sermon, and through intimacy of contact with the individual Muslim at the level of his local residential quarter or neighborhood (*mahalle*)—that is, a quarter of town with some degree of homogeneity. Altogether, then, the binary system also sets into motion a collaboration between the *ʿālim* and the individual citizen framed by Islamic ethics. This collaboration may take a number of forms, from the strongest—participation in rebellion—to the weakest—grudging acceptance of a regime.

[4] See Karl Mannheim, *Ideology and Utopia* (London: Routledge and Kegan Paul, 1936).

[5] See Pierre Bourdieu, *Outline of a Theory of Practice*, trans. R. Nice (Cambridge: Cambridge University Press, 1977). George Ritzer has described *habitus* as "'mental or cognitive structures' through which people deal with the social world. People are endowed with a series of internalized schemes through which they perceive, understand, appreciate and evaluate the social world." See George Ritzer, *Contemporary Sociological Theory* (New York: McGraw Hill, 1992), 438.

For reasons I try to explain below, the so-called free-floating intellectual who appears on the Islamic scene in the twentieth century in a number of countries does not fit into this picture. This stage—the modern, unanticipated reevaluation of Islam—is due to the simultaneous emergence of an individualistic dimension to Muslim life in the modern world and the political needs of a socially mobilized population, both of which conspire to bring back the binary, ethically based model, that, according to the rules of positivist secularism, should have been relegated to the dustbin of history.

In the most general sense, my approach to the material that follows is that ideas (and ideal-typical constructions) are good for understanding, but only if they are guides to an understanding of social structure. Finally, I would like to claim that I am bringing back an element neglected in the social sciences until recent times, that of collective memory and its combinations and permutations.

## ISLAMIC REVITALIZATION BEFORE THE NINETEENTH CENTURY

No one has described the revival of an Islamic thrust in the modern history of the Islamic world with more understanding than the late Fazlur Rahman, and I shall begin my story by using some of his insights on this subject.[6]

In the years during which Europe was experiencing the Renaissance, it had begun simultaneously to impinge on the Muslim cultural area that, as if energized by this confrontation, began to show signs of a new vitality taking a number of different forms related to the socio-cultural characteristics of each setting in which it appeared. One dimension of this revival was due to the exacerbation of an internal tension of Islam manifest from its earliest history—namely, that between the goal of a community of believers responsible for implementing God's commands and the contrasting exercise of sultanic authority modeled on a much earlier Middle Eastern tradition of kingship.[7] Islam's most common political theory modified this earlier theory of kingship and still gave the ruler a

[6] Fazlur Rahman, *Islam*, 2d ed. (Chicago: University of Chicago Press, 1979).

[7] For the Middle Eastern tradition of kingship in the role of *Sharīʿa* law, see Erwin I. J. Rosenthal, "The Role of the State in Islamic Theory and Medieval Practice," *Der Islam* 30 (1973): 1–29; A. K. S. Lambton, "Islamic Political Thought" in Joseph Schacht and C. E. Bosworth, eds., *The Legacy of Islam*, 2d ed. (Oxford: Clarendon Press, 1974), 409–24; and Halil Inalcik, *The Ottoman Empire: The Classical Age 1300–1600*, trans. N. Itzkowitz and Colin Imber (London: Weidenfeld and Nicholson, 1973).

legitimacy difficult to challenge. At the same time, however, Islam also provided theological arguments that could combat monarchic absolutism. The idealistic, platonic interface of these two theories was a late development of Islam's political thought, but was more of a rhetorical device than a dynamic element of Islamic politics.[8] The tension between the Islamic moral and political community was similar to that between the imperatives of rule and religion in medieval Christianity. The difference between the Christian tradition of rendering unto Caesar and the Islamic tradition of embracing Caesar seems to have been exaggerated compared to another development that had a much greater impact and led to a bifurcation between the socio-political system of Islam and that of Christianity. This development was Western capitalism and its peculiar incorporation of a set of dynamic, interactive relationships between the state and the middle classes regulated by the market mechanism and economic expansion. In Islam, by contrast, the tension between moral imperatives and the imperatives of rule continued to operate for a time in a pre-capitalist socioeconomic setting, where the moral and—as postulated above—social imperatives had a greater chance of steering society. These Islamic moral imperatives appeared as religious counsels aiming to transcend magical practices, as the promotion of the interests of the downtrodden, as the elaboration of identity frames transcending those of kinship, and as the founding of educational institutions forging a trans-Islamic literate culture; and sometimes they took the form of social movements questioning the legitimacy of political power. In retrospect, it seems as if the Islamic *telos* that I seek to describe in these pages was tending toward the triumph of Islamic ethical populism as the final resolution of the internal tension between the good society and the autocratic ruler.

I have elaborated Fazlur Rahman's thesis that the revitalization of Islam begun in the eighteenth century was due to the Muslim theologians' consciousness of the moral atrophy of Islam.[9] It is truly an invaluable explanation of a key substantive element in the makeup of Islamic civilization. The availability of such arguments to Muslims of all times is one of the elementary parameters necessary to achieve an understanding of Islamic history. Yet Fazlur Rahman's important and original voice fails to retrieve the variety of social settings in which the ethical substratum operated.

[8] For this theory, see my *Genesis of Young Ottoman Thought* (Princeton: Princeton University Press, 1962).
[9] Rahman, *Islam*, 213.

In North and Central Africa, where all the dimensions of Islam as an ethical populist force could operate simultaneously, Islam had been on the move since the twelfth century. Proselytizing preachers, populist agitators, literati with educational ideals, and empire-builders who harkened to these forces only to betray them later were the substance of this alternation of the ideal and the real.[10] Similar movements may be traced much later in the Ottoman and Safavid empires, the social structure of each providing the historical stage on which the Islamic passion play was performed. In both cases, the practice of kingship had to conciliate tribal traditions as well as clerics.

The earliest example of a new dimension in the general Islamic tension between the desirable and the real appeared when Islam came up against an alien culture, that of Hinduism, which it was unable to assimilate.[11] Both in this case and in the later confrontation of Islam with Western colonial penetration, the Islamic Sufi orders achieved a new effectiveness due to their potential for mobilization. The confrontation with Hinduism began under the Mogul ruler, Akbar (1556–1605), whose rule was considered morally lax by Orthodox Muslims. This was the beginning of the ascendancy of the Sufi orders in promoting religious, social, and eventually political reform. Similar activist movements were to appear throughout the Islamic world in the eighteenth and nineteenth centuries, some the direct descendants of the India-based social movements.

## MUJADDIDI REVIVAL

Hinduism threatened to rob Islam of its moral imperative—an imperative that, as Fazlur Rahman insists, was not only a catalogue of ethics, but a map for social action. It was a Muslim *ʿālim* by the name of Aḥmad al-Sirhindī (d. 1624) who started the fray. Sirhindī fought what he considered to be the betrayal of Islamic values by entering, at the age of forty, into the "mystical" Nakshbandī order.[12] This order had always

[10] For developments in Africa, see I. M. Lewis, "Introduction," in I. M. Lewis, ed., *Islam in Tropical Africa*, 2d ed. (Bloomington: International African and Indiana University Press, 1980), 1–75; R. G. Jenkins, "The Evolution of Religious Brotherhoods in North and Northwest Africa," in *Studies in West African Islamic History* (London: Cass, 1979), 40–65; and B. G. Martin, *Muslim Brotherhoods in Nineteenth-Century Africa* (Cambridge: Cambridge University Press, 1976).

[11] See Johann Friedmann, *Shaykh Aḥmad Sirhindī: An Outline of His Thought and a Study of His Image in the Eyes of Posterity* (Montreal: McGill Queens University Press, 1971); see also Sh. Inayatullah, "Aḥmad Sirhindī" in *Encyclopedia of Islam*, 2d ed., vol. 1, 297–8.

[12] See Hamid Algar and K. A. Nizami, "Nakshbandiyya," in *Encyclopedia of Islam*, 2d ed., vol. 7, 934–9.

been on the front line of the defense of orthodoxy and populist values, although it had remained so by exploiting friendly relations with the great and the powerful. Sirhindī used the networks already established by the order to mobilize opinion against what he considered the magical garden of Muslim mysticism, a dangerous area of overlap with the Hindu magical garden. His spiritual successors continued the task of mobilizing Muslims, and the extraordinary dimensions of this inheritance are only gradually becoming clear today. It established a climate of Muslim devotion and political action known as renewalist (*mujaddidī*) Nakshbandism that later produced a series of brilliant revitalizers of Islam. This movement shaped the history of Muslim India in the nineteenth century by inspiring socio-political reformers like Shāh Wālī Allāh,[13] promoting resistance against the British occupation of India as in the Sepoy rebellion, and establishing educational institutions such as the Deoband Reform College (1867) meant to shift the energies of Islam into more peaceful educational pursuits after its defeat by the British. In its later anti-colonial form, renewalist Nakshbandism also inspired Muslim clerics in the Middle East, where the confrontation with the West had assumed a cultural dimension due to the weakness of the Ottoman Empire and its gradual adoption of Western social and political ideas. Mawlanā Khālid "Baghdādī,"[14] who came to India in 1808 to study with one of the students of Sirhindī, took up the torch of renewalism and brought it to Iraq, Syria, and Eastern Anatolia at about the time when the influence of the West was beginning to acquire clearer outlines. Parallel movements aiming to mobilize Muslim masses during the late eighteenth century appear throughout the Islamic world.[15] Once again, we do not know whether this mobilizing activism, which promoted the twin aims of greater orthodoxy and resistance to heathen cultures (such as the West), was due to an emerging field of action for the mobilizers or for the mobilized. Whether it showed that *ṭarīqa* leaders had acquired new powers as popular leaders, or whether the potential for mass action had increased, we can think of it as a wager along the lines of "let us bring your masses to a deeper understanding of the operational code of Islam, and you shall see how we will breathe new fire into Islamic civilization."

[13] For Shāh Wālī Allāh, see J. M. S. Baljon, *Religion and Thought of Shāh Wālī Allāh Dihlawī*, 1703–1762 (Leiden: E. J. Brill, 1986).

[14] On Mawlanā Khālid, see Albert Hourani, "Shaykh Khalid and the Nakshbandi Order," in *Islamic Philosophy and the Classical Tradition*, ed. S. M. Stern, Albert Hourani, and Vivian Brown (Columbia: University of South Carolina Press, 1972), 89–103.

[15] For a picture of the geographical extent of these movements, see Ira M. Lapidus, *A History of Islamic Societies* (Cambridge: Cambridge University Press, 1988), 938–9.

What we know is that the Nakshbandī followers of Mawlanā Khālid were premier proselytizers throughout Asia, particularly in Russian Asia from the late eighteenth century onward and that a foundation of Nakshbandī activism antedated even their work.

## THE ARGUMENT

As in many other studies of modern Islam, the history of the Russian occupation of Muslim Asia and the reaction of its denizens is constructed and construed as a scenario in which two straw men are set against one another, one representing Muslim enlightened progress, the other Muslim religious reaction. This image of cultural pugilism relies on the polar opposites of *Jadīdism*[16] (that is, modernism: good, progressive, secular) and *Qadīmism* ("old"ism: bad, reactionary, fundamentalist). In reality, the setting is much more complex, one of its complexities consisting in an overlap of the purportedly antagonistic attitudes. Only when one can liberate oneself from the icon of a progressive, reforming West attempting to clear away the cobwebs of Muslim scholasticism can one achieve a deeper understanding of the dynamics of the modern history of the Muslims of the Russian Empire. Problems of interpretation arise more because of this overlap than because of the divergences between old and new.

In fact, the actual rift between these two components—*Jadīd* and *Qadīm*—arises late in the nineteenth century, which means late in the history of Islamic revitalization among the Muslims of Russia. This dividing line is partly due to the instructional methods adopted by the generation of Russian Muslim reformers of the 1890s, who in growing numbers set out to provide in their new schools practical instruction in "science." It was also due to the introduction of a new time dimension that intervened in the daily life of the *Jadīd*s, a time dimension that was no longer one of beginnings and endings, of the creation and the last judgment, of the "eternal return," but one of the Tatars' recollection of their own history.

I shall try to describe the many strands that enter into this process of gradual differentiation by retracing two access roads to the phenomenon of Tatar revitalization, concentrating on the biographies of two individ-

[16] For *Jadīdism*, see B. Spuler, "Djadīd," in *Encyclopedia of Islam*, 2d ed., vol. 2, 366. For an even more localized description of these two strands as contrasting, see Yahya G. Abdullin, "Islam in the History of the Volga Kama Bulgars and Tatar," *Central Asian Survey* 9, no. 2 (1990): 9.

uals, each of whom represents one of these venues: Abdurreshid Ibrahim (1857[?]–1944),[17] Qadi of Orenburg and a political agitator, and Zeki Velidi Togan (1891–1970), a modern intellectual, historian of Central Asia, president of the Bashkurt Republic between 1918 and 1920, and an exile at the time of his death.[18]

## THE MUSLIMS OF RUSSIA

Russia had wrested the town of Kazan from the successors of the Golden Horde in 1552. The ensuing years were a time of collective suffering among the overwhelmingly Tatar local population. There were five insurrections against the Russians during the seventeenth century and four during the eighteenth century.[19] Eventually, the noose around the Tatar neck was loosened. The Tatars became partners of the Russians in their commercial relations with Muslim Central Asia. The Tatars themselves began to industrialize, and a wealthy Tatar bourgeoisie arose.[20] The Islamic tradition of learning among Russian Muslims was thereby afforded new means of development. From the mid–eighteenth century onward, young Tatars were sent to Bukhara, the most prestigious center of Islamic learning in Central Asia. Graduates returned to establish a network of religious schools in the villages of Kazan. In time, these teachers abandoned Bukhara, which they now considered passé, and went to study in Istanbul, Cairo, and Medina.[21] A Tatar intellectual renaissance began to take shape.[22] While the complex origins of the Tatar cultural

[17] I have used the biography of Abdurreshid Ibrahim drawn from his memoirs in Mustafa Uzun's "Abdurreshid Ibrahim (1857–1944)," *Türkiye Diyanet Vakfi Islam Ansiklopedisi*, Fasikül 7 (May 1989): 297–8; see also Mahmud Tahir, "Abdurreşid Ibrahim, 1857–1944," *Central Asian Survey* 7 (1988): 135–40.

[18] For Zeki Velidi [Togan], see his autobiography, *Hatiralar* (Istanbul: Tan Matbasi, 1969), which I use extensively here.

[19] For these rebellions, see Nadir Devlet, *Rusya Türkleri'nin Milli Mücadele Tarihi* (Ankara: Türk Kültürünü Araştirma Enstitüsü, 1985), 3.

[20] For Tatar history in the eighteenth century, an early source is Alexandre Bennigsen and Chantal Quelquejay, *Les Mouvements nationaux chez les Musulmans de Russie: Le Sultangalievism au Tatarstan* (Paris and The Hague: Mouton, 1960), 30–1; see also Devlet, *Rusya Türkleri'nin*, 7.

[21] See Devlet, *Rusya Türkleri'nin*, 9.

[22] The first works printed in Tatar for distribution were produced under the aegis of local Russian educational institutions. Between 1801 and 1829, the total number of such volumes was 280,000. The first private printing plant was established in 1841; between 1841 and 1850, eighty-eight titles appeared in print. Between 1853 and 1859, 82,300 Qurans, 165,900 *Heftiyek* (a religious primer), and 77,500 *Imām Sharṭī* (another primer) were produced. By the middle of the nineteenth century, about two million books a year were being printed in Kazan. By 1897 literacy among the Tatars was 20.4 percent, compared with only 18.3 percent among the Russians. See Devlet, *Rusya Türkleri'nin*, 14; and Bennigsen and Quelquejay, *Les Mouvements nationaux*, 40.

revival are difficult to untangle, there is no doubt that one of them was the penetration of renewalist influences in the region.

Among the Tatars and the Bashkurt of the Volga-Ural region, the Nakshbandī order had a prestigious position dating back to the fifteenth century. The more prominent Nakshbandī renewalist missionaries emerged during the eighteenth century. The movement was renewalist not only in the sense of taking its inspiration from the original sources of Islam and from the *mujaddidī* revival, but also now in the added dimension of promoting new schools. Among them, one may count ʿAbd al-Karīm Baltay (d. ca. 1757), the Tatar disciple of Shaykh Muḥammad Ḥabīb Allāh Balkhī, who was himself a Bukharan successor of Sirhindī's son Khawāja Muḥammad Maʿṣūm. Baltay propagated the Nakshbandī renewalist path in the town of Said (Qargaly).[23]

Already in 1771 and 1781, new-style religious schools were being established in Kazan.[24] ʿAbd al-Nāṣir Qursavī (1771–1812) was a leading light in this circle; he criticized the immobility of Bukharan religious schools in his *Irshad ül-Ibad* (Guidance for God's servants).[25] Shahabeddin Merjanī (1818–89), another *ʿālim* and mosque Imām, was the author of the first book of Tatar history written at the time, the *Mustefad ul-Ahbar fi Ahval-i Kazan ve Bulgar* (Account of the reports about the conditions of Kazan and Bulgar), the "first attempt to present the Volga Tatars with their own history in their own language."[26] Merjanī had established relations with both the teachers of the Russian Gymnasium and the professors of Kazan University, having taught for nine years in the Tatar-Russian normal school. His *Wefayat al-Aslaf wa Tahivat al-Ahlaf* (The legacy of the ancestors and the response of their descendants), the first version of which was published in 1883, was a critique of the stagnation of Muslim education.[27] The intersections between these later forms of Tatar reform and the Salafi movements of Jamāl al-Dīn al-Afghānī and Muḥammad ʿAbduh have been underlined by Rorlich.[28]

[23] See Hamid Algar, "Shaykh Zaynullah Rasulev: The Last Great Nakshbandī Shaykh of the Volga-Urals Region," in *Muslims of Central Asia: Expressions of Identity and Change*, ed. Jo Ann Gross (Durham, N.C.: Duke University Press, 1992), 113.

[24] Devlet, *Rusya Türkleri'nin*, 9. One also sees a parallel development of *madrasa*-educated Turkmen south of the region we have surveyed, the latter taking a leadership role during the early eighteenth century in developing a completely new Turkmen literary language. See Walter Feldman, "Interpreting the Poetry of Mäkhtumquli," in Gross, ed., *Muslims of Central Asia*, 167ff.

[25] For Qursavī, see Mehmed Tahir, "Abdunnasir Kursavi, 1776–1812," *Central Asian Survey* 8 (1929): 155–8; Devlet, *Rusya Türkleri'nin*, 10.

[26] Azade-Ayşe Rorlich, *The Volga Tatars* (Stanford, Calif.: Hoover Institute Press, 1986), 51. See also Devlet, *Rusya Türkleri'nin*, 10.

[27] Rorlich, *The Volga Tatars*, 52.

[28] Ibid., 54. For the Salafī movement, see Albert Hourani, *Arabic Thought in the Liberal Age 1798–1939* (Cambridge: Cambridge University Press, 1983), 103–92.

An earlier step in the new historiography had been the work of Ibrahim Half (1778–1829) who, in 1819, published his *Ahval-i Cingiz Han ve Aksak Timur* (Relations of Jengiz Khan and Timur the Lame).[29] Half's historicism should come as no surprise, since he was an employee of the Russian state. Nonetheless, it was in striking contrast with the more traditional view still found in an Ottoman document of 1852 that assumed the perspective of sacred history and purported to derive the term "Turk" from Turk, son of Japhet son of Noah.[30] A follower of the renewalist Nakshbandī tradition was Shaykh Zaynullāh Rasulev (b. 1833), who also got into hot water with Bukhara authorities when his independent stand came to be considered heretical. He was the spiritual guide of the father of our second modernist, Zeki Velidi: "It was thanks to Zaynullah that Troisk now became a principal center of learning for the Russian Empire as well as a base for the further diffusion of the Khalidī Nakshbandī order."[31]

Hüseyin Fevzihanī (1828–1866), a student of Merjanī, became a lecturer in Oriental languages at Kazan University. He is known for his attempts to reform religious school teaching and for a project that he prepared with Merjanī on the teaching in the religious schools and also the establishment of a Kazan-Tatar University, the creation of which was being considered.[32] Kayyum Nasirī (1824–1902) contributed textbooks on literature, ethnography, arithmetic, physics, and geography, in addition to writing a grammar of the Tatar vernacular that was replacing the Chagatay literary idiom.[33] Many of those engaged in the revitalization of the educational curriculum of the Tatars were the same persons who wrote the first "native" histories of the Tatar past. One branch of renewalist activism took millenarian dimensions and briefly, after the Russian Revolution, a socialist cast.[34]

The new schools established under the influence of the renewalist Khālidī[35] Nakshbandī order dismissed the scholasticism of Bukhara and targeted their own program of instruction toward a clearer understand-

[29] Ibrahim Half's grandfather, Saït Half (d. 1758), had worked as an interpreter for the Russian government, as had his father; see Devlet, *Rusya Türkleri'nin*, 11.

[30] See Jean-Louis Bacqué Grammont, "Turan: Une description du Khanat de Khokand vers 1852 d'après un document Ottoman," *Cahiers du Monde Russe et Soviétique* 13 (April–June 1972): 194.

[31] See Algar, "Shaykh Zaynullah Rasulev," 121.

[32] For Fevzihanī, see Devlet, *Rusya Türkleri'nin*, 12.

[33] For Kayyum Nasirī, see Chantal Lemercier-Quelquejay, "Un Réformateur Tatar au XIXe Siècle, ʿAbdul Qajjum Al-Nasyri," *Cahiers du Monde Russe et Soviétique* 4 (January–June 1963): 117–42. In the Tatar region, the first Tatar grammar had been printed in 1778 to meet a demand for translation in Russian-Tatar.

[34] See Chantal Quelquejay, "Le 'Vaisisme' à Kazan," *Die Welt des Islams* 6 (1959): 91–112.

[35] Or Halidi, i.e., followers of Shaykh Khālid.

ing of the essentials of Islam. Whether or not promoters of these schools showed the delayed influence of contacts with Russian programs of education is an unresolved issue, but the point is that they attempted to set up modern religious schools aimed at revitalizing Islam. From the 1860s onward, the Russians re-embarked on a policy aimed at the cultural assimilation of the Tatars, and the attitudes of both personalities I study here are better understood as partial reactions against this policy.[36]

One step toward a more secular worldview among these producers and users of printed books was that the *ʿulamāʾ*, the promoters of the Tatar "renaissance," were thereby moving away from the oral character of their classical discourse in the Friday sermon in the mosque. This meant a real shift, a distantiation[37] in their communication with the "common folk," since the world of books was not accessible to the illiterate. Zeki Velidi, our second Muslim activist of the Volga-Ural region, took another step in this direction by attempting to join the Republic of Letters that post-Renaissance European intellectuals had created for themselves and that the Russian intelligentsia were replicating with a vengeance. The emerging historicism among the Tatars was no doubt in part the consequence of Russian Orientalist research carried out at the University of Kazan. Russians wanted to learn about Tatars, and Tatars began to see themselves as part of Tatar history. For an *ʿālim* like our first "revitalizer," Abdurreshid Ibrahim, however, the emphasis was still on the Muslims of Russia and eventually on the Muslims of the world.

The picture is complicated at this point by the influences of the Nakshbandī order in the Ottoman Empire and its extension into Russian Asia. We know that already in the sixteenth century the Nakshbandī Shaykh Aḥmad Bukharī (d. 1516), i.e., "from Bukhara," was a well-known figure in Ottoman governmental circles.[38] A number of Nakshband lodges in the Ottoman Empire served a Central Asian clientele. In 1784, there were four Özbek Tekke or Sufi lodges in Istanbul, and similar lodge centers for the use of visitors from Turkestan were available in Anato-

[36] This theme is extensively treated by Rorlich in *The Volga Tatars*, 44–7.

[37] For distantiation, see Anthony Giddens, *The Constitution of Society* (Berkeley: University of California Press, 1986), 203.

[38] See Cornell H. Fleischer, *Bureaucrat and Intellectual in the Ottoman Empire: The Historian Mustafa Ali (1561–1600)* (Princeton: Princeton University Press, 1986), 17. I have treated the theme of Nakshbandī influence in "The Nakshbandi Order in Turkish History," in *Islam and Modern Turkey*, ed. Richard Tapper (London: I. B. Tauris, 1991), 121–42.

lia.[39] The Sultantepe lodge, which was of renewalist persuasion, had been established by Sultan Mustafa III (1757–1774).[40] His contemporary, the great Islamic/Ottoman scholar Müstakimzāde Saadeddin Efendi, was also a renewalist.[41] It has been established that there were a number of reciprocal demands for assistance between Bukhara and the Sultan in the years 1719, 1786, and 1819.[42] Nevertheless, all of this evidence for the maintenance of links between the Ottoman Empire, Central Asia, and possibly the Nakshbandī centers in Russian Asia must be placed beside the Ottomans' suspicious and dismissive attitude towards Nakshbandī "fundamentalism,"[43] suspicions well justified, given that the Khālidī renewalists twice attempted a political "coup" in the capital, in 1820 and 1859.[44] Only later, at the time of the Crimean War, did the Ottomans begin to see the possibilities of using Nakshbandīs for their own ends.[45] Privately, however, the Nakshbandi in Istanbul seem to have had no compunction about penetrating Russian Asia.[46]

Altogether, then, in the eighteenth century, the Volga-Ural Tatar region and Western-Central Asia seem to have become part of a network of influences stemming from the new activism of Sufi orders and from early modernization in Russia and the Ottoman Empire. This primarily renewalist development within the Nakshbandī order was hardly a reactionary movement. Islamic modernization or renewalism was, at first, fully integrated; only in a second stage did it begin to differentiate into

[39] See Mümtaz'er Türköne, "Siyasi Ideoloji Olarak Islamcílíğín Doğuşu, 1867–1876," doctoral diss., University of Ankara, 1990, 110. His information was based on Atilla Çetin, "Istanbul'da Tekke, Zaviye ve Hangâhlar Hakkínda (1784) Tarihli Önemli bir Vesika," *Vakíflar Dergisi*, no. 13 (1981); and Halim Baki Kunter, "Tarsus'taki Türkistan Zaviyelerinin Vakfiyeleri," *Vakíflar Dergisi* (Istanbul, 1985).

[40] See Grace Martin Smith, "The Uzbek Tekkes of Istanbul," *Der Islam* 57 (1980): 131.

[41] For this scholar, see B. Kellner-Heinkele, "Müstakim-zâde" in *Encyclopedia of Islam*, 2d ed., vol. 7, 724–5.

[42] See Azmi Özcan, *Pan-Islamism, Osmanli Devleti, Hindistan Müslümanlarí ve Ingiltere (1877–1914)* (Istanbul: ISAM, 1992), 39–41.

[43] See Alexandre Bennigsen, "Un Mouvement populaire au Caucase au XVIIIe Siècle," *Cahiers du Monde Russe et Soviétique* 5 (April–June 1964): 159–205. The Ottomans were extremely wary of the anarchistic/millenarian dimension that Nakshbandī activities, such as those of Shaykh Mansur of Daghistan, could assume. See Ibrahim Yüksel, "Çarlík Rusyasínín Azerbaycan'í Istilasí ve Osmanli Devleti'nin Tutumu," in *Kafkas Araştírmalarí* 1, eds. Mehmed Saray et al. (Istanbul: Acar, 1988), 38.

[44] See Butrus Abu Manneh, "The Nakshbandiyya-Mujaddidiya in the Ottoman Lands in the Early 19th Century," *Die Welt des Islams* 22 (1982): 1–36.

[45] See Mustafa Budak, "1853–1856 Kírím Harbi Başlarínda Doğu Anadolu-Kafkas Cephesi ve Şeyh Şamil," in *Kafkas Araştírmalarí* 1, 52–69.

[46] On the Nakshbandī order's penetration of Asia, through the work of nineteenth-century Nakshbandis, see Irfan Gündüz, *Gümüşhanevi Ahmed Ziyaüddin* (Istanbul: Seha Neşriyat, 1984); and W. E. D. Allen and Paul Muratoff, *Caucasian Battlefields* (Cambridge: Cambridge University Press, 1953), 48–53.

religious and ideological, nationalist streams. Here I want to dwell on this early polymorphism and some of the processes leading to later differentiation.

## ABDURRESHID IBRAHIM: POLITICAL FIREBRAND

Although Abdurreshid Ibrahim was born in Siberia in the town of Tara, his family came originally from Bukhara. He studied in one of the premier religious schools of Kazan, the Kishkar *medrese*. In 1878, upon his release from imprisonment by Tsarist authorities for subversive activities, he decided to flee to Turkey. There he established contacts with leading Ottoman intellectuals. He may have been alerted to the support he would find among the intellectuals of the Ottoman capital by the officially sponsored voyage to Central Asia (1868) of Shaykh Süleyman Efendi, a Nakshbandī of the Özbek Tekke in Istanbul.[47] But other, more direct links with the Nakshbandī seem to have existed. There are, for example, his contacts in the Ottoman capital with Shahabeddin Merjanī.[48]

His next step was to go on to Medina where he found a group of Central Asian exiles who shared his distress with Russian rule. Here he made the first interesting departure from the classical Islamic moralistic line and embarked upon what may be described as the "Pan-Islamization" of his concerns. He concluded that Muslims were still weak because, as he expressed it, they did not "share a language."[49] In Medina the international Nakshbandī connection can also be followed. He returned to Istanbul in 1884 where he met a group of Ottoman statesmen who supported his incipient Pan-Islamism. Encouraged by two wealthy Tatars, he went back to Russia and established his own "new method" (*usul-u jadid*) religious school in Tara near Omsk a few years later.

His first publication, *Liva ül-Hamd* (The banner of praise), which he had printed in Istanbul (1885), was aimed at having Russian Muslims emigrate to Turkey; it appears to have been an early version of the clas-

[47] Türköne, "Siyasi Ideoloji Olarak Islamcílíğín Doğuşu, 1867–1876," 113, esp. n. 40. Shaykh Süleyman Efendi is an important contributor to the study of Turkic languages who is also considered a promoter of Turkism. For the involvement of the Özbek Tekke in the rise of language studies, see David Kushner, *The Rise of Turkish Nationalism 1876–1908* (London: Cass, 1977), 13, 60.

[48] See the comprehensive biographies in "Abdurreşid Ibrahim (1)," *Toplumsal Tarih*, July 1996: 6–27, esp. p. 8, with contributions of Nadir Özbek, Ismail Türkoğlu, Selçuk Esenbel, and Hayrettin Kaya.

[49] Ibid.

sical *Hijra* strategy later to reemerge among Egyptian fundamentalists, but a more activist stance was to emerge gradually.[50] The same year he led a group of students to Medina and secured their entrance in educational institutions. In 1892, he was appointed by the Russian government to the Orenburg Spiritual Assembly, the official body for Islam, but resigned because of a conflict with the Mufti. Two or three years later, he returned to Turkey where he published a brochure, *Çulpan Yıldızı* (The Northern Star), in which he attacked Russian autocracy and Russian rule over Muslim populations. This appeal to Muslim-Turkic populations to combat the Russian administration was placed on the index in Russia: *Çulpan Yıldızı* is therefore considered the first political document to have been produced by the Muslims of the Russian Empire. It was a far stronger cry than the more cultural-bound aims that appeared in the writing of the person considered the more secular hero of renewalism, the Crimean Gaspíralí Ismáʿíl (1851–1915), active in the 1880s.[51]

In 1896, Ibrahim traveled in Europe, establishing contacts with exiled Marxists and attempting to draw them to his side in his struggles for the Muslims of Russia. Between 1897 and 1900, he set out from Istanbul on travels that took him to Egypt, the Hijaz, Western Europe, and Chinese Turkestan. Returning to Tara in 1900, he soon began publishing the periodical *Mir'at* (Perspectives) in St. Petersburg (1902) where he once again took up the cause of the Muslims of Russia. During 1902–3, he visited Japan.[52] We see him back in Istanbul in 1904, a city from which he was extradited to Russia upon the demand of the Russian government. He was again imprisoned for a while, then released because of the uproar among Russian Muslims over his imprisonment. The very same year, he established a printing press in St. Petersburg. He promoted publications about the fate of Russian Muslims and published the *Ülfet* (Friendship) and *Tilmiz* (Pupil) in 1905.

The years 1904 and 1905 were momentous for Russia. The Russians lost the Russo-Japanese War; the Tsar announced his intention to convene a consultative assembly (March 1905); the Russian assembly,

---

[50] See W. Montgomery Watt, "Hidjra," in *Encyclopedia of Islam*, 2d ed., vol. 3, 366–7. Cf. Gilles Kepel, *Muslim Extremism in Egypt*, trans. J. Rothschild (Berkeley: University of California Press, 1985), 70–100.

[51] For Ismail Gasprinski (Gaspíralí Ismáʿíl), see Edward J. Lazzerini, "Ismail Bey Gasprinski and Muslim Modernism in Russia," Ph.D. diss., University of Washington, 1973; Rorlich, *The Volga Tatars*, 57ff; and Devlet, *Rusya Türkleri'nin*, 13, 15, 17–8, 31, 35, 37, 78, 82, 89, 91–2, 94–6, 99–100, 110, 127–8, 140, 147, 151, 154, 156, 166, 170, 188, 199–202, 205, 225, 293, and 295.

[52] See "Abdurreşid Ibrahim (1)," 9.

the Duma, was created (August 1905); the workers organized the Great General Strike (October 1905); Russia was granted a constitution; the workers in Moscow rose up (December 1905); and the first Duma met (May 1906).

By 1904, the Tatars had founded an underground political party by the name of *Hürriyet* (Freedom). Gaspíralí Ismāʿīl, already known for his own attempt to establish "new schools" and his publication of the *Tercüman* (Translator) in 1883,[53] had a widening influence, but he was being upstaged by the more radical Young Tatars. In the Kazan region, a younger generation had adopted the socialist line of Lenin's clandestine *Iskra*. These developments, however, were overshadowed by the much more striking activism of Abdurreshid Ibrahim, i.e., our qadi acting in the established, but now shifting, Nakshbandī activist tradition of renewalism. When, in the fall of 1906, there was agitation in St. Petersburg for a representative body of local institution, the so-called Zemstvo congress, Abdurreshid Ibrahim attempted to get similar concessions from the Minister of the Interior for Russian Muslims.[54] Unsuccessful, he returned to Kazan where he was able to mobilize some of the leading local businessmen, intellectuals, and *ʿulamāʾ*, as well as intellectual leaders from the Crimea and the Caucasus, with a view to petitioning the prime minister to authorize a meeting of representatives of Russian Muslims in St. Petersburg. The reaction of the Imperial Russian administration was to organize a much narrower meeting of the *ʿulamāʾ* of Russia in Ufa. Despite this diversion, when the *ʿulamāʾ* met they showed a willingness to collaborate with the uninvited Muslim secular intellectuals, and they passed resolutions that revealed a highly developed political sense. In general, many of the more sophisticated *ʿulamāʾ* of the time, such as Alimjan Barudi (1857–1921), lent their support to the Muslim movement initiated by Ibrahim.

Just before the meeting of the Ufa Congress of the *ʿulamāʾ*, Abdurreshid Ibrahim gathered in his home in St. Petersburg Ali Merdan Toptchubashi, Ahmed Aghaoghlu, and Ali Hüseyinzade—all three from the Caucasus—together with *ʿālim* Maksudov, Bunjamin Ahmed, and Gaspíralí Ismāʿīl. The group decided to establish a political party of the Muslims of Russia, to be named *Ittifak* (Alliance). On August 5, 1905, the Muslims met in Nijni Novgorod (*Mekerje* in Turkish) in what became known as the First Congress of Russian Muslims. The brochure by Abdurreshid Ibrahim entitled *Bin Üç Yüz Senelik Nazar* (A 1300 year

[53] Devlet, *Rusya Türkleri'nin*, 33.
[54] For these and succeeding developments see Devlet, *Rusya Türkleri'nin*, 81–112.

look backwards) summarized the reasons why unity among Russian Muslims was necessary.[55] In short, Ibrahim was the architect of the first attempt to build a Russian Muslim political party. Notice the emphasis on "Muslims" rather than "Turks"; as we shall see, this latter locution was to be used by our second figure as the focus of his own ideals.

The First Congress of Russian Muslims was also the occasion for the writing of the program of the Muslim Alliance by Abdurreshid Ibrahim, Ali Merdan Toptchubashi, and Ahmed Aghaoghlu.[56] The political activities of the Muslims of Russia continued with representation in the Duma, where, having agreed to work within the frame of the Kadet Party, they were not very effective. At the third Congress of Russian Muslims, Abdurreshid Ibrahim brought forth a new thesis, namely, that the ultimate goal of the group should be to secure the union of the three hundred million Muslims of the world. As one follows his career, one sees the gradual emergence of a Pan-Islamic ideology, especially in *Shirke* (Partnership), a periodical published in 1907 and closed by the Russian authorities the same year. It was now becoming clear that he was less interested in party politics than in a Muslim Grand Design that, in fact, must have energized him from the beginning of his career.

Indeed, we see him embarking thereafter on a trip to study the Muslims of Asia, the outcome of which was a two-volume work entitled *Ālem-i Islam ve Japonya'da* (The World of Islam and Japan) published in Istanbul in 1910.[57] At the time, he was collaborating on periodicals of Young Turk and Pan-Islamic orientation, such as *Türk Yurdu* (The Turkish homeland), *Türk Sözü* (The Turkish world), and *Islam Dünyasi* (The Islamic world).[58] He was in Japan in the fall of 1908 establishing political contacts with prominent figures, among whom were Prime Minister Hirobumi Ito and Shigiminobu Okuma, minister of Foreign Affairs (1887–96) and Prime Minister in 1914. He remained in Japan for six months.

His voyage was promoted by the radical nationalist Japanese organization known as the Black Dragon. In his memoirs, Abdurreshid Ibrahim

[55] See Mustafa Uzun, "Abdurreşid Ibrahim," 298.
[56] Devlet, *Rusya Türkleri'nin*, 96.
[57] *Ālem-i Islam ve Japonya'da Intişar-i Islāmiyet*, two vols. in one (Istanbul: Ahmed Saki and Kader, 1328–9 [A.H.].
[58] This information given in my source for his biography does not seem to be confirmed by the list of contents of *Türk Yurdu*. However, two articles with his name appear in *Islam Mecmuasi* in 1915. This was a periodical showing the influence of the Party of Union and Progress. See Masami Arai, *Turkish Nationalism in the Young Turk Era* (Leiden: E. J. Brill, 1992), 110–54.

speaks of a somewhat utopian goal in this connection, namely, a Japanese mass conversion to Islam, which he describes under the rubric of *Ittihad-i Shark* (The Unification of the East). His contact with Turkey continued, but his first contacts with the Young Turks were inconclusive. Only when the Young Turks attempted to counter the propaganda of their conservative rivals of the Entente Libérale Party did his position improve. His activites among intellectuals in Istanbul continued.[59]

In 1911, he engaged in Islamic propaganda in Cyrenaica in the struggle of the Sanusis against Italian invasion. At the beginning of the First World War, he was the representative of Russian Muslims in the Stockholm-based association known as the Ligue des Allogènes de Russie. During the First World War, he was engaged in creating a battalion of Central Asian Muslims taken prisoner by the Germans (*Asya Taburu*).

Between 1919–26, he was constantly on the move in Russia and in Asia establishing contacts with, among others, Mir Said Sultan Galiev, the communist whose theory that there existed no international proletariat as such but only "proletarian nations" or victims of imperialism led to his early demise in the Soviet Union. From 1926 to 1933, he was in the province of Konya, cooling his heels in a Turkey that did not wish to antagonize the Soviet Union, although he presented Mustafa Kemal with a report of his findings.[60] Later in the 1930s, we find him in Mecca and then in Japan, possibly having taken part in the Japanese propaganda for Asian independence. This certainly is the impression given by his translation two decades earlier of a Japanese brochure promoting Asian unity against Western Imperialism.[61] He died in Tokyo in 1944.

## ZEKI VELIDI TOGAN: FROM THE LITERATI TO THE INTELLIGENTSIA

Ahmet Zeki Velidi, who in Turkey later adopted the surname Togan, was born in the Bashkurt village of Küzen in 1891.[62] The Bashkurt, a warlike

[59] See "Abdurreşid Ibrahim (1)," 11.

[60] Ibid., 15–16. For Sultan Galiev's ideas, see Alexandre A. Bennigsen and S. Enders Winbush, *Muslim National Communism in the Soviet Union: A Revolutionary Strategy for the Colonial World* (Chicago: University of Chicago Press, 1979), 42–4.

[61] *Asya Tehlikede* (Asia in jeopardy), Istanbul, 1910. See the remarks of Selçuk Esenbel in "Abdurreşid Ibrahim (1)," 18–27, on the extent to which he was used as a foil by Japanese foreign policy.

[62] Togan, *Hatiralar*, 37 and 49. The year 1890 was a threshold in the Russian policy in Turkestan, which took a turn to the complete colonizing of the area. See A. Zeki Velidi Togan, *Bugünkü Türk Ili ve Yakin Tarihi* (The Contemporary Turkish land and its recent history), 2d ed. (Istanbul: Enderun, 1981), 279.

people who resisted Russian penetration with arms and organized many rebellions, were nonetheless part of the expanding Russian Empire. They seem to have had lasting relations with the Ottoman Empire: in 1667, the Ottoman traveler, Evliya Çelebi, was impressed by their "national and religious fervor."[63] Their envoys were still in Istanbul in the early eighteenth century. Nurtured in the framework of the complex Islamic revival I have described, Velidi nevertheless eventually emerged from this experience with a worldview that diverged significantly from that of Abdurreshid Ibrahim.

Zeki Velidi was a member of the Sokli-Kay Clan of the Eastern Bashkurt.[64] This is the point at which an element not visible in the case of Abdurreshid Ibrahim enters into our story, namely, tribal kinship linkages and the communications network that came with it. Indeed, one of the key elements in the ability of the Tatar region to emerge with a modern face in the late eighteenth and nineteenth centuries was the existence of already deeply etched networks of cultural interchange that also extended to the ambient Islamic world. In the case of a setting like the birthplace of Zeki Velidi, we have to add a vertical dimension of mobilized kin groups to the already existing horizontal crisscrossing network so effectively expanded by Nakshbandī activities. On the one hand, Eastern Turkistan, Bukhara, Togan's village, and the towns of Troisk, Interlimak, Ufa, and Kazan were linked more closely by Muslim *ʿulamāʾ* and intellectuals from the seventeenth century onward; but we understand from Velidi's *Memoirs* that, in addition, family, clan relatives, descendants of the Mirzas of the Golden Horde, and the scions of Timurid dynasties of the Kokand khans were all drawn into the Tatar cultural renaissance I have described and were thereby mobilized during the second half of the nineteenth century. In Velidi's memoirs, we can follow the resuscitation of their genealogical memory, which also often embodied historical information. Among the historical memories of a more general type that influenced Zeki Velidi as a child were epic poems: those of Edige, Cirence, and Isaoghlu Emet, dating from the days of the Golden Horde.

A number of Zeki Velidi's close relatives, including his father, had seen service in the Russian Army. His father's military service took place in Daghistan,[65] another Nakshbandī stronghold; while stationed there, he studied Arabic and Farsi from Dibr al-Indi [Hindi?], the secretary of the

[63] See Z. V. Togan, "Bashdjirt," in *Encyclopedia of Islam*, 2d ed., vol. 1, 1075–7.
[64] Togan, *Hatiralar*, 7.
[65] See W. Barthold (article revised by A. Bennigsen), "Dāghistān," in *Encyclopedia of Islam*, 2d ed., vol. 2, 85–9, for the religious history of the area.

renewalist Nakshbandī Shaykh Shamil who had led the resistance against Russian penetration in the Caucasus. Among the early influences in Zeki Velidi's life were Shaykh Mollakay Abdullah, another Khālidī Nakshbandī, and Zaynullāh Rasulev, his spiritual mentor. He describes the latter as having been intent on combatting "ignorant mullahs."[66] Velidi also acknowledged the influence of Shahabeddin Merjanī through this thinker's *al-Ṭarīqa al-Muthlā* (The Exemplary method) with its emphasis on mathematics and philosophy.[67] Velidi learned geometry from another Mullah from the village of Büje who used Ulugh Bey's astronomical tables to find the direction of Mecca. He learned Arabic from a number of shaykhs.

Two variants of the early Tatar revival competed to influence Zeki Velidi during his childhood and adolescence. There was, first, his father's religious school, where he studied until eleven. The setting was that of progressive but conservative revivalism. The Turkish spoken at home was reinforced by the Islamic "humanities," that is, the serious study of Arabic and Farsi. An alternative model of Islamic pedagogy was available in his maternal uncle's religious school in the village of Ütek, three miles away.

Both Zeki Velidi's father and his uncle directed local religious schools, but his uncle Satlíkoglu Habibnejjar had an easygoing, tolerant attitude toward the program of instruction. There, Zeki Velidi did not have to go through the steps of theological and Quranic studies and could choose his own subjects. This network of family relations led to a wider set of contacts with Kazan and even more distant places.

Already in the early nineteenth century Ütek had produced a renowned *ʿālim*, Kockar Oghlu Emirhan,[68] who had studied in Daghistan, Istanbul, Egypt, and the Hijaz. The entire village was a center of Tatarists, who got their name from their opposition to the theologians of Khiva and Bukhara. All of this had begun in the eighteenth century when sons of two shaykhs from the Khorezm Karakalpak region undertook extensive travels to Kazan, Daghistan, and Istanbul and returned to start a campaign founding religious schools in the Bashkurt region,[69] the tradition of which was still lively around 1900. To find the historical origins of this movement, one would have to follow its connection with revivalist activities in Istanbul, already visible in the third quarter of the eighteenth century. A point to be considered in future research is the fact that delegations from Azerbaijan's local rulers and, at the end

66 Togan, *Hatiralar*, 10.
67 Ibid., 11.
68 Ibid., 12–13.
69 Ibid., 87.

of the eighteenth century, one delegation from Daghistan repeatedly requested assistance from the Ottoman Sultan, as "Imam al-Müslimin."[70]

Velidi's uncle had studied with Shahabeddin Merjanī and was a disciple of Shaykh Zaynullāh Rasulev. This uncle allowed Velidi to concentrate on his favorite subject, the study of Arabic literature. The focus on literature was facilitated by the wider circulation of a variety of classical texts in the region at the time, evidence of which may be found on every page of Velidi's autobiography.

Velidi's uncle had accepted a new view of cosmology through a Turkish translation of what the Paris editor Flammarion had set forth concerning the solar system. His father, on the other hand, relied on the world picture of al-Ghazālī, a difference symbolizing the distance between the two religious schools. Habibnejjar was also drawn to historical studies. While he was Merjanī's assistant, he had edited a work of Islamic chronology, *Miftāḥ al-Taʾrīkh* (The Key to history) with an Arabic title and Turkish text.[71] Merjanī's circle also printed many Islamic classics. Once more, this activity demonstrates that the effect of the adoption of printing on the intellectual life of a collectivity is to mobilize their *traditional* lore: not a very conspicuous theme in studies of modernization, to be sure, but one essential for understanding the Tatar renaissance.

Habibnejjar regularly acquired the most recent publications from Turkey through Tatar booksellers in Kazan. He had a subscription to Gaspíralí Ismāʿīl's *Tercüman*, published in the Crimea. Through his uncle, Zeki Velidi became acquainted with the Turkish translation of Draper's *History of the Conflict Between Religion and Science*, the philosophical speculations of Schopenhauer (also in Turkish translation), and the works of the Salafis Muḥammad ʿAbduh and Farīd Wajdī[72] accessible to him because of his knowledge of Arabic. In his uncle's religious school, he also found the work by Mehmet Arif Bey, the Ottoman who, stunned by the Ottoman defeat in the Russo-Turkish war of 1877–8, had written a brochure directed to the lower-class Ottoman population in the style of "One Thousand and One Hadiths"; the brochure addressed the

[70] See "Abdülhamid ve Kafkasya Müslümanlari," in *Kafkas Araştírmalarí* I, 63.

[71] Togan, *Hatiralar*, 19.

[72] Note that Farīd Wajdī's stand was subtly different from that of Muḥammad ʿAbduh: ʿAbduh had argued that true civilization was in conformity with Islam. Wajdī accepted "the claim of modern Europe to have discovered the laws of social progress and happiness" and went on "to maintain that these laws are also those of Islam." Hourani, *Arabic Thought*, 162.

qualities Ottomans had to acquire in order to stand fast against such invasions and attacked Islamic scholasticism.[73] At the religious school, Velidi created a small library for the students in which he made available various newspapers published by the Muslims of Russia. In the neighboring town of Isterlitamak, he worked to improve his Russian with an autodidact Muslim tailor.

A Yesevī shaykh, a friend of his mother's family, seems to have worked in the midstream of these influences: he gave Zeki Velidi his knowledge of ʿAṭṭār (1119–1230) and Rūmī (1207–73). These representatives of the mystical tradition offered a relatively more open, secular fare compared to strictly theological sources. Velidi's fascination with the Arab essayist Abū al-ʿAlāʾ al-Maʿarrī (973–1058), who may be seen as a free thinker, indicated the new direction that his thoughts were taking.

Of all these forces, the gradual intrusion of a Tatar-historical timeframe seems to have been the most pervasive; it was encouraged by his father, who did not realize how far it would take his son, and it was promoted by family friends, such as the Tatar Murad Remzi who lived in the Hijaz and had written a two-volume work in Arabic on the history of the Muslims of Russia. This book, *Tawfīq al-Akhbār* (Reconciling the accounts), was "marked by a strong nationalist tone, the book consistently referring to the Russians as Gog and Magog, and called for the unity of the Turkic Muslim peoples."[74] Remzi encouraged Zeki Velidi to gain the means to use the Russian sources he had heretofore been unable to use. Velidi's description of his contacts with his friends underlines the enthusiasm with which these as yet scattered clues to identity were taken up by young men of his generation.

Velidi's father was one of the persons who encouraged him to learn Russian; as a result of this knowledge, Zeki Velidi was able to follow publications subversive of Russian rule. It was his father who brought him the Russian historian Yadintsev's *Siberia as a Colony* and *The Situation of non-Russian People in Siberia*.[75] The biography of Siddik Sultan, the son of the Kazakh leader Kine Sari,[76] had been included in Murad Remzi's history, the historian having received it from Siddik Sultan himself.[77] On his visits to Velidi's family, Remzi elaborated on this infor-

[73] Togan, *Hatiralar*, 28.

[74] See Algar, "Shaykh Zaynullah Rasulev," 125. Notice the interlacing of themes from sacred and secular history, indicating an intermediate stage in the timeframe shift from the sacred to the secular.

[75] Togan, *Hatiralar*, 39.

[76] For Kine Sari, see Togan, *Bügünkü Türk Ili*, 312–18.

[77] Kine Sari fought both Russians and local rivals (1837–47) and attained fame as a hero of the Kazakhs, but also one whose influence permeated the Bashkurt area.

mation. Zeki Velidi's paternal uncle taught him the poems celebrating another hero, the famous Kazakh leader Abilai Han (1711–81), the grandfather of Kine Sari. Abilai Han, after having eliminated the danger of Dzungarian Mongols and Kirghiz, had petitioned Catherine the Great to confirm him as khan of all three Hordes. "The Empress, rightly perceiving the potential danger of Kazak unification under such a vigorous and awe-inspiring leader, preferred to allot him only the Middle Horde, whereupon Abilai refused to participate in the official ceremony of installation."[78] The mobilizing character of the vivid recollection of Abilai's feats is evident in one of the quatrains Zeki Velidi remembered as having marked him:

> We attacked the enemy on all sides like a snowstorm. / Shouting Abilai, Abilai, we surrounded them and smashed them. / Where will your soul rest if you don't keep God in your heart? / How will your soul be free if you don't see your state free?[79]

In 1908, Zeki Velidi left for Orenburg, possibly because he expected to find financial support for studies in the Russian Normal School for non-Russian people in Kazan. Rizaeddin Fahreddin, the disciple of Zaynullāh Rasulev, was publishing a literary journal, the *Shūrā* (Consultation), in this city. Zeki Velidi established contact with the intellectuals in Orenburg and received sufficient assistance to go on to Kazan. Arriving in Kazan, he immediately proceeded to Merjanī's religious school, which was directed by Merjanī's son, but was disappointed by what he found.

His memoirs show that Tatar intellectuals still concentrated their effort on education, but "matters of nationality" were beginning to appear as a new concern. At the time, there was among the Kazan Tatars a group that believed in the necessity of widespread reforms in the Tatar area and, with this aim in mind, had taken up the idea of educational reform. They published a paper called *Işlāḥ* (Reform).[80] Zeki Velidi relates that this group wanted to transform the existing *madrasa* system into one of lycées (*gimnazia*), topped by an engineering school and a university. Velidi found this utopian and wrote a critical article in the *Beyan ul-Hak* (Declaration of the truth) newspaper published by Abdurreshid Ibrahim's son.

Velidi visited the Tatar thinker, Musa Jarullah, where he met Abdur-

[78] Kermit E. McKenzie, "Chokan Velikhanov: Kazakh Princeling and Scholar," *Central Asian Survey* 8, no. 1 (1989): 7.

[79] Togan, *Hatiralar*, 54.

[80] Ibid., 61.

reshid Ibrahim in person. Years earlier, Velidi's father had been on the Hajj with Ibrahim. Velidi's aim had been to go to Egypt to continue his study of Arabic literature, but persuaded by Abdurreshid to remain in Russia he soon afterward began to work for the *Beyan ul-Hak*. In 1909–10, Velidi was appointed teacher of Turkish history and the history of Arab literature in the Kasimiye religious school,[81] new subjects that indicate what an extraordinary shift in the curriculum had resulted from the cumulative effects of the intellectual streams I have attempted to describe.

It is, of course, important to understand what Zeki Velidi means in his *Memoirs* by "Turkish history." It appears he intended this term to embrace all Turkic Muslims, explaining their history as one of gradual differentiation within the frame of an ur-Türk nation. The implication was that this common Turkic trunk showed sufficient cultural uniformity to merit being revived. This certainly was to be the core of his later teaching in Turkey.[82] What he meant by "Turkish" can also be gathered from his having written a textbook of Turkish history, to the title of which his Kazan publishers objected. "Tatarism," the opposite of "Turkism," had been nourished by the uncompromising stand on Tatar as the language of Kayyum Nasirī,[83] whose followers opposed the Turkist position of Gaspíralí Ismāʿīl. The publisher and later important Tatar communist, Alimjan Ibrahimov, proposed calling Velidi's work a Tatar history, and the final compromise achieved was "Turkish-Tatar history."[84]

This was a time when Velidi began to read the works of Western historians such as Langlois and Seignobos as well as Lavisse and Rambaud on methodology[85] and Howorth on Central Asian and Mongol history.[86] Velidi had already clashed with Tatar conservatives in Astrakan, who were publishing an Islamist periodical, *Maʿārif* (Knowledge). He now

81 Ibid., 75.
82 See Togan, *Büngünkü Türk Ili*; and cf. the article, "Turks," in *Encyclopedia of Islam*, 1st ed., vol. 8, 899–972.
83 For Nasirī, see p. 69 and n. 33.
84 Togan, *Hatiralar*, 104. Alimjan Ibrahim[ov] later became a member of the Central Muslim Commissariat [around 1918] before disappearing. See Alexandre A. Bennigsen and S. Enders Winbush, *Muslim National Communism in the Soviet Union*, 28. The debate between "Turkists" and "Tatarists" can be followed in Devlet, *Rusya Türkler-i'nin*, 166–71.
85 See C. V. Langlois and Charles Seignobos, *Introduction aux études historiques* (1898; reprint, Paris: KINE, 1992); Ernest Lavisse and Alfred Rambaud, *Histoire générale du IVe siècle à nos jours* (Paris: Colin, 1893–1905).
86 See Harry H. Howorth, *History of the Mongols from the Ninth to the Nineteenth Century* (1876–8; reprint, London: Longmans and Green, 1925).

began to see himself as someone who had to find an answer to two questions: what had been the cause for the decline of Islam (and particularly of the Turks), and was it true that Islam bore the responsibility for that decline? He states that he began to get a hint of the solution to these issues in the books on Russian social history Plekhanov had published under the pseudonym Beltov. Some of the conclusions he now reached were concerned with the nature of the Quran as an instance of divine revelation. He came to believe that while the inspiration of the Quran may have been truly divine, the book was, in fact, based on the pre-Islamic beliefs and values of the Arabs in order to make the message comprehensible to them. He had become a deist, but he still saw Islam as a fulcrum that would enable Muslims to keep their distinguishing characteristics as a collectivity. It is quite clear in his memoirs that, for him, Islam and its *ādāb* (good manners) represented the pristine behavior he contrasted to the drunken slovenliness of the family from whom he was then renting a room.

In a sense, then, although Velidi had distanced himself from the beliefs of his youth and had begun to see himself as the inheritor of the Tatar historical past, he retained Islam as a frame of ethical reference. The question that comes to mind is why he did not adopt "integral" Turkishness as an overarching frame for personal and social identity. The answer surely is that the binary Islamic formula, with its attention to personal integration, its reference to an ethical universe, *and*, at the same time, its construction of social and political identity, provided a richer ideological framework than emergent "Turkism." We have seen that Zeki Velidi was not so much involved in confronting the "other"—Russian society in this case—as in trying to build a new frame of social identity. At one point, he even had to integrate himself into the culture of the "other" (that is, the culture of Russia and the Enlightenment in its materialistic form) that Abdurreshid had combatted within his own social moorings. For Velidi, Islam acted as a personal counterpoise to his acceptance of new elements of social structure. Such a delicate equilibrium between self and other, between Islam and Turkishness, could endure in the mind of an intellectual; but among the less literate Muslims placed in similar dilemmas, it was unstable enough to open the door to a full return to Islam, as has been the case in a number of instances in similar circumstances in the twentieth century.

Zeki Velidi had established close relations with the faculty of Kazan University, especially with Professor Katanov, head of Kazan University's Association of History and Archaeology. From Katanov, he heard a bitter complaint one evening that strengthened his emerging patriotic Bashkent-Turkic conscience. Katanov related his frustration with his professional life:

> Among Eastern Turks and Mongols who took up Orientalism as a career the following persons may be counted: Dorji Banzarov, Chokan Velihanov, and myself. We gave our all to Russian Culture. I left Shamanism and became a Christian, and I am now serving the Russians. Dorji and Chokan died of drink before the age of thirty-five. And that was due to the fact that the Russians never opened up wider horizons for us. Now you are the fourth one. Protect yourself from this setting. I was not raised in a culture as strong as Islam and therefore my identity was eroded. We are left as foreigners within Russian culture. You must become aware of the strength provided by your own cultural background.[87]

All the circumstances working to shape Zeki Velidi's worldview came to a focus in this statement and reinforced his culturally separatist leanings.

Zeki Velidi was now being published in Turkey, and he undertook work of increasing scope on Central Asian history. He was a recognized scholar in Russian academic circles. His plunge into politics came much later, after the Russian Revolution, but his identity had already crystallized; it is this process of identity formation that is my focus here. The most pertinent remark to be made in the case of Zeki Velidi is that, although the *materials* he used for the elaboration of his new identity were Islamic, they were also in part *ethnic* and were immediately projected onto a larger, possibly imagined[88] Turkic dimension—one shaped by the world of Western knowledge and communication. This dual process is one whose *details* find little explanation in the literature on ethnicity.

One of my main points in this chapter is that contrary to all those who have spoken of the invention of traditions[89] or imagined communities, these processes cannot take place without redrawing an existing historical memory. The latter began to appear as a consequence of an acceleration of communication modes, some of the components of which were the Nakshbandī revival working in tandem with Russian educational institutions but also with the further input of mobilized traditional materials. Islam—now understood in ideological, mobilizing terms, rather than in purely religious terms—was a second universalistic frame into which these foundational materials were projected. In short, the new

[87] Togan, *Hatiralar*, 106.

[88] For this concept, see the work of Benedict Anderson, esp. *Imagined Communities*, 2d ed. (New York: Verso, 1992).

[89] See, for example, Eric Hobsbawm and Terence Ranger, eds., *The Invention of Tradition* (Cambridge: Cambridge University Press, 1983).

*field* created by the development of modern communications affected the mode in which the materials of the binary formula were used. Islam was no longer simply a belief and a view of ethics framed by sacred history. Rather, it increasingly became a "flag" for mobilization and a means by which the intellectual established a new basis for a shattered faith. But this is by no means the end of the story.

## CONCLUDING REMARKS

The tribulations of Abdurreshid Ibrahim and Zeki Velidi appear to have a common point of departure in the eighteenth-century revival of Volga Tatar culture, that was largely inspired by the renewalist Nakshbandī movement and that prepared the ground for their careers. But they belonged to generations separated by half a century. The ambient circumstances of each were markedly different.

Ibrahim acquired the status of a learned Muslim cleric (a position conflated with that of a Muslim intellectual) at an early age. There were two dimensions to this rise. First, Islamic education, while usually very long, had always provided brilliant young men with the means of rising to positions of authority. Second, and more importantly, as a qadi, Ibrahim occupied a position that, while being primarily religious, also possessed a political dimension. The reason for this was that the *ʿulamāʾ* constituted one of the two components of the peculiarly Islamic dyadic system made up of the executive and the keepers of Islamic values. This also made Abdurreshid Ibrahim an actor in the perpetuation of the Islamic *telos*, i.e., the tension between ideal Islam and the rule of pharaoh, a role played in this instance by the Tsar's government. In that sense, the frame of Ibrahim's action was the sacred history of Islam. His life embodied the two dimensions of the Islamic system: the ethical/political and the sacred. It had no place for the "national" as such. In the end, the frame that fitted these components was Pan-Islam.

Things were quite different in the case of Zeki Velidi. Nothing alerts us better to this difference than his minimal involvement in the surge of political activities by Russian Muslims between 1904 and 1917. Only much later and in the face of overwhelming crisis did Zeki Velidi join the political fray: Zeki Velidi, though groomed in the *madrasa* system, did not step into the ready-made slot of an *ʿālim*. Instead, he attempted, during the first twenty years of his life, to discover for himself a new social and cultural position as a modern intellectual. He stepped into the shoes of a modern intellectual in the sense of taking up the role of *inter-*

*rogating* nature in both its physical and social dimensions. This detached view was completely unlike Ibrahim's, whose role as *ʿālim* focused upon legitimation, transmission, and moral contestation whenever Islamic norms were breached.

Abdurreshid Ibrahim was less inhibited in his oppositional stance because he did not live in two dissonant worlds, as did Velidi. In Velidi's discourse the legitimating dimension of the *ʿālim*'s role was replaced by involvement in a cognitive scheme rival to that of the *ʿālim*, i.e., fitting the pieces of a puzzle together or reconstituting history seen as an open time-frame to be explored.

It is no contradiction that the increased circulation of the *old* products of Central Asian culture formed part of the complex change in ambient conditions associated with the reshaping of Velidi's role. Already in the eighteenth century, the frequency of inter-Turkic contacts seems extraordinary. To this was added a new culture of books and periodicals that spread elements of traditional culture, introduced a new, Western-influenced culture, revamped the use of the vernacular language, and (as yet unstudied in this context) disseminated an acquaintance with Farsi. In part, it was the first circle in this communications revolution, namely, the wider circulation of products of his own "ethnic" culture, that sowed the seeds of a new, extra-Muslim identity in Zeki Velidi. One gains the impression that he began to see himself integrated in the frame of Turkish-Tatar history, a development that was as much the result of an intensification of communications bringing such materials within his reach as of the *contagion* of historicism originating in Kazan, although the latter certainly shaped Velidi's later development. Finally, Zeki Velidi's deistic, heuristic, and ideological *use* of Islam was not only the outcome of his having read Draper and Plekhanov, but a logical consequence of his newly activated remembering nested in a secular time frame.

In fact, it would appear as if the important changes that occurred in the identities of our two men had three interpenetrating dimensions. First, there was the shaping force of a specific social role. Abdurreshid Ibrahim had been able to realize the political potential of the *ʿālim*'s role by opposing it to the Russian pharaoh. As a non-*ʿālim*, i.e., as a free-floating intellectual, Velidi did not consider himself to be fulfilling this role. Second, Abdurreshid Ibrahim fit into the *telos* of Islam. For Zeki Velidi, the terms of the social equation were different, and the *telos* was that of a new, pristine, *untested* imagined community, the Turkish nation, underpinned by a more ideological Islam conceived in a deistic mode.

Third, Velidi, in his new role as intellectual, did not attempt to duplicate the role of an *ʿālim* providing guidance in the "everyday," nor did he reproduce the discourse that underpinned the older, political and religious role.[90] Zeki Velidi's spatial and temporal model was Utopia; i.e., in addition to using a new time frame, Velidi "distantiated" himself from the "everyday."

It would be easy to leave our actors at this point where the contrast between their worldviews is clear. However, we still have to face the fact that Zeki Velidi's deism—quite akin to that of Turkish Kemalists—has suffered a reversal throughout the Islamic world in the last part of the twentieth century. In their everyday life, Muslims have become more, rather than less, Islamic with time. The momentous changes that shaped the years between the 1920s and the 1990s cannot, of course, be followed in detail. One may approach the problem through the concept of globalization. Contemporary history shows that the increasingly globalistic dimension has become as important as local history for understanding events. A hint of how these worldwide developments apply to Islam may be found in the writing of the sociologist Anthony Giddens. According to Giddens, modern society's expectations of rule-directed behavior have disappeared. Modern society, he contends, has focused on a general goal—emancipation—defined as the pursuit of justice, equality, and participation. The ideal, here, is autonomy. Given the increasing instability of society, these tendencies—the erosion of rule-directed behavior and the pursuit of emancipation—have introduced an entirely new dimension of social action which Giddens calls "life politics," a politics of repeated life decisions into which individuals are drawn.

> What are these decisions and how should we seek to conceptualize them? First and foremost, there are those affecting self-identity itself. As this study has sought to show, self-identity today is a reflexive achievement. The narrative of self-identity has to be shaped, altered and reflexively sustained in relation to rapidly changing circumstances of social life on a local and global scale. The individual must integrate information deriving from a diversity of mediated experiences with local involvements in such a way as to connect future projects with past experiences in a reasonably coherent fashion. Only if the person is able to develop an inner authenticity—a framework of basic trust by means of which the life

[90] An interesting description of the way this discourse of the Muslim "everyday" has been structured in contemporary Iran may be found in Jann Richard, "La Fonction parénétique du ʿalem: La prière du vendredi en Iran depuis la révolution," *Die Welt des Islams* 29 (1989): 61–82. For the "everyday" or "Alltäglichkeit," see Michel de Certeau, *L'Invention du Quotidien* (Paris: Union Générale d'Éditions, 1980), and Leslie Paul Thiele, *Timely Meditations: Martin Heidegger and Postmodern Politics* (Princeton: Princeton University Press, 1995), 233–40.

span can be understood as a unity against the backdrop of shifting social events—can this be attained. A reflexively ordered narrative of self-identity provides the means of giving coherence to the finite life span.[91]

The narrative of Islamic sacred history fits this modern demand quite admirably by providing Muslims with a narrative base of identity formation.[92] Views similar to those of Giddens have often been fielded by Muslims themselves to explain the demand for a return to original Islamic practices in our time. Unlike these Muslim observers, however, Giddens sees the new demands placed on identity formation as a consequence of dynamic social expansion. Where the Islamic apologists lament the failure of modernity, Giddens celebrates the liberation of human potential brought about by the project of modernity. Yet, for Giddens, too, this new situation creates circumstances in which

religion [has] failed to disappear. We see all around us the creation of new forms of religious sensibility and spiritual endeavor. The reasons for this concern quite fundamental features of late modernity. What was due to become a social and physical universe subject to increasingly certain knowledge and control instead creates a system in which areas of relative security interlace with radical doubt and with disquieting scenarios of risk. Religion in some part generates the conviction which adherence to the tenets of modernity must necessarily suspend; in this regard it is easy to see why religious fundamentalism has a special appeal.[93]

This description is certainly true of the situation faced today by the citizens of a large majority of countries with an Islamic culture. The first clear expression of fundamentalism was political—the rise of the Ayatollahs—an outcome that can be understood in terms of a revival of the terms of the fundamental Islamic *telos*. In the conditions of today's autocratic, Islamic, ethical-cum-political regimes, it is easy to see how the binary Islamic political formula, which is also a map for everyday life and for a constitution of the self, would apply. Numerous studies, however, have shown that, with the modern transformation of society, this model now reaches to areas well beyond the political dimension. It is now common for people to deconstruct Islam's layers of meaning in order to reconstruct for themselves a new social or personal identity. The historical cunning embodied in Muslim women's strategies of self-

[91] See Anthony Giddens, *Modernity and Self-Identity: Self and Society in the Late Modern Age* (Stanford, Calif.: Stanford University Press, 1991), 215.

[92] The place of narrative in the construction of self is exhaustively investigated by the social psychologist Jerome Bruner in "The Narrative Construction of Reality," *Critical Inquiry* 18 (1991): 1–21.

[93] See Giddens, *Modernity and Self-Identity*, 207.

expression—with Sufism as one of the elements used to this end—can be followed in the recent work of Fedwa M. Douglas.[94] Turkish studies describing how Islamic dress symbolism is sometimes used as a step toward liberation from parental authority provide another aspect of the complex, modern reevaluation and revitalization of Islam.[95] Finally, and probably most importantly, in the modern setting, the *ʿālim*, as one actor in the dyadic formula, is of necessity increasingly in competition with the intellectual of Zeki Velidi's type. In Turkey, these pressures have, through the secularization of society, resulted in the appearance of a special Islamic intelligentsia, which takes the discourse of Descartes, Kant, Marx, and Heidegger seriously. This unique Turkish phenomenon is, nevertheless, an adumbration of more wide-ranging trends. For persons who are appalled by the success of a more violent type of fundamentalism, these transformations of the original Islamic *telos* are harbingers of a future that scholars cannot neglect to study and evaluate, viewing them, not as isolated events, but as *integrated* with ongoing developments in the social and political sphere.

[94] Lecture at Georgetown University, February 24, 1994.
[95] See Nilüfer Gole, *Modern Mahrem* (Istanbul: Metis, 1992).

# 4

# Muslim Opposition Thinkers in the Nineteenth Century

SAID BENSAID ALAOUI

## INTRODUCTION

The study of Islamic political thought must account for the existence of two divergent tendencies, each of which lays claim to the religion of Islam. With the first, thinking is limited to the ideal Islamic state insofar as it faithfully responds to the precepts of Islam and finds itself in perfect concordance with the spirit and letter of these precepts. The second, far less oriented toward the transcendental and more attached to the here and now, takes as its field of investigation the ensemble of actually existing social and political relations. Thus, these two tendencies are almost at odds with one another. If the first can be considered an ideology of intransigence and, consequently, of contestation, the second may well be considered an ideology of acceptance or, better yet, of justification. Islamic history furnishes us edifying examples of each of these two ways of thinking. In Aḥmad Ibn Ḥanbal, Taqī al-Dīn Ibn Taymiyya, Jamāl al-Dīn al-Afghānī, and, along with them, almost all the intransigent reformers (*Muṣliḥūn*), the ideology of refusal and contestation is incarnated with force and clarity. By the same token, Abū al-Ḥasan al-Mawardī's theory of the caliphate, Abū Ḥāmid al-Ghazālī's legal statements granting advantages to the army, and ʿAbd al-Raḥmān Ibn Khaldūn's privileging of group solidarity (*ʿaṣabiyya*) as one of the conditions of political development all most eloquently illustrate the attitude of acceptance and justification.

The nineteenth century offers the best opportunity to test the soundness of this proposition, namely, that Islamic political thought is best understood as reflecting a permanent conflict between two antagonistic ideologies. In many respects, the nineteenth century constituted a decisive turning point in the history of the Muslim world and the slow transformation of its societies through contact with the modern world. To be sure, such contact fomented a feeling of revolt and indignation: mired in depressing backwardness, Islam questioned itself while the West continued its march of constant progress. The "discovery" of "the West"—that "other"—was for the Arab-Muslim world the occasion of a bitter awakening. New political, social, and cultural conditions made possible the emergence of an Islamic political thought itself novel in form as well as in content. In the following pages, while restricting ourselves to the Arab-Muslim world, we will attempt to shed new light on the dimensions of an Islamic political thought that can be considered as one of refusal or as an ideology of intransigence. To distinguish more clearly how a political thought of opposition arose during the last century, we intend to look at a number of different thinkers yet let them speak for themselves as much as possible.

Prior to any reflection on the nature of a political thought arising from a social and political context that differs from what was previously experienced, some questions need to be asked. They will also help us grasp the extent to which classical forms of protest in Islam were affected when they so brutally came into contact with Western political thought. Thus, we must ask what it means to be an opposition thinker in Islam, examine whether any kind of opposition thinking was really possible in the nineteenth-century world of Islam, and wonder whether we are not really speaking of multiple aspects of reform rather than opposition thinking.

## REFORM (*IṢLĀḤ*) AND OPPOSITION

*Iṣlāḥ*, the verbal noun (*maṣdar*) of *aṣlaḥa*, itself the fourth form of *ṣ*l*ḥ**, is used in the Quran with multiple senses. At times, it signifies a peaceful action (*ṣulḥ*), one leading to reconciliation and accord; at other times, it signifies a pious deed (*ʿamal ṣāliḥ*), one having to do with righteousness (*ṣalāḥ*). To express the meaning of *iṣlāḥ* clearly in European languages, different translations of the Quran have used the word "reform." Other derivatives from the verb *aṣlaḥa* confirm the accuracy of such a choice. Thus, to be a *ṣāliḥ* (pl. *ṣāliḥūn*) is to conduct oneself as a righteous person: "Let me be brought in, by your compassion, among your righteous servants."[1] To be a *muṣliḥ* (pl. *muṣliḥūn*) is to be concerned with the moral perfection of one's fellow, to call for peace: "You want

[1] *Quran*, 27:19.

only to be an oppressor on earth and do not want to be among the reformers."[2] The *muṣliḥ*, then, is the opposite of the oppressor, and oppression thereby signifies all forms of wandering from the straight path traced by religion. The *muṣliḥ* is animated by the desire to assume fully the mission of the prophets who were essentially reformers. In this, he lays claim to another Islamic precept, that of enjoining good and prohibiting evil.

But can one ever rise up against an oppressive rule, raise one's voice against an injustice, without drawing upon oneself all kinds of difficulties? To be sure, throughout the history of Islam, the *muṣliḥ* has been the object of calumny and has even been charged with unbelief. Quite often, he opposes those in power, as when he judges them to be going against the spirit of the Quran and the teachings of the prophet. And he stands in opposition to society whenever, in his eyes, it succumbs to blameworthy innovation (*bidʿa*). The call for *iṣlāḥ* thus expresses, at one and the same time, an awakening of religious consciousness, social dissatisfaction, and political opposition.

In the nineteenth century, *iṣlāḥ* was the order of the day for all Muslim reformers. In its name, they forged and formulated whatever programs for action they had in mind. And the contact Muslim thinkers of the period had with the West led them to give *iṣlāḥ* a new sense, one going beyond any religious connotation it derived from the Quran and Sunna. For them, it became "an appeal to progress, a breath of renovation, and the promise of a better future."[3] As such, this appeal was combatted within the Muslim world both by the indigenous social and political forces whose interest lay in maintaining the status quo and by foreign powers intent upon bringing their domination of Muslim peoples to a successful end. The appeal of *iṣlāḥ*, with its extolling of Arabism on the one hand and of pan-Islamism on the other, went counter to their aims.

Thus *iṣlāḥ* and opposition often go together in the Islamic world, their joint action being carried out in the name of religion. To work for the purification of religion is, for the *muṣliḥ*, merely a way to express his refusal of the here and now and a means to oppose it. Thus, apologetic writings on the order of Jamāl al-Dīn al-Afghānī's *Refutation of the Materialists* or Shaykh Muḥammad ʿAbduh's *Epistle on Unity* and *Exposition of the Muslim Religion* are also highly political.

[2] *Quran*, 28:19.

[3] See Aziz Ahmad, "*Iṣlāḥ*," in *Encyclopedia of Islam*, 2d ed., vol. 4, 141–71, esp. 150–1.

## PRECURSORS AND HERALDS

Nineteenth-century Muslim travelers to Europe were the first to notice the backwardness of the Muslim world as contrasted to the Christian West. Shaykh Rifāʿa Rāfiʿ al-Ṭahṭāwī (1801–73), dazzled by everything he saw from the moment of boarding the French boat that brought him to Marseilles on through his long sojourn in Paris, expresses feelings of great admiration for the West in his *Kitāb Takhlīṣ al-Ibrīz ilā Talkhīṣ Bārīz* (Book of the refining of pure gold unto the distillation of Paris). Sometimes he dwells at length on what he considers to be a sign of progress or a major cause of it, all the while prodding his fellow Muslims to let this inspire their behavior. A careful observer who assiduously devoured the newspapers of the day, al-Ṭahṭāwī thought the 1830 revolution in France arose from the king stubbornly having wanted "to do by himself what he should have done only in concert with others" so that "certain republican newspapers incited people to disobey the king."[4] The king, duty-bound to uphold the Constitutional Charter, could overstep its provisions and allow his own will free rein only at the risk of provoking the people to rise up against him. Emphasizing the intimate link between progress and equity in the West, al-Ṭahṭāwī—the leader of the first Egyptian scholarly mission sent to France by Muḥammad ʿAlī—leaves to his reader the task of drawing the inevitable conclusion about the Muslim East, namely, that backwardness is the legitimate daughter of tyranny.

That Muḥammad al-Ṣaffār, secretary of the delegation sent to France by Morocco's King ʿAbd al-Raḥmān Ibn Hishām, also succumbed to the charms of Paris is evident from his travel account. He in no way seeks to hide his admiration for the signs of manifest liberty, especially the freedom of expression:

> among the things for which they reproach their king, Charles X, the predecessor of the one now reigning, and that caused the insurrection against him and led to his being overthrown were his having prohibited the expression of opinions, that is, of writing or publishing them without prior examination by a state official who decides [what is publishable and what is not].[5]

[4] Rifāʿa Rāfiʿ al-Ṭahṭāwī, *Kitāb Takhlīṣ al-Ibrīz ilā Talkhīṣ Bārīz*, ed., with notes and preface, Fahmī Ḥijāj (Cairo: GEBO, 1974), 348–9.

[5] Muḥammad ibn ʿAbd Allāh al-Ṣaffār, *al-Riḥla al-Titwāniyya ilā al-Diyār al-Faransiyya, 1845–1846* (The Tetouan voyage to the French regions). This work, a unique autograph manuscript (Ms. 113) held in the Royal Library of Rabat, has been edited, with an introductory study, by Umm Salmā (Tetouan, 1995); it has also been edited and translated by Susan Gilson Miller, *Disorienting Encounters: Travels of a Moroccan Scholar in France in 1845–1846: The Travels of Muḥammad al-Ṣaffār* (Berkeley: University of California Press, 1992).

Nor are al-Ṣaffār and al-Ṭahṭāwī by any means the only nineteenth-century Muslim travelers in Europe. Numerous other travel accounts from this period testify to their authors' esteem for the equity apparent in European political institutions and ascribe the West's progress to it. At the same time, more or less discernible circumlocutions and metaphors are employed to link the iniquity of governmental practices in the travelers' countries with the backwardness of their world. These travel accounts, each in its own way and according to the public it addresses, constitute embryonic forms of social and political protest. For a select group of readers—whose limited number was more than offset by the powerful positions they occupied—these accounts triggered the slow process of developing a critical political awareness.

Much less circumspect in their criticism of the political institutions of the Muslim East, the Egyptian Muṣṭafā Fāḍil Pasha (1830–75) and the Turk Namik Kamal (1840–88) called for a clean separation between religion and politics. Writing to the Ottoman Sultan ʿAbd al-ʿAzīz in 1867, Muṣṭafā Fāḍil Pasha (the brother of Khedive Ismāʿīl and grandson of the great Muḥammad ʿAlī) said:

> Sire, you know better than I that religion orders souls and provides us with perspectives on the future life, but does not regulate the rights of peoples; indeed, when it does not limit itself to the sublime domain of institutional worship, it brings about its own demise as it undermines all else.[6]

Namik Kamal, a man of far more modest social standing, drew attention to the urgent necessity of adopting a constitutional regime. According to him, such a course of action was the only means to defend the interests and resolve the problems of the Sublime Porte. "If such a regime is adopted," he concluded, "it will clearly appear that each individual is free. Europe will then treat us as a civilized nation and no longer as a scarecrow standing in front of Russia, as it treats us today."[7]

From here on, the instability of political institutions is at the center of the debate for Muslim thinkers concerned about backwardness, its causes, and the means to overcome it. The Syrian al-Kawākibī, the Afghan Jamāl al-Dīn, the Egyptian Muḥammad ʿAbduh, along with other reformers in Morocco and Tunisia, were all more or less virulent critics of the way their own countries, as well as the world of Islam taken as a

[6] As cited by Marcel Colombe, "Trois réformateurs des institutions de l'Islam" in *Études d'orientalisme* (Paris: Maisonneuve et Larose, 1962), 1:107. For the bibliography of Muṣṭafā Fāḍil Pasha, see E. Kuran, "Fāḍil Pasha, Muṣṭafā," in *Encyclopedia of Islam* 2d ed., vol. 2, 728.

[7] Colombe, "Trois réformateurs," 108.

whole and presumed to form a single nation, were governed. If, unlike a Namik Kamal or a Muṣṭafā Fāḍil, they were not always fervent supporters of a Western-style constitutional regime, they nevertheless came close to it in their programs of *iṣlāḥ*.

## REGENERATION, PAN-ISLAMISM, AND OPPOSITION

From 1880 on, the thinking of Jamāl al-Dīn al-Afghānī (1839–97) forcefully dominated the Islamic reform movement while deeply impregnating it with his militant advocacy of Muslim unity. Indeed, Muḥammad ʿAbduh (1849–1905), who with al-Afghānī founded that veritable tribune of pan-Islamism, *al-ʿUrwa al-Wuthqā* (The Indissoluble link), spoke of Jamāl al-Dīn as a master thinker "burning with zeal, so to speak, for religion and the faithful."[8] Similarly, for Ḥasan al-Bannā (1906–49), founder and supreme leader of the Muslim Brotherhood, the author of the *Refutation of the Materialists* was one of the key figures in militant Islam and the one who precipitated the Islamic revival of modern times. Yet in the eyes of his adversaries, European as well as Muslim, he was only a dangerous agitator whom it would be best to render incapable of doing any harm.

Three ideals inspired Jamāl al-Dīn al-Afghānī. First was toiling for the regeneration and purification of Islam, which he deemed the best way to end the backwardness of Muslim peoples and permit them to recover their glorious past. The whole call for going back to the origins—that is, the *salafiyya* movement engendered by ʿAbduh and his disciples—represents little more than a crystallization and extolling of this aspect of al-Afghānī's teaching.

The second was militating for Muslim unity by bringing the separate Muslim states together under a single caliphate so as to restore Islam to its former glory and Muslims to their former prosperity and vigor. To this end, al-Afghānī stood forth as a veritable opponent, one both impetuous and intractable, of all "Muslim sovereigns who opposed reforms or did not sufficiently resist European encroachments."[9] In this sense, he is the instigator of the pan-Islamic idea, and contemporary movements of what is termed "political Islam" hail him as their founder.

The third was fighting against those imperialist-minded Western coun-

See Muḥammad ʿAbduh, "Biographie d'al-Afghānī," in *Jamāl al-Dīn al-Afghānī, Réfutation des matérialistes*, trans. A-M. Goichon (Paris: Geuthner, 1942), 48.
See J. M. B. Jones, "al-Bannā, Ḥasan," in *Encyclopedia of Islam*, 2d ed., vol. 1, 1018–19.

tries that sought to seize Islamic lands, subjugate their peoples, and put Muslim states under their yoke. To give form and consistency to this struggle, al-Afghānī drew the attention of his fellow Muslims to the danger of materialism in all its manifestations, particularly as adopted by certain Muslim intellectuals in India. Encouraging the diffusion of materialist theories, especially among educated Muslims, was the best way for the colonizing power to sow doubts about religion, weaken potential opposition, and make the people bow to its will. Thus did this Afghan *muṣliḥ* strive to bring to light the goal the materialists so cleverly tried to conceal, namely, that of undermining religion and fostering doubt and anxiety among Muslims. The fruit of this anti-materialist campaign was his *Risāla fī radd ʿalā al-Dahriyīn* (Refutation of the Materialists).

It is worth focusing a bit on this epistle, not to become acquainted with its contents on the grounds that it is the only treatise al-Afghānī wrote, but to show how this Muslim reformer viewed his appeal for purifying religion and preserving it against the attacks of its sworn enemies as a subtle and effective way of waging a successful political struggle. According to the author of *The Refutation of the Materialists*, "religion is the mainstay of nations, and their prosperity comes through it; in it is their happiness, and it is their pivot."[10] Religious dogmas constitute the solid base on which the edifice of real civilization is constructed. The day a nation is taken over by the morbid teachings of the materialists marks the beginning of the end, for that nation "gives up its durability." The history of humanity from the pagan Greeks to "the socialists, nihilists, and communists" of today teaches us about the corruption of nations touched by materialism in its many forms. The history of Islam should be read with a view to this tension between religion and materialism: "The beginning of the weakness of the Muslims goes back to the day that the lying opinions and beliefs of the materialists appeared as a kind of religion."[11] In the land of Islam, each period of doubt and decline corresponds to the appearance of materialism in one form or another.

In India, the naturalists "imitate the behavior of European materialists in a comic way."[12] Other forms of materialism are to be encountered in Ottoman Turkey. The Ottoman caliphate "saw its position weakened in recent times only as the result of suggestions the materialists wheedled into the souls of its mighty and its military leaders."[13]

[10] See *Jamāl al-Dīn al-Afghānī, Réfutation des matérialistes*, 65.
[11] Ibid., 129–30. [12] Ibid., 82.
[13] Ibid., 133.

To struggle against the materialists and the propagation of their ideas in the land of Islam, to warn against the danger of these ideas for the well being of Muslims constituted for al-Afghānī the best way, in the context of modern times, of preventing the open practice of evil when it was carried out openly—this, then, in keeping with the religious duty incumbent on every legally responsible Muslim. Thus, the struggle takes the form of a political combat waged on two fronts: first, against the colonizer who seeks to conquer the minds and subjugate the people by propagating materialist beliefs in preparation for seizing Islamic countries; second, against the political regimes in the land of Islam judged to be collaborating with the colonizing enemies or to be too weak and insufficiently vigilant about resisting them. In all instances, the struggle against materialism is a crucial form of political opposition, and by his stance the *muṣliḥ* shows himself to be an overt opponent.

Al-Afghānī pushed the struggle against the colonizing powers and against weak or defective Islamic regimes as far as he could, all the while seeking to link it with the struggle for uniting Muslim nations. In so doing, he stood forth as an indefatigable opponent, one hostile to anything that hindered his purposes or threatened to nullify his appeal.

## DESPOTISM AND BACKWARDNESS: OPPOSITION AND FORMS OF STRUGGLE

The Muslim reformers of the nineteenth century were unanimous in criticizing the way Muslim countries were governed and in holding those governments directly responsible for the backwardness of Islam in modern times. All the same, the views and analyses of ʿAbd al-Raḥmān al-Kawākibī (1849–1902) set him apart. Like his peers, this Syrian reformer starts from the usual refrain of failure: he draws attention to the deplorable gap between what Muslims had been in their golden age and their current condition of decline and backwardness, especially as contrasted with the progress of other civilized peoples. Like his fellow reformers, al-Kawākibī offers a political explanation for this decline, but the underpinnings of the analysis are entirely unprecedented. He writes:

> It seems to me that the cause of our sluggishness lies in the transformation of the political regime in Islam. At the outset, it was representative and consultative, that is, completely democratic; but due to the rivalries that arose following upon the rule of the four rightly-guided caliphs, it became imperialist, though

still inspired by the principles of divine law. Afterwards, it became more nearly absolutist.[14]

By claiming that the political regime in Islam has passed through three phases, he manages, at one and the same time, to describe a historical process, hit upon an adjective—absolutist—that best characterizes the way Muslim countries are currently governed, and establish the grounds for a theory linking tyranny and backwardness. If tyranny and backwardness are intimately linked, as the history of Islam indicates all too well, it is because backwardness owes its existence to tyranny; and, whenever it needs to, it turns to the intrigues of tyrannical rule for justification and renewed strength. Thus, before speaking about ways to "struggle against subjugation," we must first discern the causes and learn to recognize "the characteristics of despotism," a task to which al-Kawākibī devoted himself wholeheartedly.

Looked at from a purely rational perspective, despotism appears to be nothing other than "carrying out the affairs of the collectivity according to the whims of the despot." To act as a despot is to deny the collectivity the right of giving its opinion and to negate the principle of representation by turning aside all popular demands, thereby reducing everyone to a state of subjugation. In this respect, the despot is comparable to an evil guardian, who, instead of seeking to protect his ward's inheritance, allows his own private desires free rein. Just as it is not in the interest of the evil guardian that "his ward reach adulthood . . . so is it not in the interest of the despot that his subjects become enlightened through science."[15]

Ignorance is servile; by his evil deeds, the despot is certain to continue his domination. Science is salutary; through the rays of light it emits, the nation finds joy and liberty once again. Thus, the path towards progress starts with the abolition of despotism. To acquiesce in the reign of a despot is to accept backwardness, to surrender to it, bound hand and foot. Worse yet, despotism is the reason for national independence being lost:

If a nation does not know how to conduct its political affairs wisely, God puts it under the authority of another nation, as do those lawmakers who place a

[14] This passage from ʿAbd al-Raḥmān al-Kawākibī's *Umm al-Qurā* (Mecca) is cited in Norbert Tapiéro, *Les idées réformistes d'al-Kawākibī* (Paris: Les Éditions Arabes, 1956), 83. The literal translation of the title of al-Kawākibī's book is "Mother of the Villages," this being the honorific name by which Mecca is denoted in Arabic.

[15] This passage from ʿAbd al-Raḥmān al-Kawākibī's *Ṭabāʾiʿ al-Istibdād* (Characteristics of despotism) is also cited in Norbert Tapiéro, *Les idées réformistes d'al-Kawākibī*, 84.

minor or a person of feeble intelligence in the hands of a guardian . . . thus it is not God who oppresses men, but men who oppress themselves.[16]

There are three principles to be taken into consideration in the combat to be waged against despotism. The first principle, from which the other two are derived, consists in acknowledging that "any nation that does not resent—unanimously or in its major part—the sufferings imposed by despotism does not deserve to be free." Thus, without the least hesitation, al-Kawākibī subscribes to the golden rule decreed by the Quran: "Verily, God does not change the condition of a people until they change themselves."[17]

The second principle is a rule of conduct we are to hold as being universally valid: "Despotism is to be fought not with violence, but with forethought and measured steps."[18] Thus, it will be overcome neither by a sudden confrontation nor a brutal uprising. Only profoundly intelligent and continuous activity will be equal to the task of eliminating despotism, and this sort of activity "can be achieved only through instruction and tenacity." Before it becomes political activity, the fight to be waged against despotism is a three-fold undertaking: cultural, because it works to spread science and to extol the way it benefits humankind; pedagogical, insofar as it draws its inspiration from the great lessons of history; and, finally, spiritual, in that it constitutes a step toward the salvation of the soul and true submission to the divine will.

The third principle is also a rule of conduct, one—as with any liberation movement—that calls for the adoption of a well-defined program: "Before combating despotism, it is necessary to prepare the regime that is to replace it." Fundamental to this regime is that its mode of government be based on the respect of the nation and the supremacy of the law, for these are the two conditions necessary for pursuing progress and guaranteeing the well being of the nation. To achieve this, legislative power must be vested in the nation—a stipulation that finds its justification in the well-known saying of the Prophet: "My nation will never come together in unanimity upon error." By the same token, the courts are to be authorized to "judge the king and the pauper on an equal footing . . . and to place those responsible for government, those called

16 This passage and the next, both from al-Kawākibī's *Ṭabāʿiʾ*, are cited by Tapiéro, *Les idées*, 91.
17 *Quran*, 13:11.
18 This and the following citations are from al-Kawākibī's *Ṭabāʿiʾ*, as cited by Tapiéro, *Les idées*, 91ff.

to handle the nation's affairs, in a position such that they cannot exceed the rights following from their duties."

In brief, to abolish despotism one must toil to bring about a political regime based on the people being truly represented and effectively consulted about all things pertaining to their political life so that they may have "the possibility of watching over and controlling the way government functions." Yet the installation of a constitutional regime along these lines is not an end in and of itself for Muslim peoples. A far greater ideal remains to be attained: that of uniting all Muslims under a single caliphate.

Is this a sort of pan-Islamism? To be sure. But the differences in tenor and tone between al-Kawākibī's and al-Afghānī's pan-Islamism must be taken into account. It differs in tenor, first of all, because the author of *Umm al-Qurā* drapes his pan-Islamism in such exalted hues of Arabism. Like all advocates of Arabism, al-Kawākibī attacks the Sublime Porte harshly, albeit indirectly:

> The greatest part of this disorder came about . . . after the empire was obliged to organize its own affairs. Former principles of governing showed themselves to be useless, and the empire was able neither to imitate the old rules nor to innovate; it fell apart . . . and lost two-thirds of its territories, while the other third was ruined and on the point of disappearing.

The "other third" was none other than the Arab world. For the decline of that world, as well as of all the Muslim countries under Ottoman domination, al-Kawākibī holds the Sublime Porte implicitly responsible. On the one hand, it failed to provide "capable men" to handle local affairs, and, on the other, "his majesty the Sultan was [so] totally preoccupied with seeking to protect his own noble person" that he did nothing to protect the territories he ruled.

The pan-Islamism of al-Kawākibī differs in tone due to the greater emphasis he places upon the democratic aspect of what is entailed by the reunification of Muslims in modern times. At the fictitious conference he holds in Mecca (not in Istanbul, the official capital of Islam), all of the Muslim states are represented in the full diversity of their languages and trappings. In his eyes, the conference would be bereft of meaning and effectiveness were such complete representation lacking. The importance al-Kawākibī attaches to having the different delegates of the Muslim peoples speak at this conference highlights even more the difference in tone between his idea of what pan-Islamism signifies and what al-Afghānī takes it to mean. For the author of *Umm al-Qurā*, a necessary condition for Muslim unity to succeed is that people be free to express themselves openly. This condition seems not to have greatly troubled the famous Afghan reformer.

In sum, al-Kawākibī calls for struggling against despotism, working to bring about a political regime that truly represents the nation and consults with it, and militating in favor of a pan-Islamic ideal that is strongly impregnated with an anti-Ottoman Arabism. These are the diverse forms through which he was able to manifest his uneasiness about the current state of affairs, express his refusal of such a transformed political world, and ally himself with an opposition thought whose broad lines had been sketched out by his predecessors.

## CONCLUSION

Religious intransigence was not the only form of opposition in the Muslim countries of the nineteenth century. Indeed, a number of thinkers attempted to reflect upon social and political questions without having recourse to the sphere of religion. After the 1870s, Christian Arab thinkers were quickly caught up in a current of thought that embraced the key words of the Enlightenment—reason, progress, liberty, and social contract—as well as the ideas that had been in vogue in Europe during the previous century. In some circles, Muslim intellectuals were no less susceptible to similar ideas—a fact that, among other influences, helps account for al-Afghānī's anti-materialist campaign. Although Morocco lay somewhat outside the influence of these ideas, a group of young *ʿulamāʾ* and intellectuals of various bents militated in favor of constitutionalism in the political life of the country. *Lisān al-Maghrib* (Voice of Morocco) was the publication that best expressed the hope animating the thoughts of the "modernists" who gathered around the new Sultan following the removal from power of Sultan ʿAbd al-ʿAzīz in 1908.

Nonetheless, reaction animated by religious conscience remained the main force behind the opposition. Calls for religion to be regenerated, for Muslim states to be reunited under a single caliphate, and, at times, for *jihād* were the multiple manifestations of one and the same wish, namely, to be part of the new era while preserving the outward signs of an older, authentic identity. At the same time, the dominant trait of Muslim opposition thought in the nineteenth century was the staunch rejection of any compromise. Concessions to necessity, as in the phrase "necessity has its own laws" (*li-al-ḍarūra aḥkām*), were never invoked, numerous as were the incidents that might have justified them. Differently stated, there was no place in the vocabulary of Muslim discourse during the nineteenth century for words like realism, political pragmatism, and national interest.

# Part II

## Twentieth Century

# Preface

## I. WILLIAM ZARTMAN

In the second half of the twentieth century and the beginning of the twenty-first, the confrontation between hardened versions of the state and religion in the Middle East was not merely the figment of an observer's Manichean imagination. The postwar period began with a gradual affirmation of the state, grown out of nationalist movements rising from the ashes of colonial collapse and nurtured by the hostile Israeli challenge and the seductive cold war rivalry. By the end of the first postwar decade, under the leadership of Gamāl ʿAbd al-Nāṣir's revolutionary Egypt, the Arab socialist Mukhābarāt state was in place.

Even against the democracy movement of the 1990s that rose with the collapse of the Soviet Union and the advancing peace process in the Middle East, the state held firm. The nationalism that inspired it and the socialism that directed it have both run thin, but it is in no danger of—according to various theories—withering away, being permeated to pieces, or sinking into civil society. Its most ironic fate is to be privatized, ending up in the hands of a small group who use its powers and perquisites for their own advantage, quite out of the reach of any public control. Even when it teetered on the edge of collapse, as in Algeria after 1988, it was pulled back by a reassertion of force before it won legitimacy, turning Weber's definition of a state on its head.

Initially in this period, the state fostered and tamed religion, using it to give positive content to its nationalism and then turning it into a sector of the civil service. But as the state lost its inspiration and its self-assurance over its leadership into the better life, a vivified Islam came to fill the gap. Islamic movements that had formerly enjoyed state protection or even sponsorship in the 1960s and 1970s turned from timid imams to avenging angels, decrying the secular authorities for corruption and impiety and proclaiming themselves human agents of the wrath of God.

There is no doubt that the causative context for the Islamic revival was the failure of the secular "-isms" to deliver, but reassertive Islam is not just a material response: it is an antidote to failings of the soul as well as of the body. And not surprisingly, in its political form, it seeks to seize and wield the same unbending rule as did the authorities it decries.

Ibn Khaldūn analyzed and predicted all this, in the late fourteenth and early fifteenth centuries, but he missed a twist of the twentieth century that complicates his story. While it is true that even today, the softening of state in the fleshpots of urban modernity calls forth a response of militant cleansing and solidarity in the name of religious revival, the twentieth-century state was not as easy a prey to the onslaught from the desert as was its predecessor half a millennium earlier. Current state response to Islamist attacks from Morocco through Egypt to Saudi Arabia has been to harden its control, clamp down in various ways on civil liberties, civic pluralism, and individual expression. Even when controls are relaxed on these items, they are loosened selectively and by degrees by a state in charge.

## INCIPIENT PLURALISM

Yet through these two slabs of concrete cracks appear, as the following chapters testify. There is vibrant intellectual exchange that takes on both religious and secular authority, translating itself as well into organized activity. In the shadow of the struggle for monolithic control rises a struggle against monolithic control. The competing orders are questioned, new reference points are advanced. With greater creativity than the apostles of monolithism, thinkers, writers, technocrats, organizers look for new ways.

Without necessarily suggesting a causative sequence, the account can begin with the penetration of controlled space by ideas and images from an outside world. Jean Leca and his associates show how new world technology in the form of satellite disks shatters comfortable images of the present and the future in the Maghrib, as in the Mashriq, creating new dysfunctions and dissonance. Focused identities are disjointed as people see themselves—or cannot see themselves—in other places; what they want to be clashes with what they are, of course, but also with what they can be.

It would be wrong—or unproven—to suggest that television parabolas open closed societies to religious and political paradoxes. It is more likely—though still unproven—that external dissonance took root because society was already restive under the clamp of religious and political orthodoxies. Quite independent of and prior to the penetration of television from north of the Mediterranean, curious minds wrestled with pluralism and reform in both fields. Asʿad AbuKhalil deals with the religious side, whose Islamic nonconformism seeks to combine religious reform and fidelity. As the democratic thinkers attack the unicity of the single-party authoritarian state, so the religious conformists seek to impart flexibility to a religion whose doors of interpretation are officially closed. Similar to the political writings, the religious reformers look for change from within, rather than turning their backs on religious goals and values.

Iliya Harik presents a number of writers who preach democratic ideals. Like the tele-spectators, their images are torn between the message and the context. Democracy is described and debated, but not as a good in itself; it is a more appropriate means to the end of unity and progress, goals appropriated from the failed orthodoxies. But since these belief systems have failed to deliver, it is their inadequacies that allow foreign ideas to penetrate and to be assimilated.

The practical translation of such ideas takes the form of opposition parties that seek to carve out political space between the state single party and the organization of political Islam. Ibrahim Karawan presents several such parties, liberal or leftist in nature, whose message is structurally condemned to be more a protest against political monolithism than an assertion of a different platform. So much programmatic space is occupied by the competing parties of the state and the religion that there is little room left for a broad appeal from the opposition, frequently locked by vulnerability and inexperience into a position of permanent minority. But their presence gives expression to different interests and philosophies in society and shakily introduces political pluralism.

The ultimate base of such pluralism in both domains is found in civil society, with its interests, organizations, and activities growing out of socioeconomic differentiation. As modernity in ideas is associated with empathy toward different experiences, so in action is it related to specialization and pluralization in the experiences themselves. Timothy Piro presents professional organizations, whose membership and interests are determined by their specific activities in, and contributions to, society. While such organizations are by nature independent of both state and religion, as part of civil society, it is their pluralism that provides the basis for the incipient pluralism in outlook that the preceding chapters have presented.

Pluralism in all its forms between state and Islam is defined in opposition, and is torn by the complexity of its relations with the monoliths it opposes. Threatened on both sides, pluralism in thought and organization is dogged by structural dilemmas. While its opposition would make it a kind of irregular sniper shooting indiscriminately at both sides, its need for sources of power and momentary advantage often makes it a hired gun. With whom to ally—the tactical question—brings it close to betrayal of its own mission. In the end, democratic thinkers and religious reformers alike are torn between an alliance with fellow secularists or religionists, respectively, or with fellow opponents of the monolith they oppose. Liberal parties and professional organizations are dependent on the state for permission to exist but often defend even religious extremists or are taken over by them in the name of pluralism.

## THE OPEN ROAD

To identify the work of synthesis as the important calling of the various groups and currents lying between the state and Islam is not to say that such a synthesizing current is sweeping away everything in its path. Its voice is timid, its actions controlled, and while it expresses irrepressible cries and reflexes from within society, they reach a level of articulation and diffusion only through the tolerance of political and religious authorities. That is in the nature of their structural position. But more important is the fact that the seekers of synthesis have not yet worked through all the directions and implications of their arguments and actions, as the following chapters show as well.

Internally and externally their work is not yet done. Professional groups of business and labor have come to be accepted as spokespersons for particular interests but have only rarely found their places together in general fora on public policy issues. As a result, the broader implications of their interests have not been pursued. Similarly for the opposition parties, the challenge of carving out an alternative position and an alternative source of support to the government party—and yet one that is not Islamist—is daunting. Previously, the government platform was a local variant of Arab Socialism; now it is a local form of structural adjustment. Alternatives are not obvious, and appeals on the part of inexperienced politicians for support from an electorate that tends to vote for power are not successful. With rare exceptions—in the monarchies of Morocco and Jordan, and possibly in Algeria in the future—secular opposition parties are not yet real players in a political confrontation still dominated by the state party and the Islamist pretender to the same exclusive role. No political or economic system in the Arab Muslim world has yet been successfully pluralized. A modernization of the religious beliefs—defined as individualization of beliefs, accommodation with science, social equality of individuals, and reevaluation of dogma—is still far off; reformers are pilloried, intolerance is reaffirmed, and reformers are still on the outside trying to look in, not working from within the religious establishment.

The challenge is as striking on the level of the ideas themselves. Proposals for a modernized religion and theories of a non-Western democracy lack coherence; many of the issues inherent in each are not yet joined, as AbuKhalil and Harik indicate in some detail. On the most popular level, local television programs have not yet been able to present a national image that is attractive and credible. But the fact that the glass is half empty indicates that it is half filled, that there is space between Islam and the state, and that there are vigorous efforts to fill it.

# 5

# Against the Taboos of Islam: Anti-Conformist Tendencies in Contemporary Arab/Islamic Thought

AS'AD ABUKHALIL

## INTRODUCTION

Reform in Islam has long been the subject of analysis and debate among Muslims and non-Muslims alike. For many Muslims, Islam is beyond reform. It is the perfect religion completed by the Prophet Muḥammad, to whom is attributed the saying "I have completed your religion for you." In their eyes, reform becomes legitimate only insofar as it is limited to matters that can be revised through interpretation—which thus excludes the Quranic text—or to rituals and modes of worship. Muḥammad ibn ʿAbd al-Wahāb, for example, views reform as seeking to purify religion from external, harmful influences. From this perspective, reform does not arise to counter inadequacies within Islam that are responsible for the social and political problems afflicting Muslim societies. The reformist movement in Islam that emerged in the nineteenth and twentieth centuries adheres to these restrictions and thus differs from the radical reformist tendencies discussed in what follows. But there are similarities between the two worth noting.

The traditional reformist movement—as exemplified by Muḥammad ʿAbduh, Rashīd Riḍā, and ʿAbd al-Raḥmān al-Kawākibī—continues to exert influence through the Muslim Brotherhood and similar conservative political groups. It is concerned primarily with religion, while the radical reformist movement discussed here is concerned with the state. For traditional reform, social illnesses are manifest signs of the weakness of the hold of Islam. The complaints people have about their lives are to be addressed by increasing, not diminishing, the role of Islam. Society does not figure in the literature of traditional reform, because no distinction between state—to the extent that it is legitimate according to Islamic norms—and society is recognized. Such a distinction is viewed as the result of Western models of secularism that could eventually signal the end of Islam as a universal religion.

The individuals covered here do not constitute a movement as such. Many are unknown to one another and differ in their political and ideological orientations. What they share, however, is revulsion over the views and interpretations of establishment Islam as well as over the champions of traditional reform. Nonetheless, in agreement with traditional reform, these thinkers consider *ḥadīth* less significant than the Quran. Unlike traditional reformers, who are willing to go no further than commentaries on the Quran, radical reformers tolerate and even encourage modern interpretations of Quranic texts. They refuse the theologically centered analysis (what Mohammed Arkoun calls *logocentrisme*) that has given religious scholars a monopoly on defining religion for the public.[1] The difference between traditional reform per se and the radical reform covered here is greater than that between fundamentalist and liberal Islam. As Leonard Binder states, "both fundamentalist Islam and liberal Islam draw on the same religious sources."[2]

The authors to be studied were not chosen accidentally. All are either only superficially known to the West (e.g., Faraj Fūda because of his assassination) or totally unknown. They represent a trend of free-thinking that has accompanied the rise and decline of Arab/Islamic civilization. However, because they eschew ideological and theoretical positions or lack shared foundations, their efforts cannot be summarized as fitting a single category. Hādī al-ʿAlawī, for example, is a Marxist and Faraj Fūda a Western liberal. Yet, in their work on Islamic history, both diverge from scriptural literalism and glorification of the Islamic past. As representatives of radical reform (which I term anti-conformism), they differ from traditional reformers like ʿAbduh and Riḍā who express unstinting admiration for the worthy ancestors (*al-salaf al-ṣāliḥ*) and regard them as the architects of a past utopia. The goal of traditional

[1] Mohammed Arkoun, *Pour une critique de la raison islamique* (Paris: Maisonneuve et LaRose, 1984). Here, and in what follows, the term "religious scholars" refers to those *ʿulamāʾ* salaried by governments in Muslim countries who overwhelmingly approve of and rationalize—on Islamic grounds—the decisions, policies, and deeds of those governments. Thus, as a group, religious scholars in Egypt supported Anwar Sadat's peace agreement with Israel, even though individual members of the same establishment had in the past supported Nasser's rejection of peace with Israel. The disenchantment with the subservience of religious scholars has helped promote the rise of a new generation of independent scholars, many of whom are now active in Islamic fundamentalist opposition groups in Egypt and elsewhere in the region.

[2] Leonard Binder, *Islamic Liberalism: A Critique of Development Ideologies* (Chicago: University of Chicago Press, 1988), 357.

reform is to establish a replica of the past in the present and future. The state is seen not as the builder of a new, original order, but as the mirror of early Islamic government. The relationship between the state and Islam is to be determined according to the political needs of Islam. Those needs are viewed, however, as unchanging on the grounds that regardless of how much people's needs and inclinations change, Islam remains the same and is always capable of solving human problems in any century and in any cultural context.

For the radical reformers, Islam is a private matter relegated to a realm outside the control of the state. Even the Quran is subject to a critical examination that considers its text subservient to science[3] and to the public interest. The pioneer in this regard is not ʿAlī ʿAbd al-Rāziq, but Ṭāhā Ḥusayn. Seeking to apply the methodology of Descartes to the study of the Quran, which he deems to be no different from other works of Arabic literature, he insists:

> Yes, when we turn to the examination of Arabic literature and its history we should forget our nationalism and all its symptoms, our religion and whatever is related to it, and whatever opposes this religion and this nationalism. We should not adhere to anything or submit to anything other than the genuine methodologies of scientific examination.[4]

In a similar fashion, the authors under study refuse to submit to the postulates of religion as defined by the consensus (*ijmāʿ*) of the religious scholars.

Conversely, the methodology of the anti-conformist writers sometimes resembles that of their enemies insofar as they seek to turn their own weapons against them. For example, in a recent book, Muḥammad Shuḥrūr dismisses the validity of *ḥadīth* in principle, yet cites a sound (*ṣaḥīḥ*) *ḥadīth* in support of this view.[5] Their objectives are nonetheless quite different from those of traditional reformers. Traditional reformers view the state as a mere tool in the service of Islam and Muslims, a means to an ideal end. The state can and should be molded to conform to the order existing at the time of the worthy ancestors. For the anti-

[3] See Ṭarīf Khālidī, *Dirāsāt fī Ta'rikh al-Fikr al-ʿArabī al-Islāmī* (Studies in the history of Arab Islamic thought) (Beirut: Dār al-Ṭalīʿa, 1979), 11.

[4] See Ṭāhā Ḥusayn, *Fī al-Shiʿr al-Jāhilī* (On pre-Islamic poetry) (Cairo: Maṭbaʿa Dār al-Kutub, 1926), 12. This remark notwithstanding, Ḥusayn accepted the accuracy of the Quranic text while questioning the accuracy of pre-Islamic poetry. Note that this book was banned soon after its publication and republished in full only recently as part of the Egyptian government's efforts to counter insurgent religious tendencies.

[5] Muḥammad Shuḥrūr, *Dirāsāt Islāmiyya Muʿāṣira fī al-Dawla wa al-Mujtamaʿ* (Contemporary Islamic studies on the state and society) (Damascus: al-Ahālī, 1994), 25.

conformists, the state is an end in and of itself, serving the public regardless of whether the period of rule of the Rightly Guided Caliphs was truly a Golden Age or not. The state is important because it can guarantee rights and freedoms not envisioned by the Quran. Nor do they see any reason to argue that the Quran negates the possibility of a democratic, or even a secular, state.

In the discourse of traditional reform, there is a debate about the desirability of reviving the Islamic caliphate, not necessarily to respond to people's needs and desires, but to ensure that those needs and desires not be met through a Western model of political organization. Traditional reformers want the state to preserve the customs and ways of life that correspond to those of the worthy ancestors. For the radical reformers, the challenge is for Muslims to continue to consider themselves Muslims even if they deviate from the standards of the worthy ancestors. In fact, the literature of radical reform contains new analyses aimed at debunking the myths of Islamic apologia and even at discrediting the very personalities hailed as the exemplary pioneers of Islamic piety. If Islam is the solution for traditional reformers, the state—a secularized, democratic (and, at least in one case, a Marxist) state—is the solution for the radical reformers.

## METHODOLOGICAL INTRODUCTION

Western studies of contemporary Islamic thought often attribute to it monolithic characteristics. The view that there exists one kind of Islam and one kind of Muslims has been reinforced by classical Orientalists such as the influential emeritus Princeton historian, Bernard Lewis. The various strands within contemporary Arab/Islamic thought have been obscured insofar as Islamic fundamentalism, hereafter denoted as Islamism, has been portrayed as consisting of a rigid bloc that allows no room for disagreements or diversity of opinions. Yet that portrait is inaccurate in that the general agreement existing about issues of principle—the desirability of imposing *sharī'a* law; insistence upon male supremacy; fear of Westernization; opposition to Israel on religious grounds; and calls for change at the social, political, and economic levels—breaks down over the practical questions of how and when these goals are to be achieved.

The emergence of critical, free-thinking trends in Islamic thought represents a long tradition of anti-conformism in Arab/Islamic civilization. Poets, philosophers, scientists, writers, and Sufis all contributed to the legacy of dissent. Yet because not all rulers were open to criticism, many free-thinkers paid the highest penalty for expressing their beliefs. Again, it sometimes happened that their personal enemies mounted successful campaigns against them under the guise of combating their nontraditional views. Ibn al-Muqaffaʿ, for example, may well have been killed for personal reasons rather than for the heresy of which he was accused.[6] Finally, in the history of Arab/Islamic civilization, rulers sometimes oppressed free-thinkers to send a message of toughness to the masses or to appease conservative elements among the hierarchy of religious scholars.

The study of reform requires attention to methodology. There are certain strands in the body of reformist thought, within and without Islam, that need to be distinguished. Not all reformers adhere to the Islamic apologetic paradigm, nor do they accept the postulates of Islam as terms of reference. Moreover, the political and religious scholarly establishments alike sometimes oppose reform for reasons not necessarily related to religion. Some, but not all, religious scholars have vehemently opposed reform in the course of Islamic history. Such opposition has been strengthened in this century because reform has asserted itself more vehemently and because religious scholars have increasingly been losing their monopolization of control over the interpretation of religious texts.

Attempts at reform within Islam have also faced opposition because such activity conjures up images both among the public and among religious scholars of the way reform works within the Christian church. There is still paranoia that Islam reformed will become Islam secularized, relegated to a private realm separate from political activity. This is anathema insofar as Islam, unlike Christianity, is viewed by the religious scholars as covering all facets of life. Thus, despite claims by strict adherents of Judaism and Christianity that their religions also cover all facets of life, the suggestion that Islam can be considered a religion like them is rejected on religious grounds. In Islam alone has this rigid, rejectionist viewpoint achieved nearly unanimous popular support after centuries of state-engineered inculcation. Opponents of reform also argue that reform will inevitably lead to religion and politics becoming separated.

Reformers within Islam have also to contend with the argument that reform will automatically lead to Westernization. What hampers the

[6] ʿAbd Allāh ibn al-Muqaffaʿ (d. 142/759) is one of the most celebrated writers of Arabic prose. The best treatment of his life and literature is ʿAbd al-Laṭīf Ḥamza's classic study, *Ibn al-Muqaffaʿ* (Cairo: Dār al-Fikr al-ʿArabī, 1965).

efforts of reformers within Islam in this century is that their predecessors did not conceal their admiration for, indeed glorification of, Europe and its ways. In a little-noticed article that Ṭāhā Ḥusayn wrote before his writings became controversial, he insists upon the necessity that "European civilization cover (*taghmur*) Egypt and Syria until these two countries become parts of Europe."[7] While reformers of his bent deemed the total Europeanization of the Arab world to be the logical conclusion of reform, others like Muḥammad ʿAbduh did not want to compromise the cultural and religious essence of the region.[8] The accusation that to reform Islam is to Westernize it assumes, then, that Islam cannot be reformed without losing its essence—that is, that Islam reformed is not Islam. Furthermore, the fear about Islam becoming Westernized is based on the mistaken association between secularism and Christianity. Yet Westernized Muslims are not necessarily less Islamic. Not even contemporary Arab Islamists question the Islamic commitment of Muslims living in secular Western countries.

But religious scholars have a lot to lose from the reform of Islam, not least their salaried positions of leadership within the community. Moreover, the breakdown of the system of official interpretation of the *sharīʿa* would undermine, if not eventually eliminate, their positions of leadership. The community of Muslims today is beginning to question the moral legitimacy of religious scholars because their subservience to political leaders has been exposed. The proliferation of Islamist groups throughout the Arab world has resulted in an increase of popularly selected religious scholars who are seen as an alternative to the salaried scholars appointed by the government.

The history of free-thinking in Islam—a subject worthy of further research and study in light of the one-dimensionality and dogmatism of Islamic historiography—will not be addressed here. We will focus, instead, on contemporary writers in the Arab world whose writings are almost as unknown to readers in the Arab world as they are to Western readers. By examining these authors, it may be possible to suggest how people living under extremely harsh and repressive conditions express dissident views on sensitive issues dealing with Islam and on the legitimacy—or lack thereof—of dominant interpretations of texts.

The study of free-thinking, or of anti-conformism, is not necessarily a study of reform. Reform is intended to revive Islam in order to apply

[7] See Ṭāhā Ḥusayn, "Fatāwā" (Legal opinions), in *al-Hilāl*, 1923, 86.
[8] See Malcolm Kerr, *Islamic Reform* (Berkeley: University of California Press, 1966), 108–9.

it more effectively in polity and society. Anti-conformist radicalism—at least those strands of it examined here—aims at marginalizing Islam to revitalize polity and society in order to move them away from the sway of religion. Anti-conformism reflects the efforts of individual Muslims who, rather than blindly accept officially sanctioned interpretations of religious texts, choose to reject those interpretations and subject the sacrosanct texts to critical examination and interpretation.

Three separate trends or schools of anti-conformism can be distinguished. The first is the school of thought that blames certain historical phenomena in religious life and understanding on the way texts are interpreted. It absolves the religious texts (namely, the Quran and *ḥadīth*) from responsibility for particular harmful practices in society. Fatima Mernissi, for example, attempts to reinterpret texts of the Quran and *ḥadīth* with respect to the gender question. She argues that the true Islamic position on women differs from the view that has come to be traditionally accepted.[9] Leila Ahmed's work on women in Islam also fits within this school.[10] Without insisting upon a problem in Islam per se, this school of thought blames religious scholars and the community for having distorted the original meaning of Quranic verses and *ḥadīth*s or for having given undue emphasis to particular *ḥadīth*s. Nonetheless, it does not call for dismissing the Quranic text either in part or in total.

The second school, which may be referred to as that of "convenient selectivity," calls for accepting parts of the Quran and rejecting others. This method of abrogation (*naskh*) was practiced in early Islamic history and later abandoned due to its potentially pernicious consequences. ʿAbd Allāh al-Naʿīm[11] and Muḥammad Shuḥrūr are both affiliated with this school.

The third school of anti-conformism, consisting in the main of thinkers who align themselves with Marxism, rejects religious thought as a matter of principle. Members of this and the second school suffer persecution more readily than members of the first. After all, to reject the authoritativeness of the Quran in Muslim society is to question the foundation of contemporary political and social institutions.

9 See Fatima Mernissi, *The Veil and the Male Elite* (New York: Addison-Wesley, 1991), 189–95.

10 See Leila Ahmed, *Women and Gender in Islam* (New Haven: Yale University Press, 1992), 79–101.

11 See ʿAbd Allāh al-Naʿīm, *Towards Islamic Reform* (Syracuse: Syracuse University Press, 1987).

## CHARACTERISTICS OF THE ANTI-CONFORMIST MOVEMENT

The study of anti-conformism in contemporary Arab/Islamic thought requires a realistic assessment of the nature and impact of the writings of the authors in question. Though the wishful thinking of secular intellectuals sometimes portrays them as a widespread and popular movement, their effect as a group is in reality very limited. Indeed, as already noted, there is no anti-conformist movement as such. There is no political party and no central program to tie the movement together in any coherent manner. Anti-conformism consists of fragmented clusters of various individuals who often are not aware of one another's writings or existence. Even when some of the anti-conformist writers within particular Arab countries are acquainted with one another, they may still be ideological rivals. Personal and political differences sometimes impair the chances for the creation of a central organization.

And, their critics notwithstanding, the anti-conformist writers cannot all be described as hostile to Islam. Most of the writings of the anti-conformists examined here, as well as those of others not discussed, are characterized by an apologetic cast. In their treatment of Muḥammad's life, the definitiveness of the Quranic text, and Islam's responsiveness to modern problems, most—if not all—anti-conformists approach the subject apologetically, even defensively. All too often, the harassment of anti-conformist writers can be traced to extrinsic forces: the pressure exerted upon those who live under governments anxious to use Islam for purposes of political legitimacy.

## BLAMING THE PAST: FARAJ FŪDA AND THE PENALTY OF DISOBEDIENCE

Of the thinkers considered here, Faraj Fūda is best known to Western readers. His June 1992 assassination in Egypt at the hands of Islamists brought his name to the attention of the media throughout the world. Trained as an agricultural engineer, Fūda devoted his efforts and writings to the subject of Islamism and Islamic history. He believed in dialogue with the Islamists and often called upon them to debate secularists. Indeed, he participated in a widely attended debate of this sort with the renowned Islamist thinker Muḥammad al-Ghazzālī during the 1992 Cairo Book Fair.

Fūda lacks extensive knowledge of Islamic jurisprudence (*fiqh*) and Arabic lexicography, but he is a careful reader of the books of the Arab/Islamic heritage and uses that knowledge to refute inaccuracies he discerns in Islamic historiography. Polemic, sometimes reaching to vulgar vilification of his rivals, marks his writings. In magazine articles, for example, he has boasted of possessing videotapes showing two Tunisian Islamist leaders in sexually compromising situations.[12] Apart from the book *al-Ḥaqīqa al-Ghā'iba* (The Absent truth),[13] his writings consist of compilations of previously published newspaper and magazine articles.

Yet, because Fūda's style and approach are more accessible, his influence exceeds that of the other writers examined here. He writes in simple, straightforward Arabic and is always daring as well as provocative in his thought. Because he so often directed his attacks against Islam while promoting secularism, he came to be demonized by many Egyptian Muslims—a phenomenon noted by the press. In addition to the enemies he gained through his views on Islam and his ridicule of Islamists, his espousal of Westernization and peace with Israel discredited him further.

For Fūda, the West (and Israel) represents an ideal type, even though his portrayal of the West is as far from reality as that found in the writings of the Islamists. In his debate with Fūda, Muḥammad al-Ghazzālī promotes the application of Quranic penal measures (*ḥudūd*) and holds the West up as lawless, singling out the United States on the grounds that murderers there are never executed "because the death penalty is rejected by them [the Americans]."[14] Yet Fūda is equally uninformed: in his efforts to discredit governments based on religion, he contends that religion has no role in Western societies. In an article originally appearing in the Egyptian weekly, *Uktūbir* (October), he insists that the West long ago abandoned religious persecution and that discrimination on the basis of gender and ideology is nowhere present in Western societies. Moreover, he staunchly denies the existence of hostility to Islam and Muslims in the West. Because he portrays the West in such utopian terms, he becomes an easy target for those who accuse Arab secularists of blind imitation and glorification of Western ways. At times, he seems to believe that the American government is absolutely neutral toward religious

[12] See Faraj Fūda, *Ḥattā lā Yakūn Kalāman fī al-Hawā'* (So that it does not become words in the air) (Cairo: Dār al-Ma'ārif, 1992), 34 and 237.

[13] Faraj Fūda, *al-Ḥaqīqa al-Ghā'iba* (Cairo: Dār al-Fikr, 1988). The title is a parody of the underground Islamist booklet entitled *al-Farīḍa al-Ghā'iba* (The Absent obligation).

[14] See the transcript of the debate published in *Miṣr bayn al-Dawla al-Dīniyya wa al-Madaniyya* (Egypt between the religious and civil state) (Cairo: al-Dār al-Miṣriyya, 1992), 14.

beliefs and he even describes the Israeli Likud party as desirous of "permanent peace."[15]

The major thrust of Fūda's writings is to strip Arab/Islamic history of the ideological and apologetic myths in which it has been shrouded. He takes the theses of the Islamists to their logical conclusions in calling for the examination of a past they consider the blueprint for a utopian future. Then, challenging the excessive pride they take in the Golden Age of Islam, he urges them to learn more about the details of that age and to do so without succumbing to writings that erroneously glorify the Islamic past. In this enterprise, Fūda relies on the writings of Islamic historians like al-Suyūṭī, Ibn Khaldūn, al-Ṭabarī, and al-Daynūrī who are largely unknown to Arabic readers today. From them, he ferrets out unpleasant facts. Noting that three—and according to some accounts, all four—of the Rightly Guided Caliphs did not die of natural causes, but were assassinated, he insists that, contrary to the way it is portrayed in school curricula and political literature, even that highly vaunted era was not one of peace and harmony.[16]

Fūda also debunks the theory that the application of the *sharīʿa* would, in and of itself, take care of all the social, economic, and political problems afflicting Muslim societies. Reminding readers of the numerous instances when injustice and oppression prevailed even though the *sharīʿa* was in force, he draws upon the history of the caliphate to show the magnitude of corruption and sedition in precisely those Muslim governments regarded as exemplary by many contemporary Muslims.[17] His reading of history thus allows Fūda to make the daring observation that, in terms of progress and humanitarian standards, the present is superior to the past. In his endeavors, Fūda is ever ready to point to sexual misconduct (defined according to the almost Victorian, contemporary Islamic standards) and to contest the claim that earlier Islamic governments adhered to strict standards of moral and ethical behavior. As hostile to homosexuals as the Islamists, he singles out for particular attention the homosexual caliphs and thus further discredits the caliphate.

Fūda's support for secularism is not, however, accompanied by firm support for human rights and democracy. His hatred of Islamist ideology and practice leads him to identify with any cause that weakens it, even those that abuse human rights. Thus he strongly identifies with the

[15] See *Ḥattā*, 40–1, 46–7, and 71.

[16] See *al-Ḥaqīqa*, 24–6.

[17] Ibid., 29–30.

Egyptian state in its war "against terrorism."[18] As long as the state continues to combat the Islamists, he is not troubled by its egregious actions.

Still, the effectiveness of Fūda's writings cannot be underestimated. He never refused an offer to debate; he always printed his personal address at the end of his books; and he painstakingly read the publications of the Islamists to expose their preoccupation with insignificant issues. For example, he cited one publication in which two major Islamic thinkers debated whether Muslim men would enjoy permanent sexual arousal in heaven.[19] Nonetheless, his concerns never strayed far from those of power politics nor can it be claimed that his influence approximated that of any of his intellectual rivals. Yet he would surely never have been marked for assassination had his writings not had some effect on others.

It can be argued that Fūda's legacy will not long survive. Though his writings may appeal to those Muslims who have not been exposed to critical writings about their religion and its role in society, his insistence upon polemic and his fixation with the interests of the Egyptian state detract from the genuine merit of his contribution. Fūda not only failed to concern himself with the question of "authenticity," but he was all too open about his belief in the need to emulate Western political and social models. This in itself will undermine the credibility of his reform, especially given his strong political views.

## THE SCHOOL OF CONVENIENT SELECTIVITY

### *1. Muḥammad Shuḥrūr and the Books of the Quran*

The work of Muḥammad Shuḥrūr would still be unknown to Western readers, were it not for a few references in the British press and an introductory article by Dale Eickelman in the *Bulletin* of the Middle East Studies Association. Shuḥrūr's first book, *al-Kitāb wa al-Qurʿān: Qirāʾa Muʿāṣira* (The Book and the Quran: A contemporary reading), met with such popular acclaim that Eickelman called it a "publishing event."[20] The descendant of an established Damascene Sunni family and a civil engineer trained in Moscow and Dublin, he was at the time generally unknown to readers in the Arab world.

18 See Faraj Fūda, *Nakūn aw lā Nakūn* (To be or not to be) (Cairo: al-Hayʾa al-Miṣriyya al-ʿĀmma li-al-Kitāb, 1992), 73.

19 See *Ḥurriyyatī* (My freedom), 19 April 1992; cited in *Ḥattā*, 199–200.

20 See Dale Eickelman, "Islamic Liberalism Strikes Back," *MESA Bulletin* 27/2 (December 1993): 163. I am grateful to Edward Said for first alerting me to Shuḥrūr's book and to Ṣādiq Jalāl al-ʿĀẓm for sending me a copy of the third edition (Beirut: Sharikat al-Maṭbūʿāt, 1993).

In the beginning of the book, he makes some observations about the field of study of Islam in general and the Quran in particular. He laments the paucity of objective, scholarly studies in the field of Islamic thought. Books on women in Islam, for example, even if well documented and researched, tend to reflect their authors' dogmatically held prejudices and to be based on passions and emotions. Thus, like Orientalists before him and unlike most Muslims living in oppressive regimes such as his, Shuḥrūr avoids the "prior judgment" approach to the study of Islam. He also urges that an authentic theory of knowledge requires a utilization of "all the accumulation of knowledge produced by human beings, including the heritage of all the sciences."[21] Thus, Shuḥrūr's approach promises to alter the way all Muslims understand Islam and the Quran. It suggests not only that the *sharīʿa* is dynamic and constantly changing, but that Islam itself can evolve to fit the needs of people in different historical eras.

This is one reason the book has been fought by Arab governments, many of which have suppressed its publication and banned its circulation. Arab newspapers completely ignore the book, although they carry articles praising the publication of books written in response to it. But in the age of faxes, computers, and photocopiers, it is impossible for the governments of the Middle East to control the dissemination of ideas to the degree they could in the past. The publication of responses to Shuḥrūr's book shows how much it has affected official circles. For example, one author was content to attribute Shuḥrūr's conclusions to "satanic sciences produced by Jewish thought."[22]

Nonetheless, and this points to the narrow parameters of religious debate among Muslims today, Shuḥrūr gives in to an apologetic bias by refusing ever to question the unique genius of Muḥammad or the superiority of Islam. This writer, who wants to free himself of all dogmatism, declares:

> I cannot imagine that an Arab and a Muslim human being could take a negative stance toward Muḥammad, because this stance is a betrayal of religion by the Muslim and a betrayal of nationalism by the Arab. And I cannot imagine an Arab human being, regardless of his religion, taking a negative stance toward the prophet and then saying that he is nationalist or Arab.[23]

Yet, this diminishes neither the daring nature of his enterprise nor his challenge to centuries-old interpretations, some of which have become integral parts of Islam.

[21] See Shuḥrūr, *al-Kitāb*, 30 and 33.
[22] See Nash'at Ẓabyān, *Dhāka Radd?* (That is a response?) (Beirut: Dār Qutayba, 1992), 13.
[23] Shuḥrūr, *al-Kitāb*, 39.

The most significant aspect of Shuḥrūr's work is his rejection of the thematic and authoritative unity of the Quran. His study is influenced by his reading of classical Arabic linguists, especially Abū ʿAlī al-Fārisī, who would not accept the existence of synonyms in the Arabic language. This linguistic approach to the study of the Quran guided Shuḥrūr's research from its very beginning in 1970.[24] He divides the Quran into several sections or books, assigning each a different religious weight and significance. One of his novel ideas is distinguishing two aspects of Muḥammad's divine mission: the first is "prophecy," which includes the universal and human theory of existence; and the second is "the message," which comprises the specific rules and regulations contained in the Quran.[25] Thereafter he divides the Quran according to these two aspects of "prophecy" or "message."

Shuḥrūr's heavily linguistic arguments and outward respect for Islam mask his call to disregard those sections in the Quran that do not conform to the interests of the community or the lofty ideals of human rights. Thus, he is in fundamental disagreement with all schools of Islamic jurisprudence and finds it has become a "burden" not responsive to the "information and circumstances" of the twentieth century.[26] Similarly, rejecting the fundamental principle of Islamic jurisprudence to the effect that "there is no independent interpretation (*ijtihād*) on what is covered by a [Quranic] text," he does not deem the Quran itself to be binding. His sophisticated and detailed analysis leads him to reject adherence to any single school of jurisprudence. Moreover, extrapolating from the prophet's prohibition on *ḥadīth* during his lifetime, Shuḥrūr insists that recourse to it is in no way obligatory. Instead, he calls for the institution of "freedom and permissiveness" as the basis for Islamic legislation and human life.[27] He also urges that natural scientists be considered "the right-hand" of the legislator and reduces the fulfillment of Islamic obligations to respecting the general philosophical and ethical values of the Quran.

Consequently, for Shuḥrūr, a state can be deemed Islamic without having to rely on the obsolete dictates of any of the traditional schools of Islamic jurisprudence. What is more, his teaching leads to the notion that a truly Islamic state should be democratic "with its basic infrastructure based on political pluralism and the freedom to express opinions."[28]

[24] Ibid., 46.
[25] Ibid., 37.
[26] Ibid., 579.
[27] Ibid., 583.
[28] Ibid., 725. The term translated here as "political" is *ḥizbiyya* and might be more literally rendered as "party."

The weakness of Shuḥrūr's work lies in his reliance on a particular linguistic school. If that school is found to be technically faulty, his system faces intellectual collapse. He also suffers from a materialistic dogmatism known as orthodox or vulgar Marxism and seems to want to replace a religion of the spirit by another rooted in materialism.[29] Yet, at other times, his attempts to reconcile Islam with modern science make him sound like contemporary Islamists. He accepts the Big Bang theory of the origin of the material universe while asserting that only God is eternal. He then proceeds to argue that the material transformation of the universe will eventuate in a transition to the hereafter.[30] The book's current appeal is primarily due to the thirst among Muslims for courageous analysis of the Quran and for any study of Islam that eschews the dogmas of traditional Islamic apologetics.

The reformist ideas of Shuḥrūr are perhaps the most original of any writer considered here. His second book, *Dirāsāt Islāmiyya Muʿāṣira fī al-Dawla wa al-Mujtamaʿ* (Contemporary Islamic studies on the state and society), clearly states the implications and limitations of his first work. That is, he wishes to allow for independent interpretation of the Quran while disregarding the body of traditional *ijtihād*. Yet dismissing the body of *ḥadīth* as a source for interpreting the Quran could have several problematic results. It may lead to a pluralistic society in which different interpretations of the Quran will compete and clash peacefully, or it may unleash forces that will insist upon the imposition of their own single, strict interpretation of the Quran. For the moment, however, his rejection of *ḥadīth* remains too much for religious scholars or lay people to accept.

## 2. *Muḥammad Saʿīd al-ʿAshmāwī and Political Islam*

Muḥammad Saʿīd al-ʿAshmāwī, an Egyptian, is a former jurist who has devoted all of his recent writings to the presentation of a critical perspective of Islam fundamentally at odds with the perspective of contemporary Islamism. His themes, even more far-reaching than those of ʿAlī ʿAbd al-Rāziq, have been borrowed by many secularist writers.[31]

[29] Ṣādiq Jalāl al-ʿAẓm tried to do the same at the end of his *Naqd al-Fikr al-Dīnī* (Critique of religious thought) (Beirut: Dār al-Ṭalīʿa, 1969), 203–30.
[30] Shuḥrūr, *al-Kitāb*, 43.
[31] Faraj Fūda was greatly inspired by al-ʿAshmāwī, and Nazih Ayubi's *Political Islam* (London: Routledge, 1991) owes many of its insights to al-ʿAshmāwī's book of the same title.

Compared to ʿAbd al-Rāziq, al-ʿAshmāwī's strength lies in his wide knowledge of the Islamic heritage combined with his use of Western writings on Islam. While ʿAbd al-Rāziq confined himself almost solely to Thomas Arnold's *The Caliphate* and to Ibn Khaldūn's *al-Muqaddima*, al-ʿAshmāwī has made extensive use of several other works from the Islamic heritage.

Like those of Faraj Fūda, al-ʿAshmāwī's books consist of collected articles, most of which were previously published in various Egyptian journals and newspapers. He has yet to develop a systematic teaching or coherent philosophical outlook. Intent above all on refuting the arguments of contemporary Islamists, al-ʿAshmāwī's main effort in his most important work, *al-Islām al-Siyāsī* (Political Islam), is concentrated in the area of re-reading and re-presenting Islamic history to deny Islamists its use for political purposes. He challenges, for example, the notion of the Quranic origin of the governance of God (*ḥakīmiyyat Allāh*) promoted by Islamists as a cornerstone of their religious and political agenda and traces the term's origin instead to the thought and practice of the Kharijites. Since this group is condemned in the historiography of mainstream Islamists, al-ʿAshmāwī concludes that the idea of God's governance is un-Islamic and alien to the Quran as well as to the practice and sayings (*sunna*) of the prophet.[32] Indeed, he argues that the notion of God's domination over the realm of politics is rooted in ancient Egyptian and Christian medieval thought.

In the process, he refutes the intellectual basis of contemporary Islamic fundamentalists and analyzes the lexicographical origins of the word "governance" (*ḥukm*). He persuasively shows, through his intimate knowledge of the Quran and its linguistic characteristics, that contrary to the way it is used now, its Quranic sense is that of arbitration and adjudication.[33] Because so much of what is set forth as the ostensible Islamic position on governance and the role of religious scholars is drawn from a handful of words in the Quran and the establishment's position on these key issues is deeply rooted in etymological discussions, the point is far from insignificant.

Muḥammad Saʿīd al-ʿAshmāwī also promotes secularism within Islam by distinguishing between two roles for Muḥammad. Drawing on the writings of his fellow Egyptian, Muḥammad ʿAmāra, who called for a secular and socialist understanding of Islam in the 1960s before turning

[32] Muḥammad Saʿīd al-ʿAshmāwī, *al-Islām al-Siyāsī* (Cairo: Sīnā li-al-Nashr, 1987), 32–3.
[33] Ibid., 37–9.

to Islamist advocacy in the 1980s and 1990s,[34] al-ʿAshmāwī refuses to put all of Muḥammad's sayings and deeds under the rubric of prophecy. He contends, instead, that Muslims should distinguish between Muḥammad's prophecy and his political leadership, the latter being independent from his divine mission. This is, to be sure, al-ʿAshmāwī's most controversial view. Indeed, in keeping with the anti-secularist opinions of current Muslim governments and their allies among the religious scholars, most Muslims today consider Muḥammad's experience as entirely divine.[35] That is, they refuse to distinguish between Muḥammad the prophet and Muḥammad the human being, although such a distinction was recognized by early Muslims and even by Muḥammad himself.[36] The point is important insofar as it relates to the question of compatibility, or lack thereof, between Islam and secularism. If Muḥammad's political leadership is indistinguishable from his prophetic role, no separation between the realm of religion and that of politics is possible.

Another major controversial opinion of al-ʿAshmāwī lies in his denial that the *sharīʿa* is based on the Quran. He maintains that the word *sharīʿa* appears in the Quran only once and then to refer in very general terms to the general path of religion.[37] Mustering other evidence from the Quran, he contends that there is no basis for promoting law based on the *sharīʿa* as obligatory. To support his point of view on the non-compulsory character of the *sharīʿa*, al-ʿAshmāwī introduces a distinction between religion and religious thought. For him,

> religion is the set of principles preached by the prophet or the messenger; and religious thought is the historical method of understanding and implementing those principles. Every understanding of the religious text and every interpretation of it after the life of the prophet are but part of religious thought. Therefore, this understanding or interpretation may or may not conform to the crux of religion.[38]

[34] See, for example, Muḥammad ʿAmāra, *al-Islām wa al-Sulṭa al-Dīniyya* (Islam and religious authority) (Cairo: Dār al-Thaqāfa al-Jadīda, 1979), 26–8.

[35] In characterizing Arab governments as anti-secular, I overlook distinctions between them with respect to the status of law based upon the *sharīʿa*. Since they all reject the notion of governmental neutrality vis-à-vis religion, they cannot be said to be secular. To one degree or another, in one form or another, they all advocate the moral superiority of Islam. Indeed, for the Islamic establishments in Arab countries, Muḥammad is considered to have been divinely inspired since birth.

[36] See, for example, *Ṣaḥīḥ Muslim* (Cairo: Maṭbaʿa Muḥammad ʿAlī Ṣubayḥ, 1963), vol. 7, 95; and Ibn Ḥanbal, *Musnad al-Imām, Aḥmad ibn Ḥanbal* (Beirut: Dār Ṣādir, 1969), vol. 6, 123.

[37] See al-ʿAshmāwī, *Uṣūl al-Sharīʿa* (Fundamentals of the Sharīʿa) (Cairo: Sīnā, 1992), 28. The single occurrence is 45:18.

[38] Ibid., 48. The "crux of religion" (*ṣamīm al-dīn*) refers to what completes religion.

Yet, reflection upon this "crux of religion" criterion reveals a weakness in al-ʿAshmāwī's argument: insofar as the distinction between religion and religious thought is artificial, it does not suffice to render law based upon the *sharīʿa* noncompulsory or to deny its Quranic origin. After all, religion is always changing. While some of what was deemed to be religion at the time of Prophet Muḥammad (e.g., temporary or *mutʿa* marriage) is no longer so viewed, nonreligious aspects of the faith (e.g., female genital mutilation in such Islamic countries as Mauritania and Somalia) have now been incorporated into the religion. Furthermore, al-ʿAshmāwī, like all advocates of the "selectivity school" within Islam, leaves unresolved the controversial question as to who is to determine whether a principle or practice is part of "religion" or "religious thought." Because his books are compilations of newspaper articles and lectures given on different occasions, with many of the newspaper articles being part of the heated polemic between the secularists and Islamists in Egypt, al-ʿAshmāwī seldom formulates a consistent, rational criterion for making such far-reaching distinctions.

His writings represent the desire of segments of the intelligentsia in Egypt and elsewhere in the Arab world for a pluralistic and tolerant political system. He calls for civil government and favors treating rulers as fallible, non-holy human beings.[39] The end of the era of the divinely inspired caliphate should, in his view, have completely nullified the notion of divine rule, which constitutes the slogan of most Islamist groups. Moreover, on the grounds that people alone are capable of ruling, even if they claim to base their rule on divine inspiration, he holds the notion of divine rule to be a corrupt principle. Divine rule absolves the ruler from responsibility and gains for him non-Quranic infallibility.[40]

Still, fitting al-ʿAshmāwī into the school of convenient selectivity is difficult: even though he questions the reliability of some *ḥadīth*s, he does insist upon the moral authority of the Quran. Still, in one press interview, he distinguishes between Quranic rules that are permanent in applicability and others that are merely temporary. Among those that are permanent in applicability, he includes rituals of worship (*ʿibādāt*) like praying and fasting. Those temporary in applicability concern human interactions (*muʿāmalāt*), that is, business transactions, interpersonal relations, and relations between human beings and the government.[41]

39 See al-ʿAshmāwī, *Maʿālim al-Islām* (The signposts of Islam) (Cairo: Sīnā, 1989), 136.
40 Ibid., 137.
41 See al-ʿAshmāwī's article in *Ṣabaḥ al-Khayr*, 30 April 1987. I am grateful to Muḥammad Saʿīd al-ʿAshmāwī for sending me an almost complete collection of his writings.

The reform proposed by al-ʿAshmāwī is deeply rooted in Western legal experience. He uses his knowledge of Islamic jurisprudence mainly to reassure those Muslims who fear the impact of secularization on their piety. At the same time, he allows for a dynamic and evolving society where the role of religion does not remain static, but reflects the changing needs of people and the state.

## MARXIST TENDENCIES

### 1. *The "Red" Shaykh: ʿAbd Allāh al-ʿAlāyilī*

Shaykh ʿAbd Allāh al-ʿAlāyilī is largely unknown in the West. The translation into English of parts of his book on Arab nationalism introduced him to students of Middle East studies,[42] but his writings on Islamic history and Arabic linguistics are still unfamiliar to Western readers. From a Beiruti Sunni family, al-ʿAlāyilī received his religious education in Cairo in the 1920s and was influenced by religious and political reformers, most notably Muṣṭafā Kāmil.[43]

The career of al-ʿAlāyilī has been very controversial. His early association with leftist causes and founding membership in the Lebanese Progressive Socialist Party earned him the sobriquet "*al-Shaykh al-Aḥmar*" (the Red Shaykh or the Red religious scholar). At the same time, the refusal of Sunni politicians to accept his views and interpretations has barred him from the structure of the religious scholarly establishment in Lebanon. Ṣā'ib Salām, a prominent member of the Sunni establishment, fought to exclude al-ʿAlāyilī from any official post. Salām's task was facilitated insofar as al-ʿAlāyilī has never had a sectarian political sponsor, something crucial for key jurisprudential appointments in a country like Lebanon.

Al-ʿAlāyilī's most important contribution in the area of contemporary Islamic thought is his 1978 book, *Ayn al-Khaṭa'?* (Where is the error?). Banned in most Arab countries, it continues to be sold through Lebanese publishers. In this work, he sets forth his disagreements with conventional interpretations of Islam. His point of departure centers on his

[42] ʿAbd Allāh al-ʿAlāyilī, *Dustūr al-ʿArab al-Qawmī* (The national constitution of the Arabs) (Ṣaydā: al-ʿIrfān, 1941). In her *Arab Nationalism: An Anthology* (Berkeley: University of California Press, 1962), Sylvia Haim published English excerpts of this work.

[43] Fāyiz Tarḥīnī's *al-Shaykh ʿAbd Allāh al-ʿAlāyilī wa al-Tajdīd fī al-Fikr al-Muʿāṣir* (Shaykh ʿAbd Allāh al-ʿAlāyilī and renewal in contemporary thought) (Beirut and Paris: Manshūrāt ʿUwaydāt, 1985) is the only study on al-ʿAlāyilī to appear, but I was able to obtain additional information through conversations with Shaykh al-ʿAlāyilī and members of his family.

objection to "the unrestrained inclination to blind imitation" (*taqlīd*). Yet, unlike other Islamic reformers, he rejects an atomistic view of Islam and insists that Islam represents a complete ideology, a "grand solution." He believes that Islam can be used to guide one's life in contemporary society, although he does not hide his displeasure with current demands in various Arab and Islamic countries for the application of the *sharīʿa*. He fears that if the *sharīʿa* is left as some fossilized totem and not subjected to interpretation based on modern standards, applying it will harm thought, society, and patterns of behavior.[44] In other words, he thinks the *sharīʿa* needs continual dynamic renewal to survive. Nor does he confine such renewal to the *sharīʿa*: relying on a nonsound *ḥadīth* (that is, one not deemed reliable by the scholars of *ḥadīth*), he calls for the renewal of Islam itself and thereby puts himself at odds with most other Islamic reformers for whom such an opinion is anathema.

The most controversial part of al-ʿAlāyilī's book and what brought down upon him the wrath of Gulf regimes concerns not his views about the *sharīʿa*, but his economic concepts. Strongly criticizing the pursuit of individual prosperity (*tharwa*), he contends that communal prosperity best fulfills those Islamic concepts of economic relations emphasizing sharing and philanthropy. He describes capital accumulation as "a criminal, greedy progression" that becomes, on the individual level, a selfish confiscation of the communal effort.[45] Because he makes no attempt in his writings to draw upon traditional authority and his views diverge from conventional standards, conservative critics often blame him for idiosyncratic interpretations of the *sharīʿa*.

Not content to oppose individual prosperity when it is divorced from communal prosperity, al-ʿAlāyilī also denies the permissibility of accumulating wealth (*kanz*). For him, wealth embodies communal effort and thus should not be monopolized by one individual. Its individual accumulation deprives the entire society of vital resources necessary for survival and well-being. Here he relies on the Quran (9:35) to support his position.

To counter the accusations of sympathy for socialism that have haunted him throughout his productive life, al-ʿAlāyilī proposes the concept of cooperativeness (*takāfuliyya*). Based on the principles of respecting individual effort and preserving balance within social groups by compulsory cooperation, it assumes the need to protect private property without social polarization and the presence of an institutionalized

[44] *Ayn al-Khaṭaʾ?* (Beirut: Dār al-ʿIlm li-al-Malāyīn, 1978), 9–10, 14.
[45] Ibid., 33.

charitable alms tax (*zakā*). Though he acknowledges that Islam recognizes two forms of property rights—one relating to the state and the other to individuals—he contends that they constitute one form in reality, state property rights being solely for public benefit and not for the enrichment of leaders and kings. In his view, citizens are members of a collective economic enterprise in which all decisions are taken on the basis of consultation (*shūrā*).[46]

Drawing upon his linguistic brilliance and extensive knowledge of lexicography, al-ʿAlāyilī sometimes uses idiosyncratic terms for his socioeconomic proposals. This allows him to avoid commonly used terms and thus to escape political controversy. Thus "cooperativeness" (*takāfuliyya*) is used in place of "socialism" (*ishtirākiyya*) and "voluntary rendering" (*al-taʾmīm al-ṭawʿī*) in place of "nationalization" (*taʾmīm*). Though he seeks to soften or even eliminate the imposing character of nationalization by inserting the adjective "voluntary," al-ʿAlāyilī nonetheless insists that it be "urged and made desirable."[47] The idea is that public utilities and interests (*marāfiq*) are to be made into social institutions.

While al-ʿAlāyilī's knowledge of Arabic philology has earned him wide respect in the Arab world, his influence in matters of religion has been quite limited because his writings find such limited circulation among the religious educators who control school curricula. Apart from his rejection by established religious scholars, his appeal has been diminished by his penchant for ideological fluctuation and political inconsistency. Among his changes on crucial issues of the day is his vacillating between support for, and criticism of, Gamāl ʿAbd al-Nāṣir. Nor does this cofounder of the ostensibly secular Progressive Socialist Party discern any conflict between his reformist ideas and his description of Muḥammad Ḥusayn Faḍl Allāh—the spiritual guide of the Party of God (*Ḥizb Allāh*)—as the one by whom the building of the nation is to be measured.[48]

In assessing al-ʿAlāyilī's reformist legacy, it is important to take into consideration that—as he himself says—most of his work is still "in the making." Nowhere does he formulate a comprehensive religious and political position. When given the opportunity by Dār al-Jadīd in Beirut to revise his earlier works before their republication, he declined. Even

46 Ibid., 40.

47 Ibid., 48.

48 See his statement in ʿAlī Ḥasan Surūr, *al-ʿAllāma Faḍl Allāh wa Taḥaddī al-Mamnūʿ* (The Eminently learned Faḍl Allāh and the challenge of the taboo) (Beirut: Dār al-Malāk, 1992), 217.

were that due to awareness of advanced age (al-ʿAlāyilī died in 1996), it does not explain why his reform writings remain preliminary. It is worth comparing him to Ṭāhā Ḥusayn who, disillusioned with the obscurantist pedagogy of al-Azhar, discovered the validity and usefulness of scientific research. Only because al-ʿAlāyilī believes that Islam and the *sharīʿa* are not static, that they need continual rejuvenation to prevent religion from becoming obsolete in people's lives, is he a reformer. Like Ṭāha Ḥusayn, he wants to discard the official curricula in Islamic schools and apply rational methods of critical examination to the study of Islamic history. Persuaded that the political origins of schisms and disputes in Islam have been ignored, he desires to pursue the link between the pre-Islamic social and political order and caliphal government beginning with the Rightly Guided Caliphs.[49] In the end, however, al-ʿAlāyilī sees the aim of reform not as augmenting religious influence, but as improving life in general.

## 2. *Hādī al-ʿAlawī and Marxist Islamic Historiography*

This is a writer unknown to most people even in the Arab world. An Iraqi Marxist affiliated with the Democratic Front for the Liberation of Palestine (DFLP), al-ʿAlawī writes for the organization's newspaper, *al-Ḥurriyya* (Freedom), which has a very limited circulation. His books are published by obscure publishing houses, and his political views and writings have earned him enemies in more than one Arab country. He has often had to move from one country to another and was last reported in Hungary.

Like Faraj Fūda, Hādī al-ʿAlawī challenges fundamentalists on their own turf and seeks, above all, to show the discrepancy between the ethical standards set forth in the Quran and the actual conduct of Muslims—including Muḥammad. Thus even though the Quran forbids espionage, Muḥammad resorted to it in order to learn about the intentions and plans of his enemies, just as he went against prohibitions in the Quran and *ḥadīth*s against lying so as to gain military advantage. With respect to the latter point, al-ʿAlawī concedes, however, that *ḥadīth* permits falsehood in three cases: warfare, reconciling people, and when used by a husband against his wife.[50] He also notes Muḥammad's will-

[49] This goal is expressed in his *Sumū al-Maʿnā fī Sumū al-Dhāt aw Ashiʿa min Ḥayāt al-Ḥusayn* (The Loftiness of meaning in the loftiness of self, or rays in the life of al-Ḥusayn) (Beirut: 1939, no publisher).

[50] See Hādī al-ʿAlawī, *Fī al-Siyāsa al-Islāmiyya* (On Islamic politics) (Budapest: Ṣaḥārā, 1991), 19–21. The book was first published in 1975 by Dār al-Ṭalīʿa.

ingness to violate the terms of contracts, like the accord of Ḥudaybiyya, although this, too, goes against precepts of the Quran. To complete the picture of transgressions and injustices in early Islam, al-ʿAlawī has written a book detailing political assassination in the history of Islam. In it, he documents those personally approved by Muḥammad.[51]

In unearthing such unpleasant incidents from Arab/Islamic history, al-ʿAlawī, like Fūda, attempts to counter the notion of a Golden Age of Islam during which peace, harmony, and justice prevailed. By drawing attention to Muḥammad in this catalogue of faults, al-ʿAlawī goes farther than Fūda. He has also written a book to document cases of torture in the history of Islam, noting that it was resorted to frequently and that Muḥammad himself sometimes approved of it.[52] Al-ʿAlawī deems arguments of moral relativism, even when interjected into discourse of cultural sensitivity, outrageous and thus criticizes W. M. Watt for seeking to excuse Muḥammad's killing of opponents by portraying that era as one in which murder and torture were commonly accepted.[53]

His most impressive accomplishment is his compilation of the poetry, anecdotes, prose, and proverbs of free-thinkers in Islamic history.[54] Though the work's title evokes al-Abshayhī's famous compilation, al-ʿAlawī's differs in that he selects from the vast body of Arabic heritage elements that express rebellion, anti-conformism, and originality.[55] From his work emerges a picture contrary to that of total popular submission and obedience appearing in the works of some Orientalists and the political literature of Islamists who promote their vision of the future by distorting and idealizing the past. Key to al-ʿAlawī's presentation of Islamic history and thought is the way he highlights the cynicism that permeated—and continues to permeate—Arabic culture.

Thus, the implications of Hādī al-ʿAlawī's writings for modern Islamic reform cannot be underestimated. His thorough critique of the Golden Age of Islam undermines the foundations of traditional reform by showing in detail how unfounded is its admiration for early Islamic models of government, even how necessary it is to reflect upon the way political considerations affected Muḥammad's conduct. That critique's

51 The book is *al-Ightiyāl al-Siyāsī fī al-Islām* (Political assassination in Islam) (Damascus: Markaz al-Abḥāth wa al-Dirāsāt al-Ishtirākiyya fī al-ʿĀlam al-ʿArabī, n.d.).

52 Namely, *Min Taʾrīkh al-Taʿdhīb fī al-Islām* (From the history of torture in Islam) (Damascus: Markaz al-Abḥāth wa al-Dirāsāt al-Ishtirākiyya fī al-ʿĀlam al-ʿArabī, n.d.).

53 See *Fī al-Siyāsa*, 22.

54 Namely, *al-Mustaṭraf al-Jadīd* (The New selection) (Damascus: Markaz al-Abḥāth wa al-Dirāsāt al-Ishtirākiyya fī al-ʿĀlam al-ʿArabī, n.d.).

55 The classic literary anthology of Shihāb al-Dīn ibn Muḥammad al-Abshayhī (d. 850/1446) is entitled *al-Mustaṭraf fī Kull Fann Mustaẓraf* (The Selection from every elegant art).

depth, combined with his powerful defense of the history of free-thinking within Arab/Islamic civilization, more than offsets any problems arising from al-ʿAlawī's candid presentation of his own religious doubts.

## CONCLUSION

While the interest in free-thinking on Islamic issues is wide, the impact of the authors under study is small—with the exception of Faraj Fūda, who fought the Islamists on their own polemical terms. The language employed by ʿAbd Allāh al-ʿAlāyilī and Muḥammad Shuḥrūr guarantees that only members of the intellectual elite will have access to their pronouncements. Although credit should be given to writers who defy conventional taboos about Islam, the study of Islam, even by anti-conformists, remains a prisoner to the apologetic approach that continues to hinder its rational study. Nevertheless, the efforts of these anti-conformist writers, and others not mentioned here, should be recognized because the constraints under which they all operate are rigid and severe. Not only do they have to contend with the political and military oppression of the state and the apparatus of oppression of the Islamist movement, but they also have to counter the legacy of official Islamic historiography. Any version of Islamic history that clashes with the official one is automatically suspect in the eyes of many Muslims.

No real challenge to official Islamic historiography is possible without a reexamination of Islam's origins and the pre-Islamic period. In her recent book, *Islam and Democracy*, Fatima Mernissi has begun to do just that.[56] Calling for a new investigation of that era, she discusses al-Kalbī's *Kitāb al-Aṣnām* (Book of idols) as part of her study of paganism and claims to find seeds of pluralism in pre-Islamic society.[57]

However, anti-conformism will not reach the popular level until thinkers in this movement make their thought accessible to the masses and they free themselves, partly or entirely, from the taboos of the traditional Islamic apologetic. There is no less a need for everyone in the Muslim world to adopt anti-conformism than for multiple, even divergent, interpretations of religious texts to co-exist.

The spread of Islamic reform, radical or traditional, depends on the attitude of political rulers in the Middle East, and they still draw on Islam for their political legitimacy and still control Islamic curricula in schools

[56] See Fatima Mernissi, *Islam and Democracy* (New York: Addison-Wesley, 1992), 85–7.
[57] See Abū al-Mundhir al-Kalbī (d. 204 or 206/819 or 821), *Kitāb al-Aṣnām* (Cairo: Dār al-Kutub, 1924).

and universities. If the campaign by radical Islamist groups in the region succeeds in threatening the stability of these states, some may well opt for the opportunistic promotion of enlightened reform. Thus, Egypt has recently embarked on a far-reaching campaign that involves officially sponsoring and tolerating the publication of daring secular writings. Only recently has it been legal to publish certain writings of Ṭāhā Ḥusayn, ʿAlī ʿAbd al-Rāziq, and Najīb Maḥfūẓ; and to reach the widest possible readership, these works have been published in popular magazines and newspapers. Yet, given the violent means always at the disposal of the state, it is unlikely that such practices will lead to strong popular pressures.

In sum, the efforts of the anti-conformist writers are important and daring because diversity of opinion about religion and politics is so strictly prohibited. Anti-conformism in the Arab/Islamic context poses a challenge to the basic assumptions and axioms of the traditional Islamic belief system, including the glorification of the past and the officially transmitted version of Arab/Islamic history. Weak as they are, the radical reformers have been noticed by the official religious scholars and by the state apparatus in many Middle Eastern countries. Worse, they have caused alarm in these circles. This summary view of the writings of a few radical reformers aims not at exaggerating their influence but at indicating how very diverse thought is within the Arab/Islamic world. It is still too early to predict whether these proponents of progress and enlightenment will prevail.

# 6

# Democratic Thought in the Arab World: An Alternative to the Patron State

ILIYA HARIK

Political thought in the Arab world today is passing through an interregnum characterized by revisionism, reorientation, and questioning. Intellectuals are cautiously looking into the future and emphasizing new directions, even as they seek to remain in touch with their heritage. Yet, in this state of flux, one can detect certain trends or tendencies.

To the casual observer, the Islamic trend is most conspicuous. There is, however, another more pervasive, though less intense, trend, namely, an awakened interest in democracy. All of the reform movements—Islamist, Arab nationalist, and leftist—avow an interest in giving the people a voice in politics. Thus, the most pervasive alternative to the patron state that has dominated Arab politics since the 1950s seems to lie in some variant of democratization. This is not to say that Islamists, nationalists, and leftists have abandoned their own basic principles in favor of a totally different outlook. They have simply added to their other political goals a greater or lesser degree of commitment to democracy. All these movements, however, share a common thread: rejection of the single-party, autocratic state.

Of these three movements, I shall leave aside discussion of the commitment to democracy among the Islamists to concentrate on democratic developments among the Arab nationalists and the leftists. Thus, the question is whether this presumed convergence toward democracy will create a structural coalition among the three reform movements and whether such a coalition will determine the current debate and struggle in favor of democracy. To emerge victorious, the democratic trend will have to overcome both the radicalism of extremist Islamists (*ghulāt*) and the hegemony of autocrats who happen to be secularists.

The increasing interest in democracy appears to result from a general trend of thought rather than to stem from individual advocates. That is, no single Arab intellectual today can be identified as leading or as having initiated the current of democratic debate. Rather, it tends to be expressed by groups of thinkers associated with a few institutions. We shall touch here on the ideas circulating among five representative groups and centers, three based in Cairo—the al-Ahrām Center for Strategic and Political Studies, the Ibn Khaldūn Civil Society Center, and the Arab Organization for Human Rights—one in Beirut, namely, the Center for Arab Unity Studies, and one in Rabat, the Thought and Dialogue Forum. Most of the intellectual leaders in these institutions are academics and/or former statesmen. All the writers to be discussed here are linked to these institutions.

The al-Ahrām Center was founded by Ḥasanayn Haykal and led initially by Boutros Boutros-Ghali. Under the leadership of Sayyid Yāsīn, it has shown a greater interest in Arab affairs and democracy, though it remains focused on Egypt. The same is true under the current leadership of ʿAbd al-Munʿim Saʿīd. It issues a quarterly journal and a yearly report or *annuaire* assessing Arab developments. It also publishes many of the writings of its researchers. Yet, wide as its influence is, the al-Ahrām Center remains constrained by limited resources and its official status as a governmental institution.

In contrast, the Arab Organization for Human Rights (AOHR), started in the early 1980s by Arab intellectuals and former statesmen from various Arab countries, is totally independent and was established to act as a watchdog over Arab regimes. While its presence in Cairo is tolerated by the Mubarak regime, it has not been able to obtain a legal status. The AOHR publishes a newsletter that draws the attention of Arab readers to the status of human rights in various Arab countries and describes the efforts of the organization to represent victims vis-à-vis their governments. It operates in association with human rights groups in each of the Arab countries, and its ideas and practices are rooted in basic democratic and civil values.

The ideas propagated by the AOHR would normally be classed as academic and thus of slight interest to most people. Yet, as ordinary people have become the beneficiaries of its activities, they have begun to subscribe to its ideas. Even Islamists have been impressed to witness the leaders of a secular organization that does not share their views nonetheless defending their right to express their religious and political ideas.

## BACKGROUND

Before discussing the perceptions particular Arab intellectuals have of democracy, it is appropriate to speak about how the current interest in democracy developed. Democracy is not entirely unprecedented in the Arab world. Indeed, in a sense, it constitutes a revival of previous principles of governance. Some of the authors to be treated here look back to the constitutional monarchy of Egypt before Nasser; they even go back to the social contract between Muḥammad ʿAlī, the *ʿulamāʾ*, and the notables. Despite being the product of such particular historical circumstances, the current interest in democracy in some Arab countries also reflects a trend toward democratization throughout much of the Third World.

The first stirring in the direction of democratic thinking resulted from the experiences of the Palestinian resistance and arose almost by default. Arab intellectuals in general and Palestinians in particular were not advocates of democracy—at least not in the Western sense of bringing together civil rights with popular representation and a modicum of social welfare. The Arab intellectuals who embraced democratic thinking shared the revolutionary goal of redefining and remaking the nation-state. The revolutionary impetus was in part dictated by the urgency of the task: transforming agrarian economies into modern industrial societies; turning weak and fragmented polities into coherent, sovereign states; and replacing outdated monarchies with populist regimes. We shall refer to this trend as modernist and nationalist.

In the Maghrib, especially in Algeria and Tunisia, nationalist modernism took a secular form reflective of the assimilated native. It was advocated by individuals who had been Europeanized during the colonial period. National modernist thought drew particularly on the authoritarian and Marxist tendencies in Western thought. In Tunisia, this modernist trend of combining liberal social ideas with an authoritarian power structure revealed itself as Bourguibism. However, Tunisian post-Bourguibists and their allies elsewhere in North Africa have been challenged by the rising tide of Islamic ideas. The Islamists claim greater cultural authenticity; and their message, conveyed by individuals steeped in Islamic scholarship, has received growing support from a new generation of young people in the provinces as well as among the urban poor. These young people, who give the popular challenge to nationalist modernism in the Maghrib its Islamic character, came of age in the post-independence school system and received their education mainly in

Arabic. Thus, the current struggle in the Maghrib is between two generations, both authoritarian in orientation—one secular, the other religious fundamentalist.

In the Mashriq, the process is similar but more complex. The struggle there between secular and fundamentalist tendencies has been associated with claims to cultural authenticity by both sides. Arab nationalism, representing the secular trend, draws its cultural ethos from classical Arab culture, which curiously enough was heavily Islamic in character. In this way, the nationalists deny the fundamentalists a monopoly on the heritage (*turāth*) or proper culture of the nation. The emergence of a democratic wing within both secular modernism and religious fundamentalism is recent. The discussion, below, will be limited to the penetration of democratic ideas among secular modernists.

As noted above, the secular democratic tendency emerged in association with the experiences of the Palestinian resistance. The conscience of Arab nationalism until the early 1980s, the Palestinian resistance movement reached its apogee after the 1967 defeat, when Nasser, who had represented the triumph of nationalist modernism, was cut down in size overnight by the military setback. For disillusioned nationalists and radicals, the Palestinian resistance emerged as an alternative to their authoritarian secular regimes. Curiously, the very triumph of the Palestinian resistance contained the seeds of its own decline. The nationalist authoritarian regimes hit back at the Palestinian challenge. The military vulnerability of the confrontation states, moreover, made control of the resistance a matter of life and death for the ruling Arab elites. When necessary, Arab regimes showed they were willing to use their armies against the Palestine Liberation Organization (PLO).

In short, the Palestinian resistance was curtailed, ruthlessly in certain cases, by the Arab regimes it challenged. It was forcibly suppressed in Jordan and had to fight a bloody war in Lebanon, where Syria showed that it was ready to meet Palestinian defiance with arms. The regime of Saddam Hussein in Iraq hunted down PLO leaders all over the world. Moreover, Palestinian sorties into Israel were blocked by the governments of Egypt, Jordan, and Syria. All this happened within the decade following the 1967 defeat.

The shock and disappointment of the secular nationalist intellectuals among Palestinians and other Arabs gave rise in the late 1970s to appeals for democracy in the Arab world. That the PLO flourished only in Lebanon suggests that the survival and success of the resistance required democratically inclined Arab regimes. This question was the subject of one of the first conferences held by Palestinian and sympathetic Arab intellectuals in Tunisia where it was strongly argued that the resistance was crushed by Arab regimes because state leaders were not accountable to the mass of their own people.

Thus the new democratic impetus stemmed from nationalist concerns. One might argue that this origin has been both a weakness and a strength for the democratic movement. A weakness because democracy has been seen, to a large extent, not as an end in itself, but as a means to achieve the nationalist ends of the resistance. A strength because its birth out of the bosom of the nationalist movement has given it a legitimacy it never quite found in the heritage.

The Palestinian resistance is not, however, the only historical source from which theorists might trace the Arab world's emergent interest in democracy. In Egypt, the issue is seen in an entirely different light. There, the idea of democracy is said to have arisen from Egypt's own national history, particularly from the pre-Nasser constitutional period.[1]

Yet a third possible origin for the interest in democracy in the Arab world, according to Saad Eddin Ibrahim, lies in the demographic growth of the middle and working classes in the last few decades.[2] Ibrahim argues that these classes have a strong interest in maintaining the Arab state system. Thus, they have acted to defend that system from internal threats, like religious fundamentalism, and from outside threats, like Israel and imperialism. Ibrahim does not tell us, however, whether mass support for democracy among the middle and labor classes is manifested in political parties or whether this support has been any stronger in Egypt in recent years than it was in Egypt between the 1920s and 1940s. That silence, plus the organizational weakness and economic dependency of both the working and the middle classes, weaken his argument considerably.

Nevertheless, whether the new interest in democracy emerged out of Palestinian or Egyptian concerns, the fact remains that it was a product of the 1967 debacle and a response to the failure of the national project of the single party, nationalist-socialist systems. In other words, the impulse toward democratization in the Arab world has grown out of the

1 See, for instance, ʿAli al-Dīn Hilāl [Dessouki] et al., *Tajribat al-Dimuqrāṭiyya fī Miṣr, 1970–1981* (The Experience of democracy in Egypt, 1970–1981) (Cairo: al-Markaz al-ʿArabī li-al-Baḥth wa al-Nashr, 1982).

2 Saad Eddin Ibrahim, "*Muqaddima*," in *Azmat al-Dimuqrāṭiyya fī al-Waṭan al-ʿArabī* (The Crisis of democracy in the Arab homeland) (Beirut: Markaz Dirasāt al-Waḥda al-ʿArabiyya, 1984).

same kinds of failures that have occurred, albeit less dramatically, in many other developing countries.

It may be noted here, that the Lebanese experience of communal democracy played an ambiguous role in all this. Though it gave impetus to the Palestinian cause, the civil war and the communal nature of the system also raised doubts about democracy. As we shall see, not one of the advocates of democratic thinking takes Lebanon as a model or deals seriously with its experience.

The new democrats in the Arab world speak as members of groups, not as individuals. Those who advocate a nationalist vision of the Arab future congregate around the Center for Arab Unity Studies in Beirut, those who favor civil society are primarily found at the Ibn Khaldūn Civil Society Center in Cairo, and the human rights proponents tend to associate with the Arab Organization for Human Rights with its headquarters in Cairo and branches in various Arab capitals. The leftist democrats participate in the dialogue sponsored by the Center for Arab Unity Studies and the Moroccan Thought and Dialogue Forum. We shall turn now to the views of leading figures associated with one or another of these organizations.

## THE NEO-NATIONALIST DEMOCRATS

Since the 1970s, Arab nationalist ideas have been put forth mainly by the Center for Arab Unity Studies in Beirut. Founded in the 1960s by a group of Arab nationalists including Qusṭanṭīn Zurayq and Walīd Khālidī, the Center for Arab Unity Studies received financial support from some Arab states, especially Iraq. Because the funds it received were invested in a trust, the Center has enjoyed considerable autonomy. Its leadership was entrusted from the start to Khayr al-Dīn Ḥasīb, an Iraqi economist and former minister in the Iraqi government. The Center's headquarters have remained in Beirut despite the war, with a branch established in Cairo.

Khayr al-Dīn Ḥasīb's importance in current Arab thought lies in his power to set the agenda, support research, hold conferences, and publish results. The Center's monthly journal, *al-Mustaqbal al-ʿArabī* (The Arab future), enjoys the highest reputation and circulation in the Arab world. Scores of quality books, all on Arab national affairs, have been initiated and then published by the Center. These diverse activities under the guidance and leadership of Ḥasīb have kept interest in ideas of Arab nationalism alive at a time when the political movement was sagging.

In 1979, Ḥasīb turned his attention to democracy as another dimension of Arab nationalism. He organized a series of lectures in Beirut and published them in *al-Mustaqbal al-ʿArabī*. Then, in 1983, he organized a conference and assembled a large number of leading Arab intellectuals from all over the Arab world to discuss the issue of democracy. A huge volume was published as a result, entitled *The Crisis of Democracy in the Arab Homeland*.[3] Since Beirut was no longer safe in 1983, the conference was held in Cyprus—a sad commentary on the conditions of freedom prevailing in Arab countries, especially given that Ḥasīb resorted to Cyprus only after having been turned down by several Arab countries. The conference may not have produced a consensus on democracy, but it did reflect a growing interest and a new moderation among the assembled dignitaries, who included Arab nationalists, Islamists, and leftists of various strains. While we are treated in the press to a flood of news on the rising number and influence of extremists and fundamentalists, the Cyprus conference shows another side of Arab intellectuals.[4]

Ḥasīb stamped his own ideas on the proceedings of this important gathering in the way he set its agenda. Thus, in the invitations for the meeting, he defined the subject of inquiry as: "a discussion of the relation of democracy . . . to the movement of Arab solidarity (*taḍāmun*), unity, and capacity to respond effectively to the challenges and dangers surrounding the Arab homeland." Ḥasīb continues steadfast in the belief that Arabs form one nation, one homeland, and should aspire to create one united state. He is willing to make only modest concessions to the territorial state and social democracy; his primary concern remains Arab unification. His importance today is that he, almost singlehandedly, holds the torch of Arab nationalism and enjoys considerable influence in intellectual circles. By turning his attention to the issue of democracy, he has given a boost to this burgeoning interest among Arab intellectuals; and by linking democracy to Arab nationalism, he has filled a serious gap in Arab nationalist concerns.

Another Arab nationalist who advocates democracy is ʿIṣmat Sayf al-Dawla, a lawyer from Egypt with a Nasserist background. He is now committed to democracy as an indispensable doctrine for the success of

[3] See above, n. 2.

[4] Leonard Binder first drew attention to moderate Arab thinkers among the promoters of religious politics in his *Islamic Liberalism: A Critique of Development Ideologies* (Chicago: University of Chicago Press, 1988).

Arab unity. The author of several books on Arab unity,[5] he is well versed in Western thought. Indeed, his understanding of democracy as a method for the solution of social problems draws heavily on Schumpeter, and, like Schumpeter, he prefaces his discourse on democracy with a critique of liberal democracy through the centuries. Weber and Schumpeter, however, were less sanguine about democracy, even in the narrow sense in which they used the term. Sayf al-Dawla, in contrast, maintains categorically that democracy is the only effective way for people to solve their problems and for societies to evolve. Free expression makes people understand their problems, and no collective or patronizing elite could substitute its own thinking for that of the people without deleterious consequences.

Another way in which Sayf al-Dawla displays his independence from most theorists who speak about Western democracy has to do with the central role individuals and groups occupy in that literature. Far from imitating them, his references are almost always to the people (*al-nās*) and to society (*al-mujtamaʿ*). Yet he does accept the familiar safeguards for democratic government: majority rule, accountability of elected officials to the electorate, and the rights of the opposition to function without harassment. Nor does he claim that once a democratic system is in place, problems will be solved smoothly and routinely; rather, he argues that all democracy can do is provide the framework for arriving at solutions to such problems. He accepts the assumption that a certain cultural level in society is required for the success of democracy but insists that there is no way other than democracy for a people to rise from cultural under-development. Such under-development must be overcome by education, knowledge, and experience with the democratic process of solving problems. He attacks intellectuals who claim that democracy is not suitable for under-developed countries, accusing them of denigrating the people in order to justify a desire to impose their own will.

The idea that democracy provides practical solutions to specific problems and is necessary for the development of nations reflects a new way of thinking among intellectuals from developing countries, a way of

[5] See, for example, *Usus al-Waḥda al-ʿArabiyya* (The Foundations of Arab unity) (Cairo, 1965); *Usus al-Ishtirākiyya al-ʿArabiyya* (The Foundations of Arab Socialism) (Cairo: al-Dār al-Qawmiyya, 1965); *Naẓariyyat al-Thawra al-ʿArabiyya* (The Theory of the Arab revolution) (Beirut, 1972); *al-Ṭarīq ilā al-Waḥda al-ʿArabiyya* (The Path to Arab unity) (Beirut, 1979); and many others.

thinking Sayf al-Dawla skillfully relates to the idea of Arab unity. Democracy and Arab unity must be realized together, for neither one is fully meaningful or attainable without the other.

Though Sayf al-Dawla's ideas of Arab nationalism are expressed with intellectual sophistication, he retains some of the old classical principles, such as the objective existence of the "nation," its precedence over the state, the responsibility of imperialism for the fragmentation of the Arab nation, and the territorial state as an incomplete entity. He argues, moreover, that the separate territorial state is structurally unable to establish democracy or solve the problems of the people. The cultural evolution of the future Arab state will depend on both unity and democracy, for they alone make possible the conditions for growth. All hopes for a future Arab state will be dashed if the new structure does not take a unified, democratic form. Were the unified national state to adopt an autocratic system, that would constitute the greatest failure in Arab history. In the literature regarding the necessity of democracy, it is rare to find statements as categorical as those made by Sayf al-Dawla.

In short, he argues that democracy is the best way for solving problems, that it is a prerequisite for the evolution of societies to a higher standard, and that combined with national unity it will provide the best path to a better life for the Arabs. He bases his case for Arab political unity on that principle, which he claims supersedes the familiar ideas about the subject. Finally, one cannot but be impressed by Sayf al-Dawla's perseverance in maintaining these ideals at a time when Arab nationalism has become a matter of indifference among most Arabs.

Needless to say, new ideas on Arab nationalism are currently quite rare. Even Ḥasīb has recently resorted to re-publishing the old classics, such as those of Sāṭiʿ al-Ḥuṣrī. Sayf al-Dawla's novelty seems to consist in his having made a strong pitch for linking the fate of Arab nationalism with democracy in its more or less social-liberal sense.

The prominent Moroccan writer, Muḥammad al-Jābirī, shares most of Sayf al-Dawla's ideas about Arab nationalism and its link to democracy, with one major exception. He believes that the territorial state has much more strength and credibility than Sayf al-Dawla is willing to concede.[6] Al-Jābirī is a cultural historian and a philosopher, and the space in his

[6] See Muḥammad ʿAbid al-Jābirī, *Wujhat Naẓar: Naḥwa ʿIyāda Binʾ Qaḍāyā fī al-Fikr al-ʿArabī al-Muʿāṣir* (Point of view: Toward a fundamental reconsideration of issues in contemporary Arab thought) (Beirut: Markaz Dirāsāt al-Waḥda al-ʿArabiyya, 1992).

prolific writings devoted to democracy is relatively limited. However, like Sayf al-Dawla, he has a conventional understanding of democracy and a strong faith in its benefits.

Another author whose intellectual heritage is grounded in Arab nationalism is Saad Eddin Ibrahim, an American-educated sociologist from Egypt, professor at the American University in Cairo, former head of the Arab Thought Forum in Amman, Jordan,[7] and current head of the Ibn Khaldūn Civil Society Center in Cairo. He was associated with, and continues to participate in, the activities of the Center for Arab Unity Studies. Widely involved in Egyptian and Arab affairs, Ibrahim unsuccessfully sought to form a political organization during the Sadat period with like-minded Egyptian intellectuals, such as Sayyid Yāsīn and ʿAli al-Dīn Hilāl [Dessouki].

Ibrahim, too, has expanded his original focus on Arab nationalism to include democracy. Unlike Sayf al-Dawla, Ibrahim makes no categorical judgments regarding either democracy or Arab unity. He has publicly criticized the basic assumptions of Arab nationalism and has found room for the territorial state within the future, united or unified, Arab state. Again, unlike Sayf al-Dawla, he does not insist upon trying to make reality conform to fixed moral or intellectual ideals. His empirical and pragmatic bent tempers his ideological enthusiasm, but one should harbor no doubts about his genuine commitment to Arab nationalism and democracy.

Ibrahim sees democracy as a function of a strong civil society. His view of civil society excludes organizations and associations based on primordial ties; nevertheless, Ibrahim played a significant role in highlighting the issue of minorities in the Arab world. Almost alone among Arab Muslim writers, he deals with the issue of religious and ethnic minorities in the light of the Arab nationalist project. Notably, he has recently published a book on the subject in which he tries to introduce a spirit of tolerance and acceptance of the full rights of minorities within the Arab fold.[8] Classical Arab nationalist views on minorities, which tend

[7] One of his achievements there was the convening of a conference for Arab intellectuals on pluralism in the Arab world, the proceedings of which were published by the Forum in a volume called, *al-Taʿaddudiyya al-Siyāsiyya wa al-Dimuqrāṭiyya fī al-Waṭan al-ʿArabī* (Political pluralism and democracy in the Arab nation), ed. Saad Eddin Ibrahim (Amman, 1989). Another volume of the same nature on intellectuals and the state was published as *al-Intilijinsiyya al-ʿArabiyya: al-Muthaqqifūn wa al-Sulṭa* (The Arab intelligentsia: The bearers of culture and authority), ed. Saad Eddin Ibrahim (Amman, 1988).

[8] *Taʾammulāt fī Masʾalat al-Aqalliyyāt* (Reflections on the problem of minorities) (Cairo: Markaz Ibn Khaldūn, 1991).

to be patronizing and assimilationist, deny ethnic minorities the right to be themselves and to preserve their distinct identities. Ibrahim reverses this order, calling for their integration, but not their assimilation[9] and certainly not their oppression. Moreover, he has tried to impress upon the Arab majority the significance of these minorities, insisting that Arab nationalists must face the problem squarely if they hope to establish a stable, unified state.

Ibrahim's special contribution lies in his civil society approach to democracy. As a sociologist in close contact with current academic trends in the United States, he immediately became attracted to the idea of civil society as useful for the Arab nation. His ultimate goal, of course, is the establishment of democracy in the sense intended by social democrats, where freedom, equality, and rule of law prevail side by side with the economic and social rights of the people. However, as a sociologist, he is impressed by the diversity of Arab societies and by the weak social base they provide for a democratic order. Tribalism, sectarianism, landlordism, familism, and so forth prevail in many Arab countries. As a person of secular convictions, Ibrahim finds such centrifugal tendencies working against democratic practice and against Arab unity. The idea of civil society appeals to him as a means to strengthen modern aspects of society along with the agencies that mediate between the government and the people as well as to encourage the assumption of greater responsibility by citizens in countries where government hegemony is the rule. In his eyes, to build civil society in the Arab world is to prepare the way for a democratic system of government.

Ibrahim's promotion of civil society is consistent with his interest in human rights in Egypt and throughout the Arab world. He was active in the Arab Organization for Human Rights in its early stages. His most notable contribution to the promotion of civil society and the study of this concept has been to establish the Ibn Khaldūn Civil Society Center. In 1992, the Center began disseminating *Civil Society: Democratic Transformation in the Arab World* about civil organizations and associations. By promoting research, holding conferences, and publishing books, the Ibn Khaldūn Civil Society Center helps to spread Ibrahim's ideas. The center was closed and Ibrahim and its staff arrested by the government in June 2000.

[9] For a clarification of the difference between the two concepts, see my article, "The Ethnic Revolution in the Middle East," *International Journal of Middle Eastern Studies* 3, no. 3 (July 1972).

## THE LEFT AND DEMOCRACY

In much the same way as with the nationalists, an impressive number of Arab communists and socialists have moved to put a liberal version of democracy at the head of their concerns. Among them are Samīr Amīn and Ismāʿīl Ṣabrī ʿAbd Allāh from Egypt as well as Burhān Ghalyūn from Syria. We shall focus here on ʿAbd Allāh and Ghalyūn, since Amīn's writings in Arabic are now rare and no longer innovative.

A French-trained economist, ʿAbd Allāh has been one of the leaders of the leftist coalition, *al-Tajammuʿ*. A former communist who had experienced jail under Nasser before the reconciliation of 1963, he became Minister of Planning under Sadat and is currently the head of the Third World Forum in Cairo. He has written numerous articles, and one of his major books is on the new international economic order.[10]

The ideas on democracy now expressed by Marxist-Leninists such as ʿAbd Allāh no longer reflect the ideological stamp of Leninism. The same is true of Nasserists among those Arab nationalists who have dropped the populism of single-party democracy. Indeed, Sayf al-Dawla repudiates ideas based on the single-party system, as does ʿAbd Allāh, who goes further and rejects the notion that providing socioeconomic rights for the masses is a substitute for their direct and free involvement in politics. The cornerstone of his thinking is that political pluralism in the widest sense is the *sine qua non* of democracy.

ʿAbd Allāh also emphasizes the need for citizens to serve an apprenticeship in the practices of free choice and public involvement. He wants political parties, trade unions, businesses, and all other civil and political associations to be run democratically in order to instill the culture of democracy in Arab citizens. He wants party and trade union leaders to be subject to periodic election by the members of their organizations, for both political parties and trade unions bear a major responsibility in supporting and instilling democratic ideas and practices among the people. In addition, a democratic attitude must prevail in the way these organizations relate toward one another. ʿAbd Allāh takes political parties in Egypt to task in particular, because while not running their own operations democratically, they nonetheless demand that the regime comply

[10] *Naḥwa Niẓām Iqtiṣādī ʿAlāmī Jadīd* (Toward a new world economic order) (Cairo: al-Hay'a al-Miṣriyya al-ʿĀmma li-al-Kitāb, 1977). See also Ibrahim Karawan's discussion of ʿAbd Allāh in "Political Parties Between State Power and Islamist Opposition," (Chapter 7, this volume).

with democratic principles. Indeed, political parties would strengthen their position vis-à-vis the authoritarian regimes against which they are struggling if they were simply to provide an example of democratic practice. By showing that they support the democratic rights of rival political parties, they would demonstrate the seriousness of their commitment.[11]

The new ʿAbd Allāh is very consistent on the issue of pluralism, as can be seen from his syndicalist line of thought. He criticizes the authoritarian Arab regimes for having co-opted trade union leaders. Nor do opposition parties escape his scathing reproach for having tried to behave in the same way as the government. He wants to see trade unions not tied to a political party, but independent and free to pursue their particular interests within the national context.

According to ʿAbd Allāh, if society is to accomplish the transition to democracy, it must retain what is valuable from the past while cleansing itself from former errors. He admits that the "progressive and nationalist forces" sacrificed democracy in their efforts to achieve the ostensibly higher goals of socialism and national unity. When progressive and nationalist forces came to power, their practices were far from democratic. Devoid of democratic content, national Arab liberation movements failed. Rather than having them persist in these failed ideologies, he urges the elite to follow the example of the masses who have shown their repugnance to tyranny, suppression, and arbitrary government.

ʿAbd Allāh's adherence to democratic principles is proven by his handling of sensitive issues, such as the treatment of ethnic minorities in the Arab world. He would grant minorities the right to maintain their culture, identity, and local government within a democratic, national system. To be sure, he stops short of granting such minorities the right of secession. That is sound, for no state—no matter how democratic it might be—could be expected to do that. Here, one can hardly avoid thinking of the great and salubrious relevance of such ideas to the situation in Iraq, not to mention other Arab countries—especially Algeria and Morocco.

While ʿAbd Allāh acknowledges ethnic minorities, he is less charitable to sectarian ones or to tribalism and other traditional forces. Like other modernists, he considers traditional associations to be reactionary and divisive, citing Lebanon as an example.

[11] See ʿAbd Allāh's article, "*al-Dimuqrāṭiyya Dākhil al-Aḥzāb al-Waṭaniyya*" ("Democracy within the national parties") in *Azmat al-Dimuqrāṭiyya*.

Burhān Ghalyūn, a Marxist Syrian scholar who lives in France, is widely known in Arab intellectual circles and participates in the activities of many of the centers mentioned in this article. His rejectionist language, though quite opaque, appeals to the young and to less sophisticated Arab readers. In his various books and articles he has addressed the central issues confronting the Arabs, including democracy and nationalism.[12]

One very clear line of thought in Ghalyūn's works is his vehement denunciation of the oppression and violation of human rights common to most Arab regimes. Even if what he has to say about democracy is somewhat muddled, he is utterly clear on one point: human rights and mass participation in state affairs are the essentials of a modern and progressive state. Ghalyūn's often blunt language shakes up some of the basic assumptions of Arab intellectual life. His criticism of Arab nationalism might serve more as a provocative gesture than as a project for Arab nationalists to see their way out of their political crises.

He makes, for example, the following two observations: despotism is linked to the rise of Arab nationalism, and the Arab masses have always opposed the intellectual projects of the elite. Conventional Arab nationalists, he maintains, camouflaged the narrow interest of the upper bourgeoisie, a class subservient to foreign capitalist and imperialist nations. He repudiates the nationalists' claims to be nation builders: what they built was class supremacy. In effect, they were anti-nationalist. As representatives of class hegemony tied to foreign capitalistic interests, it should not be surprising that when nationalists of this sort come to power they rule despotically. Ghalyūn views them as being a band (*ṭughma*) of compradores. The same applies, according to Ghalyūn, to Islamic reform movements and those who wish to develop the socialist secular state. The nation-state will not become a reality until the minority ruling class is destroyed. His reproach to Islamists is that a return to Islam will not succeed in freeing the Arabs from Western ideologies. Instead, it is intellectual liberalization, cultural flourishing (*izdihār thaqāfī*), and the formation of an educated nationalist elite that will permit a return to Islam in a way that integrates the old with the new.

12 See Burhān Ghalyūn, *Bayān min Ajl al-Dimuqrāṭiyya* (Declaration for the sake of democracy) (Beirut: Dār Ibn Rushd, 1980) and *Ightiyāl al-ʿAql al-ʿArabī* (The Assassination of the Arab intellect), 3d ed. (Cairo: Maktaba Madbūlī, 1990). See also his article, "*Mā Warāʾ al-Dimuqrāṭiyya wa al-Istibdād*" (What is behind democracy and tyranny) in *al-Tajārib al-Dimuqrāṭiyya fī al-Waṭan al-ʿArabī* (Democratic experiences in the Arab nation) (Beirut: Arab Thought and Dialogue Forum of Morocco, 1981).

True nationalism, like true democracy, must include the mass of people in an alliance with the powerful ruling class (*al-ṭabaqa al-qāʾida*). Unfortunately, the nature of such an alliance and the role of the masses and the elite in it are difficult to fathom from his writings, which contain anything but clear Arabic. He repeatedly uses the term, the "populace" (*al- shaʿb*), by which he apparently means the productive forces in society, such as workers and other lower income people. Nasser's coalition, for example, was made up of workers, peasants, national bourgeoisie, intellectuals, and soldiers. In Ghalyūn's language, we have the vague substitute, the populace, and find in his texts repeated reference to the bourgeoisie in general and sometimes to the workers. He rejects Nasserism, however, and maintains that it is a corrupted Marxism.[13]

For Ghalyūn, the populace, the vast majority of the nation, represents the authentic culture unadulterated by Westernization. It opposed the so-called progressive nationalists in their revolt against the Ottomans; it took a stand against secularism and against the modern, hegemonic state. Of its original culture, the populace has preserved the norms reflecting its interests—namely, a spirit of cooperation; a distaste for mimicking the West; an attachment to humanist ethical values in self-defense against government oppression; an opposition to the modernist state; and an antipathy toward conspicuous consumption, exploitation, and injustice.

One of the interesting points he makes is that nationalists should seek the development of the populace (*bināʾ al-shaʿb*) rather than the state. In his analysis, he tries to show that all Arab nationalist efforts have been directed toward building the state (the government apparatus), something he views as serving the class interests of the minority. Though couched in Marxist class terms, the observation is interesting insofar as it tries to divert the elite's usual focus upon aggrandizing the government system and redirect it toward society. In many places, he comes close to the language of civil society.

In *Declaration for the Sake of Democracy*, Ghalyūn sets down what he stands for under four headings. First, the nation is the populace, the productive classes who form the majority in relation to the ruling class and the state. Ghalyūn sometimes appears to want the ruling class destroyed; but in other places, he seems to assign it a lasting role in coalition with the populace.

Second, the Arab bourgeoisie is culturally, politically, and economically dependent; it is a rentier class characterized by consuming what

[13] See Ghalyūn, *Bayān*, 119.

others produce. Its survival is linked to the achievement of real independence and the formation of an alliance with the masses by meeting their needs and integrating them into the system. Democracy would entail uniting the various class interests in a coalition that ensures the balanced distribution of the benefits of growth. It is difficult, however, to see how this differs from Nasserism, which also sees democracy in terms of the social interests of a class coalition.

Third, the creation of a nationalist culture can be achieved by creating a popular culture in content and structure, free from modern, Western, capitalist influences. Consequently, there should be an end to cultural borrowing and an increased reliance on Arabization. Dependency on, and fear of, Western culture naturally tend to characterize intellectuals in developing countries.

Finally, the emphasis in economic growth is placed, not on institutions and production, but rather on controlling consumption, a policy that would be possible if the basic needs of the masses were being met. Prevalent consumer habits should be brought into balance with a country's resources. An independent nation limits its consumption to what it produces.

Ghalyūn's intellectual heritage lies in a perplexed Marxist and *dependencia* theory. Despite his protests to the contrary, his advice would require the aggrandizement of the government apparatus, for how else would society control consumer habits among the various classes, meet the needs of the masses, and follow an economic policy of self-sufficiency without applying authoritarian measures? Moreover, how can Arab thought move forward in isolation? His contribution to Arab thinking today may be confined to his value as challenger and gadfly, rather than as path-breaker. Yet his denunciation of tyranny is compelling, and his analysis linking it to prevailing ideologies is persuasive. Likewise, his emphasis on the authenticity of the culture of the populace versus that of the elite undoubtedly touches on a critical problem at this juncture in the political history of Arab countries.

## A CRITICAL NOTE, BY WAY OF CONCLUSION

It is tempting to dismiss these groups and authors as intellectuals addressing intellectuals, but that would be a mistake. Their thought and writing constitute a genuine and promising trend toward the establishment of democratic thinking as part of the lives of the Arab people. The convergence of diverse and often hostile currents of thought around one issue, democracy, is itself significant. Having come through bitter divisions, at least a few Islamists, Marxists, and Arab nationalists have concluded that democracy must be a major pillar of national reconstruction. Yet not all have reached this conclusion. Some Islamists are openly opposed to Western democracy, and the same can be said of some leftists and nationalists. However, the number of intellectuals who have come to terms with democracy is quite impressive.

While these intellectuals and groups do indeed seem, for the most part, to talk among themselves, many have also begun to expand their reach. The Center for Arab Unity Studies is highly respected among politicized Arabs from the Gulf to the Atlantic. The Center's journal, *The Arab Future*, has one of the largest circulations in the Arab world, and the Center's books are in great demand. Moreover, conferences have socialized young intellectuals into the new ideas of democracy. Almost all of these individuals are linked to some center or political party that they use as a vehicle to reach ordinary citizens. They may not be winning the battle, but they are definitely creating a most promising current of thought.

As an act of allegiance, the democratic protestations of our authors are as impressive as they are heartening. Still, apart from their statements and the prominence they give democracy in their writings, it is hard to determine the intensity of their commitment. Sayf al-Dawla, who makes the most categorical statements about the necessity of democracy for Arabs, thinks democracy possible only if Arabs unite into one state. For him, the territorial state is an incomplete entity, and its people fall short of forming a nation. The implication is that democracy has to await the achievement of Arab unity, and, at most, the two values must be the simultaneous subject of the struggle.

Of concern also is the growing fear and hesitation on the part of many intellectuals in Egypt regarding the democratization process in the face of the threat from Muslim extremists. One should not, however, entertain the idea that the Mubarak regime and the junta in Algeria are suppressing Islamic extremists in the name of democracy, for those regimes are anything but democratic. It is more accurate to say that they are acting in defense of secularism and autocracy.

Profession of allegiance to democratic principles is a good beginning, but unfortunately, it is not sufficient. We have seen many generalizations and impressive retellings of the history of the liberal idea; we have also been assured that democratic liberty must be coupled with equality and that socioeconomic rights must accompany democratization. All this is encouraging and reassuring, but it remains bookish. The issue is debated without reference to specific political experience. Turkey, for instance, has had more experience with democracy than any Arab country, and its society and culture are quite comparable to Arab societies; yet the Turkish experience is almost never mentioned, let alone studied. We have yet to find an Arab intellectual who relates the intellectual principles of democracy analytically to actual democratic experiences in particular Arab countries or to the forces that exist in Arab societies.

Though one may find democratic principles in Arab and Islamic thought, democracy remains a Western ideology and form of government. What implications will that have? How can democracy be adapted to the Arab environment? Some Islamists claim that democracy is not, in fact, alien to the Arab tradition. Ḥasan al-Turabī, among others, has provided brief, but significant, indications of how Western democracy may be adjusted to the Islamic setting. Nationalists and leftists, on the other hand, draw heavily on Western experience; they appear to regard Arabs and Arab civilization as potential participants in an enlightened world civilization. What they have not done is to relate the ideas of democracy to their own societies. Ideological statements about democracy and social forces in Arab societies abound; with all due respect to the authors, we can only judge these to be the expression of beliefs, ideals, or aspirations, rather than empirical generalizations.

ʿAbd Allāh has tried to be quite specific regarding pluralism, syndicalism, and parties, but he stopped well short of exploring the implications of his ideas. The same may be said of Ibrahim, who has, to be sure, followed his own counsel and established a center to put his ideas on civil society in place. But again the implications of these ideas have not been explored. What if these liberal ideas were suddenly accepted by leaders and put into effect? Are Arab societies ready for them, and are there ways consistent with Arab culture in which they could be introduced? One wonders if these well-meaning Arab scholars and intellectuals are poised to suffer the same disappointment from democracy as from the previously imported ideas of nationalism and socialism.

To be more precise, have these enthusiastic democrats thought about the consequences of free elections in the types of societies we encounter in the Arab world? In societies where traditional forces remain prominent, whether tribal shaykhs as in Yemen or sectarian leaders as in Lebanon and many other Arab countries, free elections generally bring to power conservative leaders. Where there is economic and status inequality, such as one finds in Arab countries, free elections will also bring in a conservative legislature and, in turn, a conservative government. Algeria in 1992 is just one reminder.

Moreover, where there is widespread poverty and relations of dependency among citizens, electoral fraud runs rampant. What will our authors' position be in the face of such an eventuality? Will they be willing to say publicly that they concede to a "reactionary" government brought about democratically? To judge from current writings, the answer has to be "No." All have denounced traditional forces in society as reactionary and divisive. Traditional leaders, groups, and practices are seen as the historical obstacle to democratization in the Arab world. Ibrahim leaves them out of the civil society, implying that pluralism does not include people who have a strong attachment to primordial ties or traditional institutions. In his view, only voluntary organizations constitute a legitimate part of civil society.

But is freedom not indivisible? Should not people with sectarian or tribal loyalties be represented? Are traditional cleavages more divisive than, say, political party cleavages? There may be legitimate reasons why such forces must be ejected from the political process, but to do so under the guise of democracy is to be guilty of not understanding democracy or, in fact, not being a democrat. If the object is to bring about a progressive government with modernist leanings, then our authors should seek an ideology other than democracy. Democracy is a process; it brings about change decisively, but slowly. Initial results are often disappointing. Diversity is integral to the democratic process. The founder of a democratic system does not select and discriminate; rather, he tries to craft proper ways to manage diversity, not to judge or eliminate it.

Then there is the question of such a basic and simple democratic principle as majority rule. What if majority rule is found to violate the political rights of minorities? The issue here is not the tyranny of a parliamentary majority, for constitutionalism may take care of that issue. The problem is that, in divided societies and especially in traditional ones where majorities do not change periodically, the social majority—be it an ethnic group, religion, class, or other long-standing affiliation—tends to become permanent, thereby excluding the minority from ever having its views and interests accommodated or implemented. Only advocates of civil society, such as Sayf al-Dawla, may be said to avoid this dilemma, because they see democracy as contingent upon the transformation of society into a civil one. That is, democracy can be implemented only after traditional forces have disintegrated, giving way to modern, secularist, social relations. According to some, even social classes should be reduced or eliminated in preparing society for democracy.

One of the paradoxes of the progressive Arab thinkers is their ambiguity regarding the concept of the individual—the cornerstone, after all, of liberal democracy. As we have already seen, they speak of the people or populace, the nation, classes, political parties, and trade unions. Yet the relevance of these broad concepts to democracy is left unclear. These intellectuals decry communalism, but collective terms such as "the populace" constitute their main conceptual currency. The individual does, however, emerge under the rubric of elections as the only legitimate elector in the process of representation. Insistence on the individual voter reflects almost universal rejection by these thinkers of any form of group representation and, with it, any legitimacy of traditional associations. None has touched on the issue of corporatism and democracy in modern society. It is almost as if they are not aware that in advanced industrial countries the major competing units in the councils of government are made up of corporations of one sort or another. Meanwhile, Yemen has been threatened with being broken apart on the rock of majority rule that is based on a strictly individualist voting system. South Yemen, quite distinct from the North in many ways, feels slighted by majority rule and wants representation as a group. What do these authors have to offer the Yemenis in the way of a solution to their democratic transition crisis?

Putting democracy on the shelf until the proper conditions for it are present is a disturbing proposal. Though totally free from the cynicism found among the ruling Arab elites, democratic authors, whether they know it or not, seem to be making the same argument. Indeed, to make the preparation of society prerequisite to the institution of democracy is to delay indefinitely the introduction and practice of democracy, an approach with obvious attraction to incumbent regimes.

The above are just two examples of the complications that arise from adapting democracy to Arab societies; yet they are sufficient to show that professions of allegiance to the idea of democracy are inadequate unless accompanied by serious studies of the issues and solutions to real political problems within a democratic framework. Here I must admit some concern, for many of the authors considered above have shown lingering vestiges of their former positions, which makes one doubt that they really have creative and democratic ways in mind to solve such problems.

ʿAbd Allāh still speaks of the need to "liquidate" (*taṣfiyya*)[14] traditional and exploitative forces and assumes that a democratic society will

[14] See ʿAbd Allāh's article "*al-Dimuqrāṭiyya*," in *Azmat*, 467.

be a modern society. Not only does he seem to hang on to old preconceptions from Marxism, but he places himself with those who want first to create the preconditions for democracy. Were ʿAbd Allāh to keep his slate clean of Leninism, he would inspire more confidence. When he defends Leninism, as he does in the "Democracy" article, claiming it was democratic, concern is truly warranted. Still, in his case, I am prepared to take such statements as indicative of a lingering defensiveness, and I continue to believe in the genuine democratic spirit expressed in his writing.

Ibrahim, as seen, leaves traditional associations and groups outside civil society; and apart from excluding them, he gives no indication of what he plans to do with them. To the extent that he acknowledges and seeks a civilized solution to ethnic and religious minorities, he is a step ahead of the others. More serious, however, is his conspicuous silence on the issue of privatization. This is an outstanding issue currently in Egypt, as in the rest of the Arab world, and for an advocate of civil society to underplay it or ignore it leaves a serious hiatus in the ideas and relevance of the civil society approach to current events and Arab societies in general.

The idea of civil society is posited as a counterpoint to government hegemony, bestowing more political and economic responsibilities on nongovernmental agencies. Privatization would obviously help correct the imbalance of political power in favor of civil society. So why is it overlooked? The question is directed not only to Ibrahim, but to the rest of our authors as well. Elsewhere, for example, ʿAbd Allāh has conceded the importance of the private sector and expressed an attitude of tolerance toward limited privatization, but has as yet nowhere treated us to a discourse on the relation of privatization to democratization. Since businessmen expect a meaningful measure of decision-making autonomy under privatization, it is important to know whether future political leaders will interfere administratively in the economy, as recent regimes have been doing, or whether they will allow business entrepreneurs to dominate government policy. What role are businessmen to play in a democratic system? Are they a social group likely to have a vested interest in democracy, or the contrary? What is their relation to other groups who may also have a vested interest in democracy? Our authors do not enlighten us regarding the groups in Arab societies who have a vested interest in democracy and can thus be expected to support it. Can they in clear conscience say that most Arab intellectuals agree with them in favoring democracy?

Again, the issue of vestiges comes back to haunt us. Egyptian intellectuals remain attached to socialist ideas. For them, anyone who attacks the public sector is labeled a conservative reactionary who is insensitive to the needs and interests of the impoverished masses. The advocate of privatization is likely to find himself accused of supporting the greed of unbridled capitalism. Ibrahim's sound political instinct has prompted him simply to ignore the subject of privatization. That will not do. Intellectual pacesetters must be expected not only to face the issue squarely, but also to provide creative ways in which a strong private sector can exist within a democratic system that is cognizant of and sensitive to social welfare.

What is being asked for here is not simply an expression of preference, a taking of sides; for it is easy to say one is for both businessmen and workers. Single-party Arab regimes have always maintained that they will take care of both economic growth and social welfare, with the result that they achieve neither. The question is how to manage social forces effectively under democratic rules in such a way as to allow reasonable shares for both working and entrepreneurial classes. Intellectuals who advocate democracy need to explore means whereby justice may be rendered to the large number of poor people in Arab societies without creating the conditions for civil war. The issue is vital because in most Arab countries the poor constitute the majority. Although historical comparisons are of doubtful usefulness, we may nonetheless legitimately ask where among Arab intellectuals is the intellectual clarity of James Madison who wrote on the problems of instituting a new democracy more than two hundred years ago?

It would be unwise to ignore or deny that democracy has the potential to aggravate social divisions and increase the unequal distribution of income in developing societies. The point is how to devise democratic ways to minimize such undesirable consequences. Modernization and political competition frequently revive and inflame primordial sentiments and divisions.[15] It is better to anticipate and thus to be prepared to deal with such problems rather than to become frustrated and, in disillusion, to abandon democracy in the same way that many have abandoned the patron state because of its apparent failure. In short, democracy, while clearly part of the solution, is also part of the problem. The challenge for Arab intellectuals and peoples is to accept democracy with full awareness of its problems.

[15] Since 1972, when I first raised this point, we have seen events give it credibility and strength in the actual course of Arab and Third World politics; see my article, "The Ethnic Revolution."

Arab democrats must realize and come to terms with one hard fact: democracy is its own reward. One wants it for itself, or one does not really want it at all. It may be helpful, but not necessary, for Arab unity; and it is unlikely to bring to power progressive and enlightened forces, at least for a long time. It is, though, dynamic and flexible; and, given a conducive regional environment, it tends to be self-correcting. It holds the promise of inevitable change—change eventually for the better.

It should now be clear why no Arab democrat has yet made use of democracy as experienced in Lebanon between the 1940s and 1970s, though it is less clear why Turkey has been studied so little. In the literature surveyed, Lebanon is referred to only to provide cursory lessons on how not to bring about democratization or to demonstrate the futility of segmentary and traditional attachments.

The fact remains, however, that the Lebanese political system was a functioning Arab democracy. Lebanon remains the only Arab country that, for at least thirty years, had a genuine democratic experience,[16] one in which democratic principles were adjusted by its founders to local conditions. Lebanese democracy provided Arab intellectuals the only place in the Arab world where they could freely discuss ideas critical of governmental authority. When Beirut was closed off by war, Arab democrats had no other Arab city where they could freely debate and publish. They had to turn to Cyprus, London, or Paris. Even Khayr al-Dīn Ḥasīb, a prime mover in many of these discussions who stayed in Beirut[17] throughout the war years, has nothing to say about the Lebanese experience; nor do any of his conferences or publications on democracy or civil society include a study of the Lebanese example.

Have Arab intellectuals no curiosity to investigate how freedom can actually come about? Have they not wondered how a reactionary and sectarian Lebanon provided the only genuine freedom the Arab people has enjoyed in modern times? Is freedom something that grows on trees? No one thinks so, but Arab intellectuals have suppressed the issue and seem wounded and shamed by what happened in Lebanon during the civil war. Their contempt for Lebanese democracy, it must be said, predates the war. Without understanding it, they saw in it the prima facie embodiment of the sectarianism and traditionalism they abhor. They are

[16] This is not intended to belittle the Egyptian experience under the constitutional monarchy. The fact remains, however, that Egypt was not independent during that period and was actually ruled by an autocratic and corrupt king, not by elected officials.

[17] Indeed, Ḥasīb has adamantly refused to move the Center from Beirut despite the dangers and inconveniences of fifteen years of war, explaining to his friends that nowhere else would he have the necessary freedom.

also reluctant to deal with the Lebanese civil war for fear of having to come to terms with the shortcomings of the Palestine Liberation Organization, whose role in the Lebanese civil war was, as Edward Said obliquely observed, "not a very happy thing."[18]

Lebanon offers a rich political terrain where the paradoxes and opportunities of democracy can be examined to the benefit of all concerned. Complexity and ugliness are no strangers to democracy, and a scholar or intellectual who advocates democracy should not shy away from facing them. Indeed, politics, all politics, is as dirty as it is sublime. Why can the same not be said of democracy? It is doubtful that Arab democrats know what they are embarked upon and equally doubtful that they are prepared for the rough-and-tumble of competitive politics. I would feel much better if I saw them mustering their courage to encounter the Lebanese experience head on, leaving behind their bias in favor of preparing a sanitized society to be the democratic bride.

Lebanon tested several principles of democracy in an underdeveloped setting, tried to adjust them to local conditions, and experienced successes as well as failures. It provides a learning experience of enormous relevance and perhaps a model. Nothing could be more timely than a dispassionate inquiry into the Lebanese civil war and democracy.

Leading Arab intellectuals have made a beginning—but only a beginning—in coming to terms with Western democracy. Now, we wait for them to show their creativity in dealing with this all-too-thorny and difficult subject.

[18] See his interview in *al-Majalla* (The Magazine) (December 1993): 49.

# 7

# Political Parties Between State Power and Islamist Opposition

IBRAHIM A. KARAWAN

## INTRODUCTION

Much of the proliferating literature on the contemporary Arab world leaves its readers with the distinct impression that the most salient feature of the politics of that region can be reduced to a confrontation between two camps: retreating state machineries and expanding Islamist challengers. A closer look, however, reveals that such a characterization is oversimplified and misleading. Not only are the two camps themselves far from monolithic, but there is between them a changing political space occupied by coalitions of political movements and groups. Factional divisions are also to be found within the ranks of the ruling elites, such as the one in Algeria between the "eradicators" who want to eliminate the Islamists and the "accommodators" willing to compromise with moderates. Conflict also persists within the Islamist camp between militant and legalist approaches to doctrine, strategy, and tactics. Thus, the overly simple image so prevalent in discussions of the politics of the Arab world needs to be made more complex. One step in this direction is to examine the political realm situated between the Party of the Government (*Ḥizb al-ḥukūma*) and the Party of God (*Ḥizb Allāh*). Occupying this middle ground are political parties and movements associated with neither the state power nor the Islamist opposition.

Such parties reject a political system based on the hegemony either of the state or of political Islam. They oppose state elites, whom they characterize as being incompetent and as stifling political alternatives; they also oppose the dominance of Islamist movements that adopt exclusionary ideologies that threaten to splinter the nation along sectarian lines. The thrust of their political action is to expand an area of politi-

I am grateful to Marius Deeb for his helpful comments on an earlier version of this essay.

cal autonomy for citizens free from control by the institutionalized power of the state or religion. These parties thereby set themselves apart from statist authoritarianism imposed from above in the name of maintaining order and from Islamist authoritarianism supported from below under the banner of safeguarding authenticity. Freedom of expression, constitutional accountability, competitive politics, popular sovereignty, human rights, equal citizenship, and the reconciliation of authenticity and modernity are among the major political and ideological concerns of these parties.

To maintain such an intermediate position between the institutional powers of the state and the political weight of Islamist movements, these parties must make many difficult choices. They frequently come under attack from both sides. In a number of countries, state authorities accuse them of advocating social hatred and class warfare, threatening domestic stability as well as law and order, and having ties to radical external forces. Islamist movements have painted them as believers in alien, imported ideas—dubbed *al-afkār al-mustawrada*—and as mere extensions of the Western sociocultural contamination threatening the moral fabric of the Islamic nation (*umma*). Faced with this dual assault, these parties have had to develop varied and complex strategies. It is against this backdrop of shifting alliances and complex political discourse that one can best explore political liberalization in three countries, each representing a subregion of the Arab world: Egypt in the Nile Valley, Jordan in the Mashriq, and Tunisia in the Maghrib.[1]

Concurrent economic crises and social tensions have generated strong societal pressures for political change in these countries. Movements, known by some as restricted political pluralism (*al-taʿaddudiyya al-siyāsiyya al-muqayyada*) and by others as controlled and incremental

[1] More attention will be devoted to the case of Egypt, given that its political parties and experimentation with political pluralism have a longer history than those in the surrounding countries. Still, those Egyptian parties that have received ample treatment in the available literature will not be examined in this chapter. Much has been written, for example, on the Wafd Party, a liberal secularist party under the monarchy that entered into an electoral alliance with the Muslim Brothers in the mid-1980s. For the earlier era, see Marius Deeb, *Party Politics in Egypt: The Wafd and Its Rivals* (London: Ithaca Press, 1979), and Afaf Marsot, *Egypt's Liberal Experiment* (Berkeley: University of California Press, 1977). For the New Wafd, see Raymond Hinnebusch, "The Reemergence of the Wafd Party: Glimpses of the Liberal Opposition in Egypt," *International Journal of Middle East Studies* 16 (1984): 99–121; and ʿIṣām Fawzī, "Ḥizb al-Wafd" (The Wafd Party), in Fu'ād Murṣī et al., *al-Intikhābāt al-Barlamāniyya fī Miṣr* (Parliamentary elections in Egypt) (Cairo: Maktabat Ibn Sīnā, 1990), 97–108. With the New Wafd's and the labor Socialist Party's boycott of elections in 1990, the National Progressive Unionist Party (*al-Tajammuʿ*) became the only opposition party represented in the Egyptian parliament.

Arab *glasnost*, reflect the realization among some members of the ruling elite that the old statist formula could no longer be maintained in light of the state's inability to garner mass support or political acquiescence by meeting its social contract obligations. A degree of political pluralism was introduced to provide a legitimate outlet for mounting societal discontent. Despite the persistence of significant restrictions, parliaments were allowed more institutional latitude to criticize domestic policies. Professional associations, labor unions, student organizations, as well as clubs of judges and university professors have become increasingly pluralistic. The spectrum of opinions reflected in the press has broadened, and the judicial system has become less subservient to the state. Many political exiles have been allowed back, and human rights organizations have been formed and more or less tolerated. In short, compared to the recent past, institutional structures have become less monolithic and the capricious use of power less frequent.

Liberalization from above, however, has been carried out by state managers determined to maintain control over the political process and minimize any real transfer of power or uncertainty about the outcome of semicompetitive politics. These managers set the parameters of permissible political action, manipulated the electoral system, suspended (but did not abrogate) the legal restrictions on the activities of citizens with "oppositional pasts," practiced state-centered clientelism, maintained control over radio and television, and unleashed repressive campaigns to demonstrate that the regime could still use its sharp teeth if its political opponents failed to discipline themselves or if they ceased to qualify as a "constructive opposition."[2]

Within this context, the political parties under discussion here did not find it realistic to pursue power through electoral means. Rather, via their newspapers and publications, they tended to function as platforms (*manābīr*) dedicated to challenging the Islamist influence among the populace in the "political street" and among the intelligentsia, as well as pressuring the state to broaden the existing limits of legitimate political

[2] See Michael Hudson, "After the Gulf War: Prospects for Democratization in the Arab World," *The Middle East Journal* 15, no. 1 (Summer 1991): 407–26; Kevin Dwyer, *Arab Voices: The Human Rights Debate in the Middle East* (Berkeley: University of California Press, 1991); Ibrahim A. Karawan, "Re-Islamization Movements According to Kepel: On Striking Back and Striking Out," *Contention* (Fall 1992): 161–79; Laurie Brand, "Liberalization and Changing Political Coalitions," *The Jerusalem Journal of International Relations* (December 1991); Rex Brynen, "Economic Crisis and Post-Rentier Democratization in the Arab World: The Case of Jordan," *The Canadian Journal of Political Science* 25, no. 1 (March 1992); and Jill Crystal, "Authoritarianism and Its Adversaries in the Arab World," *World Politics* 46 (January 1994): 262–89.

action. Accordingly, by focusing public attention on these issues, the party newspaper has often become more significant politically than the party organization itself. The literature published by leaders and theoreticians of this "third force," including their political statements to party cadres, is indeed a rich source to examine. At times, it presents a critique of strongly held positions inherited from a past era when nationalist or socialist causes were deemed the only real struggles worth fighting and even dying for. Some of these critiques recorded the depressingly numerous failures produced by postcolonial states in the Middle East, failures for which the colonial legacy cannot be held entirely accountable. At times, the authors of this literature took major risks in going public with their ideas. But the move toward liberalization never fully deprived the state elites of diverse physical and economic means of intimidating and repressing opponents.

Equally problematic was the threat of cultural intimidation directed against those who dared to criticize the prevailing notions about the Islamic heritage (*turāth*) and its mythologization, the invocation of tradition by religious and political institutions to censor ideas, and the infringement of the basic rights of women and ethnic minorities in the polity. Societal intolerance and the threat of opposition violence could be as great an obstacle to pluralism as repression by the state. Defeating the authoritarian structures in Arab polities was not politically feasible in the short run. It became necessary, therefore, to work toward the long-term development of civil society by exposing the ideological foundations of authoritarianism.[3] In short, different ideas and different societal attitudes were needed to pave the way for alternatives to statist and Islamist authoritarianisms.

## THE EGYPTIAN *TAJAMMUʿ*

The National Progressive Unionist Party (NPUP), known as "The Alliance" (*al-Tajammuʿ*), came into existence in the mid-1970s as part of Sadat's restructuring of Egyptian politics, which did away with the Arab Socialist Union (ASU) inherited from Nasser's era. In 1975, along with the Open Door Economic Policy (*Infitāḥ*), this restructuring sanctioned the creation of three political tribunes—left, center, and right—

[3] For a clear and recent articulation of this position, see Samīr Amīn, "Maṭlūb: Quṭb Thālith Qawī Mustaqill ʿan al-Ḥukm wa al-Islām al-Siyāsī" (Wanted: A powerful third pole independent of the regime and of political Islam), *al-Yasār* (The Left) 48 (February 1994): 65–9.

which were turned into political parties the following year. The fact that the NPUP owed its legal existence to a president whose domestic and foreign policies it vehemently opposed led to vigorous internal debate. Some party activists raised fundamental questions: What were Sadat's motives for legalizing leftist opposition? How significant was the margin of action permitted by the regime? How much of the state's monolithic and repressive power could realistically be expected to wither away as the new political experiment evolved? Who would be using whom under such a climate of relative political decompression and the relaxation of restrictions on political expression? Did the NPUP have other and perhaps better options? And what were the costs of remaining outside the boundaries of political legitimacy?

Obviously, no clear answers could be found to such questions. The process of political transition was fraught with uncertainty.[4] The memories of the Nasserist experience were still fresh in the minds of many NPUP activists. Nasser had agreed to allow communists to join the ASU and its "Vanguard of Socialists," provided they disband their own organizations and abide by the principles of "Arab Socialism," particularly what was dubbed the "nationalization of class conflict." This "licensed infiltration" provided leftists access to the state-controlled media and some political institutions, such as the Socialist Youth Organization (SYO),[5] and put an end to an era marked by ruthless violations of the human rights of hundreds of leftists and their torture at the hands of security agencies.[6]

The post-Nasser era offered new political opportunities to the leftists, who aspired to take advantage of the relative opening of the political process to reach wider segments of the population. The shift toward economic liberalization promised to escalate class conflict, providing a conducive setting for leftist activism, or so they thought. Their logic can be formulated as follows: the society was not yet "ripe" for a genuine socialist revolution, and the state remained capable of restricting leftist political participation. Yet, a regime that was both less authoritarian and less "progressive" might, in a certain sense, be better for leftists to work with than a regime, such as Nasser's, that was more progressive but also

4 Adam Przeworski, "Democracy as a Contingent Outcome of Conflicts," in *Constitutionalism and Democracy*, ed. J. Elster and R. Slagstad (New York: Cambridge University Press, 1988).

5 Shimon Shamir, "The Marxists in Egypt: The Licensed Infiltration Doctrine in Practice," in *The USSR in the Middle East*, ed. Michael Confino and Shimon Shamir (Jerusalem: Israel Universities Press, 1973).

6 Rifʿat Sayyid Aḥmad, *Thawrat al-Jinirāl Jamāl ʿAbd al-Nāṣir* (The Revolution of General Gamāl ʿAbd al-Nāṣir) (Cairo: Dār al-Hudā, 1993), 619–42.

more closed to leftist participation. In fact, some leftists who later became leaders of the NPUP, such as Ismāʿīl Ṣabrī ʿAbd Allāh and Fu'ād Murṣī, found it prudent to cooperate actively with Sadat in his power struggle against the Nasserist left led by ʿAlī Ṣabrī and Shaʿrawī Jumma. So, like Nasser, Sadat managed to co-opt leftists within his political system.[7]

In both cases, leftists were aware not only of the political limits imposed on their role, but also of the shortcomings and objectionable aspects of the regimes with which they ultimately cooperated. Some were too glaring to be missed. In Nasser's era, the leftists were critical of the social and political privileges enjoyed by the top military strata, the expansion and proliferation of the security services, the "fat cats" who benefitted from the public sector, and the ascendance of "bureaucratic feudalism."[8] In Sadat's era they opposed the regime's encouragement of Islamist movements, the widening gap between the haves and the have-nots, the deepening political and economic dependency on the United States, and the regime's obsession with anti-Sovietism. However, what tipped the scale in favor of involvement in the political system was the leftists' perception that the range of alternatives was quite narrow and the costs of not participating high.

Under Nasser, some leftists maintained that the Communist Party should not have disbanded itself as the regime stipulated. For them, no truly communist party should agree to put an end to its own independent existence in order to become part of a political structure dominated by a military directorate and its technocratic affiliates. The Soviet testimony that Nasser's regime was advancing along a "noncapitalist road to development" did not convince this group. However, the prevailing conclusion within the left was that participation within the existing system made more sense than either fighting or boycotting it. That system introduced certain socioeconomic measures to change the class structure in the country—measures leftists had advocated for decades. It fought American-backed military pacts and improved Egypt's relations with "the mother country of socialism." Moreover, to be imprisoned in desert camps would only deprive leftists of the opportunity to influence rising generations and shape state policies; it would not serve to destabilize such a strong and popular regime.

During the mid-1960s, such a perspective seemed to have something going for it. Leftists held important positions in the newspaper *Akhbār*

[7] See Leonard Binder, "The Failure of the Egyptian Left," *Asian and African Studies* 14, no. 1 (March 1980): 21.
[8] See Fatḥī ʿAbd al-Fattāḥ, *Shiyūʿiyyūn wa Nāṣiriyyūn* (Communists and Nasserists) (Cairo: Maktaba Rūz al-Yūsuf, 1975).

*al-Yawm* (News of the day), whose editor, Maḥmūd Amīn al-ʿĀlim, was a well-known Marxist. Two monthly publications, *al-Ṭalīʿa* (The vanguard), edited by Luṭfī al-Khūlī, and *al-Kātib* (The scribe), edited by Aḥmad ʿAbbās Ṣāliḥ, were also controlled by the left. A portion of the material used for the ideological orientation of members of the Socialist Youth Organization was prepared by Marxist intellectuals, such as Muḥammad Anīs, Muḥammad al-Khafīf, and Ismāʿīl Ṣabrī ʿAbd Allāh. From these fora, they denounced the religious conservatism of the Muslim Brotherhood and its alliance with the Saudi and Jordanian regimes as well as Western powers. In this regard, the left had a common interest with the state—a point that became especially apparent in 1965, the year in which a radical wing of the Brotherhood tried, under the doctrinal guidance of Sayyid Quṭb, to bring down Nasser's regime. The leaders of that wing saw Nasser as a communist agent and sought to end what they characterized as the "communist cultural invasion and ideological domination" of Egypt. In response, the leftists advanced a socialist interpretation of Islam stressing economic egalitarianism and social justice. ʿAbd al-Raḥmān al-Sharqawī's major work, *Muḥammad Rasūl al-Ḥurriyya* (Muhammad the messenger of freedom), focused not on divine revelation, but on the class nature of the Muslim revolution in seventh-century Arabia.

Though they accepted the notion that the Nasserist regime had a progressive, populist orientation, the leftists maintained that those who understood the "laws of scientific socialism" were uniquely qualified to help the regime move along the path of socialist transformation. For instance, they attacked the influence of rich families in the countryside during what came to be known as the Kamshīsh Affair.[9] Even Nasser seemed to have been initially persuaded by their position. Recently published transcripts of one of his semisecret meetings with members of "the vanguard of socialists" in March 1966 reveal his concern that the rural bourgeoisie still controlled agricultural cooperatives and local councils in the villages in a way incongruent with the requirements of the transition from capitalism to socialism.[10] The left advertised its common interest with the state in opposing both the Brotherhood's threat in urban centers and the influence of rich rural notables. They offered to assist the regime in combatting such threats on the political and ideological levels while, at the same time, radicalizing the sole legitimate political organi-

[9] For a good analysis of that period, see Hamid Ansari, *The Stalled Society* (Albany: State University of New York Press, 1986).

[10] Quoted in Rifʿat Sayyid Aḥmad, *Thawrat al-Jinirāl*, 778.

zation—the ASU. They drew attention to toppled populist regimes in Algeria, Ghana, and Indonesia as warnings of future developments that might unfold in Egypt if such internal and external threats were not countered immediately and effectively.

The regime's response, however, was true to its military and bureaucratic nature. Field Marshal ʿAbd al-Ḥakīm ʿAmr's office and military intelligence took charge on both fronts. Instead of the political and ideological confrontation that leftists hoped would increase their influence and significance in the eyes of the regime, the military police arrested members of the Brotherhood and then dominated their interrogations and trials. The regime formed the Higher Committee for the Liquidation of Feudalism, also under ʿAbd al-Ḥakīm ʿAmr, who was never considered sympathetic to leftist causes. The committee subjected a sprinkling of wealthy landowners to certain administrative penalties, but refrained from the social and political restructuring suggested by the left. As Leonard Binder has justly pointed out, these events did not "open thousands of Egyptian villages to the ministrations of militant leftist cadres."[11]

After Egypt's humiliating defeat in 1967, some leftists thought that both the masses and the "progressive leadership" might be persuaded that the corrupt military bourgeoisie was behind the disaster, paving the way for a radicalization of the regime through reorganizing "the vanguard of the socialists." Within the ranks of the ASU and via the mass media, they called for launching a "protracted people's war" against Zionism and imperialism and for mobilizing the masses to engage in a revolutionary struggle similar to that taking place in Vietnam. The regime put an abrupt end to such hopes by stipulating that the only way to respond to defeat was to enhance Egypt's regular army. "No sound," it proclaimed, "should become louder than the sound of the battle" for which the regular army was to be prepared.

This is the background against which the role of the NPUP during the 1970s is to be understood. The experiments in the populist restructuring of society from above during the 1960s reached their limits with the military defeat in 1967 and Nasser's death in September 1970. The magnitude of Egypt's defeat convinced many that restrictions on democratic practices by the military elite were responsible for the disaster. After Sadat so easily eliminated his rivals who controlled the ASU in May 1971, it was obvious that the party's institutional structure and the van-

[11] Binder, "The Failure," 23–4.

guard within which leftists were incorporated represented no more than a paper tiger. As the "socialist transformation" had been introduced by presidential decrees in the early 1960s, it was possible to reverse it in the same way via the Open Door Economic Policy a decade later with little resistance.

All this created an interest on the left in relaxing restrictions on political expression and association. It led some well-known leftists to cooperate with Sadat soon after his ascendancy to the presidency on the assumption that his de-Nasserization program would bring about a loosening of state control over society and the creation of limited "bourgeois democracy."[12] Even those leftists who did not have much confidence in Sadat's intentions tended to think that his economic policies might paradoxically prove helpful for leftist causes, given that these policies would intensify "antagonistic class contradictions." Stated differently, though they opposed Sadat's policy of economic liberalization, they "dialectically" appreciated its potential for radical impact in de-nationalizing class conflicts and creating an opportunity to mobilize the masses for social and political struggle. Leftists hoped that capitalist transformation might bring about conditions conducive to revolution, which Nasserism with its "distinctly petty bourgeois vacillation" had not provided. Given that the incorporation of leftist segments in the ASU had denied the left an autonomous organizational presence and an ideological identity, it was thought that Sadat's relative political liberalization might provide an opportunity to achieve real political influence among the populace.

The decision to accept Sadat's offer and work within the system was adopted by the Marxist core of the NPUP. Due to its small numbers, however, it could not hope to achieve any significant measure of success without establishing a coalition with other groups, including Nasserists and the self-proclaimed Islamic left, *al-Yasār al-Islāmī*, that had not been given legal permission by the state to form distinct parties. The forma-

[12] See Muḥammad ʿAbd al-Salām al-Zayyāt, *al-Sadāt: al Qināʿ wa al-Ḥaqīqa* (Sadat: The mask and the truth) (Cairo: al-Ahālī, 1990); Ṣalāḥ ʿĪsā, "Mustaqbal al-Dimuqrāṭiyya fī Miṣr" (The Future of democracy in Egypt), *al-Ṭalīʿa* (December 1974); Raymond Hinnebusch, "The National Progressive Unionist Party," *Arab Studies Quarterly* 3, no. 4 (Fall 1981): 325–51; Raymond Baker, *Sadat and After: Struggles for Egypt's Political Soul* (Cambridge: Harvard University Press, 1990), chap. 4; Muṣṭafā Kāmīl al-Sayyid, "al-Tajriba al-Thāniyya li-al-Taʿaddud al-Ḥizbī" (The Second experiment with multipartyism), *al-Ṭalīʿa* (November 1986): 70–83; and Gehad Auda and Daniel Brumberg, "The Phenomenon of Liberal Marxism in Egypt: The Second Transformation," paper delivered at the Conference of the Middle East Studies Association, Baltimore, November 1987.

tion of such coalitions has been a major concern of the leftists since the opening of semicompetitive politics in Egypt during the mid-1970s. Concerning the Nasserists, their strategy was to reverse the situation that prevailed under Nasser by making the more numerous Nasserists the rank and file, while Marxists acted as the vanguard of the party.

In such a setting, some NPUP theoreticians watered down explicitly Marxist beliefs and proclaimed Nasserism as the Marxism of the Arab world.[13] However, this position created divisions within the left, since it was strongly criticized by other Marxist cadres who had denounced the dominance of the Nasserist managerial bourgeoisie in the 1960s and who now saw Sadatism not as an apostasy from Nasserism but as a continuation of trends begun under Nasser's presidency. That position also failed to convince many Nasserists that the NPUP was truly Nasserist; hence, they continued to pursue the objective of forming their own party to prove that Nasserism after Nasser and outside the NPUP could be a viable political force.[14]

The NPUP's attempt to address the Islamist issue turned out to be even more complicated. One dimension of its interest in developing its own leftist-Islamist discourse was to limit its vulnerability to damaging accusations of atheism. That is why it went to great lengths in the party's political program to emphasize adherence to the genuine principles and teachings of Islam. It associated Islamic religiosity with the promotion of social progress and equal opportunity among all citizens, including non-Muslims. The NPUP leadership was aware that the regime tolerated and even encouraged radical Islamist groups and the Muslim Brothers in order to weaken the left.

Many leftists were also concerned about the increasing appeal of Islamist currents at the expense of the left. According to Ismāʿīl Ṣabrī ʿAbd Allāh, the "social base of the Islamic movement is essentially a revolutionary base stolen from the revolution."[15] What should be the leftist response to that challenge? According to Luṭfī al-Khulī's address to party cadres

> no political party can ignore the Islamic issue and not use it in the political struggle without suffering a tremendous loss by being isolated from the broad masses

[13] See, for example, the statements by Fu'ād Murṣī and Muḥammad Sīd Aḥmad in *al-Ghad al-ʿArabī* (The Arab morrow) 1 (September 1990): 140–2.

[14] An interesting example is the resignation of Yaḥyā al-Jamāl, a former cabinet member under Nasser, from the NPUP for similar reasons. See ʿAbd al-Ḥalīm Qindīl, "Suʿal al-Ḥizb al-Nāṣirī" (The Question of the Nasserist Party), *al-Ghad al-ʿArabī*, 7–18.

[15] Quoted in Nadia Ramsis Farah, *Religious Strife in Egypt* (New York: Gordon and Breach, 1986), 40.

> . . . as long as religious forces are dominant in the street. . . . Otherwise, you hav to import another non-religious people to help launch the desired revolution![16]

Not surprisingly, NPUP ranks included some cadres whom the part identified as "enlightened Islamists," while its opponents referred t them as "the red shaykhs." One of these was Khalīl ʿAbd al-Karīm, a member of the party's Secretariat, who was arrested in 1954 and 196 for belonging to the Muslim Brotherhood. His ideas were influenced b the early works of Sayyid Quṭb: *Social Justice in Islam* and *The Battl between Islam and Capitalism*.

ʿAbd al-Karīm argued that the essence of Islam is social justice for th downtrodden, not the formal implementation of religious legal codes Islamic and leftist positions are not irreconcilable, as some have suggested. The task is how to interpret the Islamic heritage in a revolutionary way so as to reveal its opposition to capitalist monopolies an exploitation. What is known as *sharīʿa* is not a single, eternal, immutabl body of rules and regulations. In other words, Islam is what Muslim decide to make of it. Political Islamists who call for the implementatio of *sharīʿa* strive to seize state power and establish a repressive system under the guise of divine sovereignty. But for ʿAbd al-Karīm and othe Islamic leftists, such as Shaykh Muṣṭafā ʿAsī, Islam is primarily abou defending the interests of the dispossessed (*maḥrūmūn*).[17] ʿAbd al-Karīm warned against political Islamists who pose a serious threat to the fundamental notions of citizenship and national integration in a way that regardless of their intentions, cannot but help the forces of social conservatism as well as the imperialist powers and Israel.[18]

The Islamic left within the NPUP called for adopting flexible an enlightened positions based on rationalist interpretations of core Islami values. Central to such a call is its emphasis on societal tolerance towar

[16] See "Nadwat al-Taṭarruf al-Siyāsī al-Dīnī fī Miṣr" (The Workshop on religious an political extremism in Egypt), *Fikr li-al-Dirāsāt wa al-Abḥāth* (Thought for studies an research) (Cairo, December 1985), 100.

[17] See Khalīl ʿAbd al-Karīm's article, "Mā Huwa al-Yasār al-Islāmī?" (What is the Islami left?), in *al-Ahālī* (The Populace)—which is the NPUP newspaper—5 June 1985, 5, an also his book *Li-Taṭbīq al-Sharīʿa lā li-al-Ḥukm* (For the Application of the *Sharīʿa* no for governance) (Cairo: al-Ahālī, 1987). His line of argument builds on writings o earlier thinkers, such as Aḥmad ʿAbbās Ṣāliḥ's *al-Yamīn wa al-Yasār fī al-Islām* (The Right and the left in Islam) (Beirut: al-Mu'assasa al-ʿArabiyya li-al-Dirāsāt, 1972). Fo ideas similar to those found in "Liberation Theology," see Muḥammad Riḍā' Muḥarram *Taḥdīth al-ʿAql al-Siyāsī al-Islāmī* (The Renewal of the Islamic political mind) (Cairo Dar al-Fikr, 1986) and "al-Ṣawāb wa al-Khaṭa' fī Mas'alat al-Yasār al-Dīnī" (The Righ and wrong concerning the issue of the religious left), *al-Ṭalīʿa* (March 1977); and Ḥasan Ḥanafī, "Mādhā Yaʿnī al-Yasār al-Islāmī?" (What does 'Islamic Left' mean?), *al-Yasār al-Islāmī* (The Islamic left) 1 (January 1981): 5–48.

[18] ʿAbd al-Karīm writes a regular article under the title "*al-Islām wa lākin bi-dūn Qasūsa*" (Islam but without a priesthood) in *al-Yasār*, a monthly periodical published by the NPUP.

non-Muslims, as well as toward Muslims who understand Islam differently from the dominant religious institutions. In other words, this was a call for ideological pluralism in Muslim societies and a rejection of the literalist positions that claim to hold a monopoly on what is Islamically sanctioned. This perspective was critical of those Islamists who claim to be the only ones saved from Hell, known as *al-Firqa al-Nājiyya*.[19] Islam, according to its leftist interpreters, sanctions neither hostility to reason nor the excommunication of Muslims who adopt new interpretations.

One of the issues emphasized by NPUP activists and writers was the threat of sectarian rifts in Egyptian society escalating as a result of the tide of Islamic militancy and the misguided policies of the state itself. Rifʿat al-Saʿīd, in particular, argued in no uncertain terms that any talk about promoting democratization and national unity would be completely meaningless without first safeguarding the civil and religious rights of Egypt's Coptic community. Islamists, or as he calls them, *al-Mutaʾaslimūn* (literally, the would-be Muslims), threaten to transform Egypt from a "national community" based on the principle of equal citizenship into a "religious community" predicated on the unvarnished political supremacy of the adherents of one particular religious faith. In such a setting, the subordinate religious community is bound to suffer from strong feelings of alienation and anxiety about the future, and may even be tempted to seek external help should it become available.[20]

He holds the state responsible for the deterioration of communal relations. After all, until the recent past, it encouraged and then appeased the Islamists. It failed to defend the Copts against their militant assailants. It ignored the principle of equal citizenship by discriminating against Copts in the state bureaucracy and restricting their right to build places of worship. The state also tolerated attacks on Coptic religious beliefs on state-run television and in governmental as well as non-governmental publications. To oppose this climate of division and repression created by political Islamists and the state apparatus a coalition must be built of "enlightened, liberal, and rational forces" that are concerned about national unity. Such a coalition would "restore the Egyptianness of Egypt," including its traditions of tolerance, and broaden the democratic space in society.[21]

[19] See Muḥammad Aḥmad Khalaf Allāh, "al-Shaykh al-Ghazzālī Bayn al-Sharīʿa wa al-Qanūn" (Shaykh al-Ghazzālī Between the *Sharīʿa* and the Law), *al-Ahālī*, 4 August 1993, and also a much earlier article by Ḥasan Ḥanafī, "al-Islām wa al-Muʿāraḍa" (Islam and opposition), *al-Ahālī*, 5 April 1978.

[20] See Rifʿat al-Saʿīd, "Munāqashāt Bārīsiyya Ḥawla Masʾalat al-Aqalliyya" (Discussions in Paris on the minority issue), *al-Ahālī*, 25 May 1994.

[21] See Rifʿat al-Saʿīd, "Munāqashāt Bārīsiyya."

According to the NPUP, violence by Islamic militants intended to bring down the regime at any price, together with counter-violence by the regime to crush the Islamic militants at any cost, creates a vicious cycle that must be broken before it undermines "the essence of society and national unity."[22] Islamist violence cannot be contained through statist counter-violence. It often does, however, provide state authorities with a rationale to impose or extend restrictions on political expression and association. In other words, Islamist violence may be used as an excuse to paint all opposition as subversive and justify the reluctance of state managers to relinquish their massive powers. Only a vibrant civil society

> represented by its various parties, unions, and social organizations can isolate the proponents of violence. The state security measures by themselves can only be temporary and of limited effect. . . . Violence is a social phenomenon which requires a comprehensive treatment[23]

identified by the NPUP as a change-oriented "national salvation program." This program would include social and economic reforms to fight corruption and promote national unity. It would be based on respect for the human rights of all citizens; the liberation of labor unions, student organizations, and professional associations from statist control; a genuine political dialogue; and popular participation in the political process.

The escalation of Islamist violence in Egypt since the early 1990s[24] brought a shift in emphasis on the part of the NPUP leadership. Clearly, they continue to denounce state-imposed restrictions on free expression, peaceful assembly, organization, demonstration, and strikes; to call for the cancellation of the military court system; and to criticize corruption and the excesses of state security agencies. But they now reserve their harshest condemnations for "terrorism in the name of Islam." For many leftists, the turning point came when Islamists began using bullets and ideological terrorists resorted to denouncing those who hold different views as unbelievers.[25]

[22] "*al-Taqrīr al-Siyāsī min Lajnat al-Tajammuʿ al-Markaziyya*" (The Political report of the NPUP Central Committee), *al-Safīr* (The Diplomat), Beirut, 19 January 1982.

[23] See *al-Safīr*, 19 January 1982, 11. More recently, the leftist Egyptian Center for Labor Union Studies called for ending state control of labor unions on the basis that "no one has interest in keeping labor unions weak except those who want to open the door to terrorism"; see *al-Yasār* (May 1993): 10. See also a summary of the discussion sponsored by the Egyptian Organization for Human Rights in *al-Ahālī*, 4 August 1993, 7.

[24] On the extent and significance of that escalation, see Saad Eddin Ibrahim, "The Changing Face of Egypt's Islamic Activism," paper presented to the workshop on U.S.–Egyptian Relations after the Cold War, Washington D.C., April 1994.

[25] See the interview with the spokesperson for the Islamic Group Abroad in *al-Ahālī*, 9 February 1994, 3.

The reasons behind such a shift are not difficult to discern. NPUP publications reflected a realization that an Islamist alternative would be far worse for them than the current regime. Islamists of the jihadist type threatened secularists with death, a threat already carried out in the case of Faraj Fūda.[26] The NPUP also noted the economic losses resulting from Islamist violence and the impact on public opinion made by the state's media campaign against the militants. Putting equal blame for the violence on the shoulders of the state and the radical Islamic groups (*Jamāʿāt Islāmiyya*) would not do, at least not for the present.

For now, the NPUP has elevated the reconstruction of political and religious thought to the top of its agenda. Violent actions in the name of Islam are inspired by a "selective, biased, and fanatical ideology" that has to be confronted and replaced by a system based on the values of rationality, tolerance, and enlightenment.[27] Radio and television programs and school textbooks have to be reshaped to serve that purpose, instead of indirectly nourishing the "intellectual wing of terrorism." The distinction made by some between moderate and radical Islamists is seriously questioned in the new leftist campaign. After all, Shaykh al-Ghazzālī, who issued the legal decree (*fatwā*) justifying the assassination of Faraj Fūda, was considered to be a moderate Islamist and had even been accused earlier by some militants of religious deviation.[28]

As the NPUP leadership sees the current situation, their dual opposition to state policies and Islamist terrorism must continue, but it must also be modified to reflect shifting priorities. In the words of the general secretary of the party, Rifʿat al-Saʿīd, the wrong strategy can lead to political disasters.

[26] See the published account of such threats given by ʿAbd al-Ḥamīd Ḥasab Allāh, a leader of "the Vanguards of Islamic Conquest" as published in *al-Ahālī*, 8 September 1993.

[27] See *al-Ahālī*, 23 June 1993, and Muḥammad Riḍā' Muḥarram, "*al-Irhāb al-Siyāsī Yuqātilunā bi-Tahaddud al-Ridda*" (Political terrorism fights us by threatening apostasy), in *al-Ahālī*, 21 July 1993.

[28] See the critical statement by the Egyptian Organization for Human Rights in *al-Ahālī*, 30 June 1993 and 4 August 1993; Ṣafwat Luṭfī et al., *Taṭbīq al-Sharīʿa al-Islāmiyya: Bayn al-Ḥaqīqa wa Shiʿārāt al-Fitna* (Applying the *Sharīʿa*: Between the truth and slogans of sedition) (Cairo: al-Hay'a al-ʿĀmma li-al-Kitāb al-Miṣriyya, 1993); Rifʿat al-Saʿīd, "Hākum Shaykhukum al-Muʿtadil?" (This is your moderate sheikh?), *al-Ahālī*, 30 June 1993; Muṣṭafā ʿAsī, "al-Mustanīrūn: Hal Yaftaḥūn Bāb al-Takfīr?" (The Enlightened: Are they opening the door for accusations of unbelief?), *al-Ahālī*, 7 July 1993; Muḥammad Aḥmad Khalaf Allāh, "Narfuḍ al-Qawl bi-Qatl al-Murtadd" (We reject the argument that the apostate is to be killed), *al-Ahālī*, 7 July 1993; Aḥmad S. Manṣūr, "al-Ghazzālī yarudd ʿalā al-Ghazzālī" (al-Ghazzālī replies to al-Ghazzālī), *al-Ahālī*, 14 July 1993; and Muḥammad Nūr Faraḥāt, "Radd ʿalā Fatwā al-Ghazzālī" (Reply to al-Ghazzālī's legal decree), *al-Muṣawwar* (The Illustrated), 2 July 1993.

> We are finding out that the civil society that Egypt has spent the last one and a half centuries building—a society that embodies Egyptian accomplishments . . . in freedom of thought, free expression, constitution, parliament, theater, press, cinema, music, art, innovation—all this is threatened . . . by elements that want to push us back to the dark ages of the Mamlukes or of the Ottoman occupation. . . . What kind of an opposition sacrifices Egypt for the sake of continuing to oppose? . . . The problems in civil society should be corrected through institutions of civil society, not through terrorism. . . . A broad front should be established by all who want to defend the civil society including politicians, academics, writers, artists, liberals, industrialists, and national bankers.[29]

It is important to keep in mind that the NPUP is a coalition of various political forces, some of which do not share the above assessment. Thus, its publications devote considerable space to discussing various viewpoints within the NPUP concerning its alliance policy.[30] A lengthy interview with the prominent Marxist thinker, Maḥmūd Amīn al-ʿĀlim, is telling in this regard. Al-ʿĀlim argued that the left has to act on the basis of rational thinking that does not confuse abstract ideologies with political interests. Some Nasserists seek an alliance with the Islamists against the state on the basis of mutual hostility to imperialism and Zionism. Al-ʿĀlim called that an exercise in "foggy thinking" (*al-ḍabābiyya*). The clash of interests between Nasserists and Islamists is fundamental. Nasserism is based on a secularist, progressive program; it never opposed imperialism or Zionism on religious grounds. The Islamist movement, on the contrary, is conservative and anti-rationalist; its roots are associated with fanaticism and rigidity.

Accordingly, three types of political fronts may exist: first, a strategic front between communists, socialists, and Nasserists; second, a practical front between leftist forces and others, including the state, against terrorism and violence in the name of Islam; and third, a partial front with a narrower focus against torture in state prisons, as has happened already between the NPUP, the Wafd, the Labor Socialist Party, and the Muslim Brotherhood. For al-ʿĀlim, there is no contradiction whatsoever between the NPUP joining the regime against Islamic militants and, at the same time, opposing all state policies that create a setting conducive to terrorism.[31]

29 See his lengthy statements against Islamists who distorted Islam and some Nasserists who misunderstood Nasserism, "Ṣafḥa min Ta'rīkh Miṣri" (A page from Egypt's history), in *al-Ahālī*, 22 September 1993, 5.

30 For a detailed analysis of the divisions within the party concerning its strategy toward the state and political Islamists see ʿIṣām Fawzī, "Ḥizb al-Tajammuʿ wa al-Yasār" (The *Tajammuʿ* Party and the left), in Fu'ād Murṣī et al., *al-Intikhābāt al-Barlamāniyya*, 109–53.

31 Interview with Sulaymān Shafīq in *al-Ahālī*, 1 September 1993, 7. See also an article by Ismāʿīl Ṣabrī ʿAbd Allāh in which he denounces Islamist violence, but points out that

Others draw lessons from past experiences inside and outside Egypt. They argue that when political action is not based on sound political learning it is bound to become self-defeating. According to Ṣalāḥ al-Maṣrī and Ibrāhīm al-Badrawī, a leftist attempt at coalition-building with the Muslim Brotherhood was made in the 1940s, but that group suddenly shifted to an alignment with the Ṣidqī government. In the 1970s, they collaborated with Sadat's regime against Nasserists and leftists. The NPUP must also reflect on the lessons of the Iranian and the Sudanese experiences. Although the Iranian revolution was launched by a broad political coalition, the clerics in power have subsequently crushed, killed, tortured, and exiled their leftist, nationalist, liberal, and even Islamic allies in opposition. The record of the military-Islamic Sudanese regime in tolerating even limited political pluralism is not any better. The same is true of Zia al-Haq's regime in Pakistan and Islamist rule in Afghanistan. These regimes recognize the right of "religionists" to be religious; they do not recognize the right of leftists to advocate secularism. Indeed, they equate secularism with atheism and even apostasy, sins that sanction murder by fanatics. If there is to be a credible end to this repugnant Islamist position and not mere dissimulation, then let the political Islamists proclaim it from the same tribunes they now use to spread their teachings and recruit their followers.[32]

Al-Maṣrī warns those whom he refers to as the "well-intentioned" that the apparent conversion of some Islamists to the virtues of pluralism is motivated by instrumental purposes similar to those of their counterparts in Iran and the Sudan when they were in the opposition. Clearly, they believe in the absolute justice of their cause and enjoy a considerable popular following. But so did the fascist leaders of Italy and Germany during the 1930s and 1940s. That is why, according to al-Maṣrī, the conflict between the left and the "Islamic fascists" is the most pressing and antagonistic issue at this historical juncture.[33]

Less clear, however, is the extent of the differences within the Marxist left, represented by other cadres, such as Ḥusayn ʿAbd al-Rāziq, Ṣalāḥ ʿĪsā, and Nabīl al-Hilālī, concerning how to deal with the Islamists. Obviously, they, too, denounce religious violence and call for a broad front

77 percent of militant Islamists on trial at the time were unemployed, which leads him to blame the regime for creating a fertile ground for despair, irrationality, and violence; *al-Ahālī*, 1 September 1993, 5. For more on ʿAbd Allāh's views on democracy and pluralism, see Chapter 6 in this volume.

[32] Ṣalāḥ al-Maṣrī, "Narfuḍ al-Ḥiwār maʿa al-Uṣūliyyīn" (We reject dialogue with the Fundamentalists), *al-Yasār*, May 1993, 83–4; Ibrāhīm al-Badrawī, "ʿAn al-Irhāb wa al-Dimuqrāṭiyya wa al-Jabha" (On terrorism, Democracy, and the Front), ibid., 42–4; and Khalīl ʿAbd al-Karīm, "Al-Sharṭ al-Raʾīsī li-al-Ḥiwār" (The Principal condition for dialogue), *al-Ahrām*, 5 May 1993, 8.

[33] Ṣalāḥ al-Maṣrī, "Narfuḍ al-Ḥiwār," 85.

against it comprising all interested parties, human rights organizations, and trade unions. But they stress that primary responsibility for the menace of religious terrorism should be placed upon the regime, due to its IMF-inspired economic policies, persistent toleration of corruption, misguided attempts to "out-Islamize" the Islamists in the media, and its "war of attrition" against nationalist and leftist parties and intermediary associations.[34] While al-Maṣrī and those who share his views challenge the Islamists to change their core beliefs by accepting the basic political and cultural rights of secularists in a civil, not a religious, system, ʿAbd al-Rāziq and others challenge the regime to indicate its readiness to resist terrorism by changing its policies which are the taproot of the political violence and the societal crisis.[35] What they all agree on is that oppositional Islamists are only nominally religious and state managers only nominally secular; both are politically authoritarian. But while the neo-Marxist trend stresses the relative autonomy and even primacy of the ideological roots of Islamist violence, others focus on the social and economic causes of violence, emphasizing the sins of the "parasitic classes" that have captured the state since the 1970s.

## THE JORDANIAN *TAJAMMUʿ*

Since the early 1990s, Jordan, like Egypt a decade and a half earlier, has witnessed a measure of political liberalization dubbed by some "controlled glasnost." Caught between the statist limitations on political liberalization and the societal appeal of Islamists, Jordanian secular leftist parties, like their counterparts in Egypt and Tunisia, had to grapple with the dilemmas of political transition. For these parties, the growth of Islamist influence, particularly when associated with political violence, posed a threat in itself; it also provided the state with an excuse to restrict opposition movements and, thereby, arrest the whole process of political liberalization.

In the 1989 parliamentary elections, an official ban on political parties was maintained. Only the Muslim Brotherhood, as a movement and not

[34] See Ḥusayn ʿAbd al-Rāziq, "al-Iṣlāḥ al-Siyāsī wa al-Dustūr . . . wa al-Irhāb" (Political reform, the constitution . . . and terrorism), *al-Yasār*, 46 (December 1993): 4–5, and "Tawḥīd al-Juhūd ḍidd al-Irhāb" (Uniting efforts against terrorism), *al-Yasār* (April 1993): 4–5; Ṣalāḥ ʿĪsā, "Dawlat al-Mukaffirūn!" (The State of those charging with unbelief!), *al-Yasār* (May 1993): 90; and the views of Nabīl al-Hilālī in *al-Yasār* (June 1993): 51–2.

[35] See Ḥusayn ʿAbd al-Rāziq, "Tawḥīd al-Juhūd," 5 and also Aḥmad Ṭāhir, "Marra Ukhrā: Man? . . . Ḍidd Man?" (Once again: who? . . . against whom?), *al-Yasār* (May 1993): 87–8.

yet as a party, enjoyed certain political advantages over its rivals due to its close ties to the regime. Secular nationalists and leftists had long been targets of state repression. In fact, many of their leaders had just been released from prison or allowed back home from exile and, hence, did not have time to mobilize popular support.[36] They had nothing that approximated the resources available to the social, economic, and cultural institutions developed by the Muslim Brotherhood and sanctioned by the state, in part, as a reward for their moderation, if not outright collaboration. These institutions acted as networks to mobilize political support in mosques, schools, and via welfare organizations. In the cabinet during the six months following elections, the Brotherhood occupied five seats. Leftists and nationalists saw this as a strategy to structure political competition against them. As one of their cadres sarcastically put it: "If we had thousands of offices where people met five times a day to hear political sermons, we would have mass support, too."[37]

During the second Gulf crisis of 1990–1, the broad political coalition known as the Jordanian National Front put leftists, Arab nationalists, and Islamists in the "same ditch" under the guidance of the King. Aside from that exceptional instance, political competition among these groups over expanding and mobilizing civil society has continued in earnest. One group that adopted positions distinct from those of the state and the Islamist opposition was *al-Tajammuʿ al-ʿArabī al-Qawmī al-Dimuqrāṭī al-Urdunnī* (The Jordanian Arab Nationalist Democratic Alliance). This alliance denounced the accelerated economic liberalization, the unemployment rate that exceeded 20 percent, and the widening gap between the haves and have-nots. It also criticized the state's slowness to institute the political liberalization desired by wide segments of society, as shown by large-scale riots in April 1989.[38]

However, the parties in the alliance agreed to participate in state-sponsored deliberations about the principles of the Jordanian National Charter (*al-Mīthāq al-Waṭanī al-Urdunnī*). Ratified in June 1991, at a time when the King was still at the peak of the popularity he gained during the Gulf War, the Charter sanctioned a measure of political

[36] See Leonard Robinson, "*al-Dawla wa al-Islāmiyyīn fī al-Urdunn*" (The State and the Islamists in Jordan), *Qirāʾāt Siyāsiyya* (Political readings) 4, no. 2 (Spring 1994): esp. 41–2.

[37] As quoted in Laurie Brand, "Liberalization," 19.

[38] See Lamis K. Andoni, "The Five Days That Shook Jordan," *Middle East International*, 28 April 1989, 3; Jamāl Zayda, "*al-Urdunn wa Ṣandūq al-Naqd*" (Jordan and the Monetary Fund), *al-Ahrām al-Iqtiṣādī*, 11 June 1990, 64–6; Robert Satloff, "Jordan Looks Inward," *Current History* 89 (1989): 57–9; and Rex Brynen, "Economic Crisis," 72–5.

pluralism in return for the opposition's strict allegiance to the monarchy. The opposition was permitted to criticize governmental policies, particularly in the domestic arena, as long as the monarchy's legitimacy remained beyond question.[39] Though cadres of the parties constituting the Alliance had opposed the monarchy as a reactionary lackey of imperialism in the past, they had apparently reached two new conclusions by the early 1990s. First, the Alliance was forced to admit that the monarchy was capable of taking positions contrary to the policies and expressed wishes of Western powers, as shown during the second Gulf crisis. Second, they realized that noninvolvement in the first competitive elections since the banning of political parties would mean losing an opportunity to gain legalized access to the popular classes.

Thus, the Jordanian Alliance pursued a strategy of participating in the political process within the existing parameters of permissible action while, at the same time, working to extract some concessions from the state to change the rules of the game to increase their political participation and influence on policies. For instance, it opposed the state's practice of dissolving the Parliament and postponing elections when that suited official purposes. It also called for reducing the fees for candidacy in parliamentary elections, redrawing the electoral districts to reduce rural bias, ending the veto exercised by security agencies against citizens suspected of membership in underground organizations, and conducting a free dialogue about modifying the electoral laws to enhance fair political representation for all parties and political movements in Jordan.[40]

The Islamic Action Front (IAF) viewed the 1993 modification of the electoral law from a bloc-voting system to one based on the principle of "one person, one vote" as a move to weaken its influence. After briefly toying with the idea of boycotting the elections,[41] the Alliance declared its approval of the "one person, one vote" formula[42] and its intention to

[39] Mary Wilson, "Jordan: Bread, Freedom, or Both?" *Current History* (February 1994): 88.

[40] ʿAlī al-Rantīs, "*al-Urdunn ʿalā Abwāb al-Intikhābāt al-Niyābiyya*" (Jordan at the threshhold of parliamentary elections), *al-Yasār* (September 1993): 44–5; see also Philip Robins, "Politics and the Electoral Law in Jordan," in *Politics and the Economy in Jordan*, ed. Rodney Wilson (London: Routledge, 1991); and John Roberts, "Prospects for Democracy in Jordan," *Arab Studies Quarterly* 13, no. 3 (Winter/Spring 1991).

[41] See the statement by Ziyād Abū Ghunayma, member of the IAF Executive Bureau, in *al-Sharq al-Awsaṭ* (The Middle East), 2 November 1993, 1; and *Jordan Times*, 4–5 November 1993.

[42] ʿAbd al-Rāziq Banī Hanī, "*al-Dimuqrāṭiyya: Injāzātuhā wa ʿAtharātuhā*" (Democracy: Its accomplishments and false steps), *al-Mustaqbal al-ʿArabī*, no. 174 (August 1993): 99.

form a list of candidates from its constituent parties. The Popular Unity Party and the Jordanian People's Democratic Party entered into a coalition.[43] In the election that followed, the IAF lost some of its previous support, but the Alliance did not gain as a result. The seats of leftists declined from eight in 1989 to three in 1993.[44] Most parliamentary gains were made by conservative forces traditionally on good terms with the palace. Some observers concluded that political parties did not make much difference in the 1993 elections; most candidates ran and won as independents. The regime enacted its version of a modified electoral law, without ratification or deliberation by the parliament.[45]

What explains the poor performance of the Alliance in the most recent elections, despite the relatively higher voter turnout (68 percent of registered voters in 1993, compared with 49 percent in 1989)?[46] First, the Alliance consists of a broad coalition of political parties and could not manage to put together a unified list of candidates. Some of its component parties were divided on important domestic and foreign policy issues.[47] Among these issues was how to deal with Islamists at a time when cases of Islamic militancy were rising (including a reported plot to assassinate the king in June 1993).[48] Given that the regime has (with tacit PLO backing) embarked on a policy of reducing Islamist influence (*taḥjīm*), exemplified by its accusation of terrorism against the Islamic Liberation Party and the army of Muḥammad,[49] the Alliance faces the question whether it should support the regime's endeavor or join the single largest bloc in the parliament, the Islamic Action Front, against the regime's march toward a settlement with Israel.[50] Social progress and

43 *The Star*, 4–10 November 1993, 4, as quoted in *FBIS*, 5 November 1993.
44 *FBIS*, 9 November 1993, 45.
45 Mary Wilson, "Jordan: Bread," 90. For the regime's perspective, see the king's press conference as reported in *FBIS-NES*, 10 November 1993, 30–7.
46 Pam Dougherty, "Election Result Cheers Hussain," *The Middle East Economic Digest*, 19 November 1993, 8.
47 See *al-Yasār*, no. 46 (December 1993): 48–50. On the roots of these divisions, see Ranad al-Khaṭīb ʿAyyād, *al-Tayyārāt al-Siyāsiyya fī al-Urdunn* (Political currents in Jordan) (Amman: al-Maktabat al-Waṭaniyya, 1992), vol. 2; Kathrine Rath, *The Process of Democratization in Jordan* (M.A. thesis, University of Exeter, September 1992); and interview with the secretary general of the Jordanian Democratic People's Party in *al-Ra'y* (Opinion), 6 February 1993, 26–7.
48 See the cover story in *al-Ḥawādith* (Events), 19 November 1993, 18; and Mazin Muṣṭafā, "*Marḥalat mā baʿd al-Dimuqrāṭiyya wa mā Qabl al-Salām*" (The Stage after democracy and before peace), in ibid., 16–17.
49 Peter Gubser, "Jordan and Hussein," *Middle East Policy* 2, no. 2 (1993): 114–15; and *Jordan Times*, 8 November 1993, 1, 3.
50 On the Jordanian role in the peace process, see Robert Bookmiller, "Approaching the Rubicon: Jordan and the Peace Process," *SAIS Review* 14, no. 2 (Summer/Fall 1994): 109–23. A joint leftist-Islamist statement accused the government of going back on the

the status of women as actors in civil society are other troubling issues that must be weighed in a political environment where, on the one hand, the state has supported moderate liberalization, while, on the other, Islamists attempted in 1989 to have the liberal feminist, Ṭūjān Fayṣal, declared an apostate for opposing their segregationist agenda.[51] In other words, the Alliance could reach no consensus about the relative weight of foreign policy and domestic issues.

Second, the Alliance had little influence in the election on major issues that were local or regional in scope. Due to severe economic hardships faced by many citizens, particularly after the sudden inflow of returned migrants from Kuwait, many voters seemed to be looking for candidates who could deliver badly needed services and work with the regime rather than defy it. Leftists and nationalists did not fit this description. Their electoral strength was also diminished by their lack of social, educational, and economic resources comparable to those administered by the Islamic Action Front.[52]

Finally, there was the impact of the deepening Jordanian-Palestinian divide in the aftermath of the Israeli-PLO accords of September 1993 and the subsequent Israeli-Jordanian peace treaty.[53] A telling case of such impact is that of Fāris al-Nabulsī, who ran in the November 1993 elections supported primarily by Arab nationalists, leftists, and liberals. Al-Nabulsī tried to represent the positions of all the constituencies that supported him by rejecting the settlement with Israel, stressing social justice, and advocating liberal causes. He lost. Many of the winners had

march toward democracy by engaging in unfair electoral practices (i.e., security and media pressures and vote-rigging) designed to consolidate its hold on the parliament and pave the way for an American-Israeli settlement, "in conformity with the dictates of the International Monetary Fund." Among the nationalist and leftist parties that circulated the statement were the Jordanian Democratic People's Unity Party, the Jordan Socialists' Arab Baʿath Party, and the Jordan Democratic People's Party; see *Jordan Times*, 24 November 1993, 3. One leftist leader stressed that "Jordan is not a private estate, so any individual can make unilateral decisions that concern its fate . . . by keeping talks and agreements with the Israelis within the framework of private bilateral relations," *al-Ahālī*, 15 November 1993, 5. See also condemnations of Jordanian-Israeli negotiations and agreements in *al-Majd* (The Splendor), 18 July 1994, and in *al-Ahālī* (Amman), 14 and 21 July 1994.

51 Michael Dunn, "Islamist Parties in Democratizing States," *Middle East Policy* (1993): 19, 20–1. The Islamist Minister of Education, ʿAbd Allāh al-ʿAkayra, caused an uproar among secular segments of society when, among other restrictions, he issued a ruling "forbidding fathers from watching their own daughters' basketball games (lest they see other girls immodestly dressed)."

52 *Jordan Times*, 4–5 November 1993, 10.

53 Reportedly, many Jordanians of Palestinian origin, especially in the refugee camps, lacked enthusiasm for participating in the 1993 elections because, after the Israeli-Palestinian Agreement, they felt unsure about their future in Jordan. See *Jordan Times*, 8 November 1993, 1, 3.

emphasized one identity and adopted a clear mobilizational strategy on that basis (i.e., local tribalist, East Jordanian, or political Islamist).[54]

## TUNISIA'S SOCIAL DEMOCRATS

Like Jordan in the late 1980s, Tunisia has witnessed a relative political opening. In Jordan, however, the opening was initiated under the continuing leadership of King Hussein; in Tunisia it was introduced after a "constitutional" coup in November 1987 against the elderly—and, by then, somewhat senile—president, Habib Bourguiba. Initially, the new president, Zine Labidine Ben Ali, led his own process of restructuring. Parliamentary elections were held in April 1989, 1994, and 1999. As in Egypt and Jordan, the liberalization of the regime in Tunisia was launched from above after accumulating societal pressures from below had broken the consensus at the top of the pyramid of power. In the late 1970s, liberal groups had broken away from the nationalist single party to form opposition parties, but their votes were not counted in the first multiparty elections in 1981. While these pressures were not sufficient to wrest control over the transition process from the elite, they did justify the decision to "dethrone" Bourguiba and to realize the opening to political pluralism that he had begun and then aborted.

During the last years of Bourguiba's rule, the regime had become quite repressive toward the opposition at the same time as the government was losing much of the political legitimacy it formerly derived from political patrimonialism, charismatic leadership, and its nationalist legacy. The dominance of the Socialist Destourian Party (PSD) was increasingly challenged by a younger breed of activists who were no longer impressed by nationalist tales about the "glorious struggle against colonialism." The machinery of this dominant party, which I. William Zartman has called "the ministry of mobilization," with its "pretensions to ideological justification" and claims "to incarnate the nation,"[55] lost its appeal under the influence of corruption and economic hardships. Riots against austerity measures in the mid-1980s and protests against the ruling party

[54] *Jordan Times*, 13 November 1993.

[55] I. William Zartman, "The Conduct of Political Reform: The Path toward Democracy," in *Tunisia: The Political Economy of Reform*, ed. I. William Zartman (Boulder: Lynne Rienner, 1991), 10–11; see also Lisa Anderson, "Liberalism in Northern Africa," *Current History* (April 1990): 145–8 and 174–5. On the Tunisian one-party system under Bourguiba, see Clement Henry Moore, *Tunisia since Independence: The Dynamics of One-Party Government* (Berkeley: University of California Press, 1965) and "Tunisia and Bourguibisme: Twenty Years of Crisis," *Third World Quarterly* 10, no. 1 (January 1989).

by abstention from voting were two clear signs that the regime's legitimacy had been eroded, and the Islamist movements were the major beneficiaries of such erosion.[56]

The transition to semi-competitive politics in Tunisia after November 7, 1987, shared many of the features of relative political opening discussed at the beginning of this essay. It was an incremental rather than a total or sweeping transition. Moreover, it was experimental and initially lacked a detailed blueprint for transforming the polity. It selectively identified actors to be licensed by the state for political competition and set the boundaries of their permissible action. The laws governing the liberalization experiment were socially constructed and were contested by diverse and uneven political forces within the Tunisian state and society. The struggle for "Ben Ali's soul"—the struggle to determine the direction and pace of the political transition—was set in motion.

This political struggle involved the dominant party, the PSD, renamed the Democratic Constitutional Rally (RCD), and the political opposition—including the Islamists, half a dozen secular parties, and civic-minded individuals. The RCD political machine tried to maximize elements of continuity and limit democratic reforms. Opposition forces pushed for a sharp break with the past and called upon Ben Ali to relinquish his post as head of the ruling party so as to become truly the president of all Tunisians.[57] The presidential center engaged in a complex balancing act to keep Ben Ali's position as party leader while persuading leftists and liberal academics to accept a Nasser-like "licensed infiltration" into the ruling party with the hope of reforming it and widening its appeal among the intelligentsia. Most of those academics came from the ranks of the Social Democratic Movement (MDS), the earlier liberal offshoot of the ruling party itself, and from the Tunisian League for Human Rights.[58] They abandoned their party to participate as individuals in the ruling party.

It should come as no surprise that other cadres of the MDS condemned their defections, which were seen as weakening the movement. Moreover, these critics doubted the ability of their former comrades to effect any radical change in a party whose leadership was still dominated

[56] See Susan Waltz, "Islamist Appeal in Tunisia," *Middle East Journal* 40, no. 4 (Autumn 1996). On Islamist assessments of these developments, see ʿAbd al-Fattāḥ Muru's article in *al-Mujtamaʿ* (The Society), no. 931, 5 September 1989, 43, and the interview with Rashed al-Ghannouchi in *The Middle East*, September 1991, 19–20.

[57] See Mark Tessler, "Tunisia's New Beginning," *Current History* (April 1990): 169–72 and 182–4. The Egyptian NPUP has also asked President Mubarak to step down as the head of the National Democratic Party, but he has thus far refused.

[58] See Zartman, "The Conduct," 19.

by holdovers from Bourguiba's years of stagnation. The MDS and other parties, including an Islamist representative, did participate in the discussions leading in November 1988 to the Tunisian National Charter, which identified the avenues of transition to post-Bourguibism and the parameters of "loyal competition."[59] The Charter contained a ban against political parties based on religion along with support for reforms that would emphasize Islamic modernism while keeping the "houses of God out of political struggles," measures directed against the Renaissance Party (*Ḥizb al-Nahḍa*) that was then seeking recognition. At the same time, the MDS favored liberating labor unions from governmental control and changing the electoral system to proportional representation. After failing to achieve either or even to gain 4 percent of the vote in the first free and fair competitive elections of April 1989, the MDS accused the ruling party of tailoring the electoral system to suit its interests at the expense of democracy and of intimidation as well as of rigging election results.[60]

The dilemma of secular opposition parties in Tunisia is immense. They have little experience in governing (a few leaders are former PSD members) and little to offer in the way of realistic program alternatives. Furthermore, the Tunisian electorate, after decades of training, has a proclivity for voting for power and so supports the dominant government party rather than waste its vote. Independent financial sources do the same.

By the early 1990s, the opposition parties were in danger of disappearing into their salons, leaving the field to the RCD and the unrecognized Islamists, to the great embarrassment of the government and its democratizing claims. After a common list that would assign seats to everyone but leave voters no choice was rejected by the MDS in 1989, the government came up with a new solution for the 1994 elections: to add another nineteen seats to the 144-member parliament and distribute them to the leading losers in the election.[61] The government also

[59] See Lisa Anderson, "Political Pacts, Liberalism, and Democracy: The Tunisian National Pact of 1988," *Government and Opposition* 26, no. 2 (1991): 244–60; also *al-Ḥayā* (Life), 24 February 1994.

[60] See I. William Zartman, "The Conduct," 23–4, and Clement Henry Moore, "Political Parties," in *Polity and Society in Contemporary North Africa*, ed. I. William Zartman and William M. Habeeb (Boulder: Westview Press, 1993), 54–60.

[61] See *FBIS-NES*, November 1993, 23, and *Africa Confidential* 35, no. 10 (20 May 1994): 7. According to one observer, secular opposition parties remain distrustful of the ruling party in Tunisia, "but their fear of the Islamist trend makes them view the status quo as the lesser of two evils." Obviously, the greater the Islamist threat to the regime, the stronger the incentive of the latter to build or rebuild its bridges with secular oppositionists. See Saad Eddin Ibrahim, "Crisis, Elites, and Democratization in the Arab World," *Middle East Journal* 47, no. 2 (Spring 1993): 295–303. On MDS support for nominating President Ben Ali for another term until November 1999, see *FBIS-NES*, 24

undertook to subsidize the opposition parties. When this did not ensure their docility, the government arrested their leaders—one, who dared run in the presidential elections, was jailed for criticizing the incumbent; another was jailed for having dealings with neighboring Libya.

Paradoxically, the life of the opposition in a democratizing, former single-party state is not easy. Independence and integrity are needed in order not to appear as the offspring of the dominant party, yet both come at a high cost. None of the Tunisian parties presents any credible alternative to the RCD. At best, they are gadflies, consciences, safety valves; at worst, they are salon clubs, ego trips, window dressing. Most ironic of all, the government need do nothing repressive to keep them in that ambiguous status. Indeed, the greatest shame for the Tunisian government is that its periodic repressive measures were so unnecessary. Yet the minor parties have had their role to play in keeping the dominant party on its toes, the system more open than it would be otherwise, and the possibility for an eventual pluralization ever present.

## CONCLUSIONS

What conclusions can one draw based on the cases covered in this chapter? In all three, secular, leftist forces were far less powerful than the parties of the regime or those of the Islamist opposition. They lacked the material and social resources available to their political rivals. They have often been on the defensive because of their ideological positions, which state authorities suspected of being subversive and political Islamists condemned as being contaminated by imported ideas. Their leaders have been subjected to diverse forms of harassment, their publications censored, and their access to the society at large restricted. Even where there has been political opening and such repressive measures have been halted or, at least, relaxed, doubt has been cast on the secular leftists' commitment to political pluralism by the sorry record of pan-Arabist and communist regimes in power.

These parties and movements are not without blame for their current state of affairs. In particular instances, as in Nasser's Egypt and Ben Ali's Tunisia, the regime has succeeded in recruiting some of the most able minds of these parties to perform specific tasks in service to the ideological apparatus of the state, while real decision-making powers con-

November 1993, 22. See also I. William Zartman, "The Challenge of Democratic Alternatives in the Maghrib," in John Ruedy, ed., *Islamism and Secularism in North Africa* (New York: St. Martin's Press, 1994).

tinued to be monopolized by the top military, party, or state bureaucracy. Such cooperation with state power has weakened the credibility of these parties as a meaningful political alternative among the increasingly politicized and restless segments of younger generations. A look at the parties under discussion in the three countries reveals considerable fragmentation, which makes it difficult to achieve consensus on policies and priorities. Division creates opportunities for outside manipulation. And, like their statist and Islamist opponents, the leftist parties tend to be controlled from the top; hence, they lack adequate internal democracy.[62]

The rise of Islamist political influence is quite problematic for such parties. To start with, the Islamist populist movements usually target social constituencies formerly sympathetic to the leftists and nationalists. In that sense, as Abdelbaki Hermassi has pointed out, for the left, Islamist movements represent "a dangerous and even formidable competitor."[63] Since they use a familiar religious language, their discourse tends to be more effective in mobilizing the popular classes of the urban centers. The success of Islamist movements has added yet another source of division among secularists and leftists in Egypt, Jordan, and Tunisia over which strategy of political alignment to employ in light of differing perceptions of what constitutes the greatest political threat—the regime or the Islamists. Their predicament, caught between a recalcitrant regime and a dangerous new foe, is accentuated when outspoken secular writers and intellectuals in those countries are threatened or even killed by Islamists intent on invoking a new jihad.

As confrontation escalates between state institutions and Islamist movements, the predicament of secular parties may be summed up in three questions: How meaningful is the familiar distinction between moderate and radical Islamists? How much can the current protracted crisis be traced to the past failures of the state? How can secular parties construct a viable consensus within their own ranks on a prudent position without becoming vulnerable to accusations of being puppets of the state or apologists for religious violence? From all indications, the controversies surrounding these questions remain unresolved.

[62] For the case of Egypt, see Waḥīd ʿAbd al-Majīd, *al-Aḥzāb al-Miṣriyya min al-Dākhil* (Egyptian parties from within) (Cairo: Markaz al-Maḥrūsa li-al-Nashr, 1993).

[63] Abdelbaki Hermassi, "The Islamicist Movement and November 7," in *Tunisia: The Political Economy of Reform*, 195.

# 8

## Liberal Professionals in the Contemporary Arab World

TIMOTHY J. PIRO

### INTRODUCTION

Throughout the Arab world liberal professionals have been instrumental in establishing many types of linkages between the state and society. The category of liberal professional is a broad one encompassing disparate elements from the various strata of society. Those falling within it may be Muslims who adhere strictly to the tenets of Islam while learning the latest scientific techniques in medicine or engineering, expatriate managers who have returned to their native countries from the oil-rich states of the Persian Gulf to establish and operate their own businesses, or technocrats in civil service whose specialized knowledge and skill contribute to the functioning of the numerous government ministries that run Arab states. Whatever their function, they are not necessarily part of the elite structure of power nor of the lower echelons of society. In general, they can be classified as part of the professional middle classes of entrepreneurs and government employees who have worked their way through government ministries, been educated within the Arab university system, and exercise power by virtue of their vocational function in society.

As a group, these liberal professionals—who congregate in a country's labor unions, chambers of commerce, business associations, and think tanks—are meaningful actors in the political life of Middle Eastern countries. In the oil producing states of the Persian Gulf, chambers of commerce as well as consultative councils (*dawāwīn*) have mediated discussions and created linkages between the state and society. In the non–oil producing states of the Middle East, a more dramatic process of economic retrenchment has increased the activities of mid-level bureaucrats and entrepreneurs. In Algeria, Egypt, Syria, and Palestine (the West Bank and Gaza), these groups have been able to function outside the purview of the state, providing alternate points of view and services in lieu of the government. In the economic realm, the growth of informal economies has become an important part of the daily operation of some economies, particularly the rentier economies of Jordan, Yemen, Tunisia, and Egypt.[1]

The more open political discourse during periods of economic and political liberalization illustrates how widely these liberal professionals range across the political spectrum and how much their activities have contributed to a greater dialogue between the state and the society. Analyzing the activities of these professionals will elucidate the vibrancy of associational life in the Arab world.

This chapter draws on themes developed in the preceding ones. It argues, first, that these professionals involved in chambers of commerce, labor unions, and think tanks are in many ways more suited to articulate and aggregate the interests of their constituencies than the traditional institutions of political parties or legislatures. Second, the activities of these professionals have increased regardless of the depth of economic and political liberalization. Indeed, they have contributed to a continuous dialogue over the changing nature of the political and economic contract between the Arab states and their societies. Third, kinship ties and ethnicity continue to play important roles in the activities of these groups. However, notions of kinship and ethnicity have been changing over time, and their differing connotations must be taken into account. In sum, new methods of political articulation and aggregation are circumventing more usual paths of political activity.

Informal groups, defined as "noncorporate, unofficially organized collectivities that articulate their interests in a relatively diffuse manner,"[2] are at the heart of associational life in the Arab world. The associational group is usually a highly organized structure formed to articulate a specific interest.

1 See Rebecca Miles Doan, "Class Differentiation and the Informal Sector in Amman, Jordan," *International Journal of Middle East Studies* 24, no. 1 (February 1992): 27–38; Kiren Aziz Chaudhry, "The Price of Wealth: Business and State in Labor Remittance and Oil Economies," *International Organization* 43, no. 1 (Winter 1989): 101–45; I. William Zartman, ed., *Tunisia: The Political Economy of Reform* (Boulder: Lynne Rienner, 1991); and Yahya Sadowski, *Political Vegetables: Businessman and Bureaucrat in the Development of Egyptian Agriculture* (Washington, D.C.: Brookings Institution, 1991).

2 See James A. Bill and Robert Springborg, *Politics in the Middle East*, 3d ed. (Glenview: Scott, Foresman/Little Brown, 1990), 87, who rely on the schema originally developed by Gabriel Almond and James Coleman in *The Politics of Developing Areas* (Princeton: Princeton University Press, 1966); see also Gabriel A. Almond and G. Bingham Powell, *Comparative Politics: System, Process and Policy*, 2d ed. (Boston: Little, Brown, and Company, 1978).

State capitalism has been the dominant mode of production in the Middle East and North Africa,[3] and it is only in the late 1980s and early 1990s that the efficiency of state-led development in Arab countries has come to be challenged. The movement toward market reform is sweeping through the developing world, as well as the former communist states of Eastern Europe and the Soviet Union; business associations and chambers of commerce stand poised to play a much larger role in the political economy of these countries. Throughout the Arab world, liberal professionals have been active through commercial associations, such as chambers of commerce, as well as through labor unions, in articulating differing points of view on their role in economic development. Their effectiveness in challenging prevailing government policies has met with mixed results. Nonetheless, they have become an important factor linking state and society.

## BUSINESS ASSOCIATIONS

Organizations representing the interests of the private sector arose in Jordan in 1949 following the passage of Law No. 41 that allowed the establishment of a chamber of commerce and industry in any governate, pending the approval of the Ministry of National Economy. Since then, the principal business associations in Jordan have included the Amman Chamber of Commerce, the largest and oldest private sector body in Jordan; the Amman Chamber of Industry, established in 1964 with approximately four thousand members; the Union of Farmers; the Bankers Association, established in 1979; the Union of Construction Contractors; the Jordanian Businessmen's Association; and the Federation of Jordanian Chambers of Commerce, Agriculture and Industry.[4]

Since the mid-1980s, when Jordan's economy collapsed, these associations have played an important role in lobbying the government and pushing for economic liberalization. In 1990, the Jordan Banking and

[3] According to Bill and Springborg, the state in the Middle East emerged independently of the bourgeoisie or any other class, namely, "as a result of the efforts by ruling elites to defend territories against the West"; see *Politics*, 69. Lisa Anderson discusses that political process in *The State and Social Transformation in Tunisia and Libya, 1830–1986* (Princeton: Princeton University Press, 1986); and John Waterbury highlights some of the historical forces that helped create state bourgeoisies throughout the Middle East and North Africa, and the analytical utility of the state defined in terms of "class," in his article, "Twilight of the State Bourgeoisie?" *International Journal of Middle East Studies* 17, no. 1 (February 1991): 1–17.

[4] See Zayd Shaʿsha, "The Role of the Private Sector in Jordan's Economy," in *Politics and the Economy in Jordan*, ed. Rodney Wilson (London: Routledge, 1991), 79–84.

Insurance Employees Association (JBIEA) spearheaded a petition to the prime minister, the Central Bank of Jordan, and the parliament requesting management reforms at the Petra Bank to end corruption and bring about higher and fairer wages. During this incident, the association side-stepped the management of the Petra Bank and went directly to the government with their demands. Eventually, the JBIEA engineered a three-day sit-in at the main office of the Petra Bank (the largest such protest in Jordan to occur since 1970) that resulted in increased wages for some workers.[5]

Other important instances of such professional influence include the Jordan Supply Merchant's Association lobbying the Ministry of Supply to increase profit margins on imported products from 15 to 22 percent[6] and the establishment on December 19, 1989, of the Jordanian National Consumer Protection Society under former Prime Minister Aḥmad ʿUbaydat to protect consumers from price manipulation and exploitation. ʿUbaydat remarked that the new organization was necessary to safeguard consumers' rights since "politics has its other channels."[7] In February 1990, the Federation of Jordanian Labor Unions held a sit-in of one thousand people to protest businesses that gave preference to non-Jordanian laborers.[8]

Two of the more prominent associations, the Amman Chamber of Industry and the Amman Chamber of Commerce, have come to the forefront of much of the political activity concerning economic policy. In 1991, businessmen lobbied against a government tax through the Amman Chamber of Industry. The lobbying contributed to the demise of the government of Mudar Badran. Additionally, these two groups led attempts to bring corruption charges against many former ministers. One of the more prominent cases was that of Maḥmūd Hawamda, former public works minister, who was charged with misusing funds designated for certain local projects while head of that ministry.

In Tunisia, the state took the lead in the overall development of the economy when, in 1962, it published its first five-year plan and tried to set the country on a socialist development path.[9] Prime Minister Aḥmad

[5] See Sana Atiyeh, "Petra Bank Staff Threaten Strike," *Jordan Times*, 3 February 1990, 1 and 4; also "Petra Bank Staff Return to Work," *Jordan Times*, 26 February 1990, 3.

[6] *Jordan Times*, 29 January 1990, 3.

[7] As reported by Serene Halasa, "New Society Aims to Protect Consumers from Exploitation," *Jordan Times*, 31 January 1990, 1.

[8] Samir Hiyari, "Job-seekers Stage Sit-in to Protest Employers' Attitude," *Jordan Times*, 15–16 February 1990, 1.

[9] For a brief overview of this period, see John Entelis, *Comparative Politics of North Africa* (Syracuse: Syracuse University Press, 1980), 133–7.

Ben Ṣalāḥ's quiet shift to encourage the country's private sector led to Prime Minister Hādī Nū'ira's explicit encouragement of the private sector in the 1970s. Thus, by 1983, Tunisia's Institut National de Statistique reported that 2,608 private-sector industrial enterprises with more than ten employees had been established. And the large de-nationalizations of the economy, as well as the implementation of an IMF structural adjustment program begun in 1986, have further loosened the constraints under which the private sector operates.[10]

In her analysis of Tunisian industrialists, Eva Bellin remarked that the largest fortunes in the industrial community were made in businesses that had no special relationship to the state.[11] Many professionals in the private sector are not members of the ruling Destour Party. During the 1960s, much of the political activity of these businesses was carried out within the Union Tunisienne Indépendante des Commerçants et Artisans (UTICA). Since the ascension of Zine Labidine Ben Ali to the presidency in 1987, UTICA has provided independent information to the business community. Another organization that has adopted a similar role is the Institut Arabe des Chefs d'Enterprise (IACE). Formed in 1985, this association conducts economic research, organizes conferences, and serves as a channel of communication between the state and the business community. While this activity is free from state control, the state continues to dominate many aspects of the economy and society.[12]

In Syria, professional associations have undertaken a much more active role in Syrian political life since the country's economic liberalization of the 1980s and 1990s, a movement spurred by the country's foreign exchange crisis and dwindling foreign aid. The ultimate reason behind the push to economic liberalization has been to broaden the political base of Hafez al-Assad's regime and to reinvigorate Syria's state-run economy. Thus, the concerted effort under way since the 1980s to allow the private sector a much larger role in the running of the economy means that private sector elites have become an important component of the regime's economic strategy. In Syria's May 1990 elections, for

10 See Eva Bellin, "Tunisian Industrialists and the State," in Zartman, ed., *Tunisia: The Political Economy of Reform*, 49 and 52; also Iliya Harik, "Privatization and Development in Tunisia," in *Privatization and Liberalization in the Middle East*, Iliya Harik and Denis G. Sullivan, eds. (Bloomington: Indiana University Press, 1992), 215–20.

11 These included ʿAbd al-Waḥīd Ben ʿAyyād in poultry, Hādī Jalanī in textiles, and ʿAbd al-Salām Aftes of STPA, a major customs manufacturer; see Bellin, "Tunisian Industrialists," 53–4. For what follows, see ibid., 60.

12 See Dirk Vandewalle, "Ben Ali's New Era: Pluralism and Economic Privatization in Tunisia," in *The Politics of Economic Reform in the Middle East*, ed. Henri J. Barkey (New York: St. Martin's Press, 1992), 105–26.

example, two members of the Damascus Chamber of Commerce were elected to parliament. Were such a trend to continue, the commercial class might well begin to use parliament as a forum for more economic reform and liberalization.[13]

By the end of the 1980s, industrial laborers accounted for approximately 15 percent of Syria's economically active population.[14] The labor force in trade has increased from 139,002 in 1970 to 338,061 in 1989. Associational membership in trade unions, housing cooperatives, the Lawyers Syndicate, the Engineers Syndicate, and the Agronomists Syndicate has also increased from 275,564 in 1974 to 848,893 in 1990.[15] By the end of the 1980s, a new class of entrepreneurs in construction and transportation had arisen.[16] Fred Lawson noted that:

> Privileged members of the state bourgeoisie actively collaborated with individuals belonging to the new commercial-entrepreneurial elite to advance their mutual interests in expanding the role of foreign capital and private subcontracting within the local economy through the 1970s and early 1980s.[17]

Additionally, independent tradespeople and shopkeepers in the larger towns benefited from deregulation. They had become powerful enough that, at the 8th Regional Conference of the Baʿth Party, labor advocated greater deregulation in commerce and agriculture.[18] The Syrian bourgeoisie has been instrumental in establishing the Prime Minister's Committee for the Rationalization of Imports, Exports, and Consumption. This committee includes members of the chambers of industry and commerce and maintains a role for the bourgeoisie in the overall economic decision making process. Syria, long known for its entrepreneurial tradition, has in place a private sector interested in facilitating the pace of

13 In "Domestic Transformation and Foreign Steadfastness in Contemporary Syria," *Middle East Journal* 48, no. 1 (Winter 1994): 47–64, Fred Lawson argues that Syria's economic liberalization is not a result of dwindling foreign aid; see also his "Political-Economic Trends in Baʿthi Syria," *Orient* 29, no. 4 (December 1988): 579–94. And see Volker Perthes, "The Syrian Economy in the 1980s," *Middle East Journal* 47, no. 1 (Winter 1992): 37–58, as well as "Syria's Parliamentary Elections," *Middle East Report*, no. 174, January–February 1992, 15–18; also Steven Heydemann, "The Political Logic of Economic Rationality: Selective Stabilization in Syria," in Barkey, ed., *The Politics*, 20.

14 Fred H. Lawson, "Divergent Modes of Economic Liberalization in Syria and Iraq," in Harik and Sullivan, *Privatization*, 129.

15 Raymond Hinnebusch, "State and Civil Society in Syria," *Middle East Journal* 47, no. 2 (Spring 1993): 251–2.

16 Volker Perthes, "The Bourgeoisie and the Ba'th," *Middle East Report*, no. 170, May–June 1991, 35–7.

17 Lawson, "Divergent Modes," in *Privatization*, 130.

18 See Elisabeth Longuenesse, "The Class Nature of the State in Syria," *Middle East Report*, no. 77, May 1979, 9–10, and Lawson, "Divergent Modes," in *Privatization*, 132.

economic reform. While the Alawi-military leadership has allowed incremental political liberalization, the Syrian regime is still structured to wield substantial economic power.

Although in the cases of Jordan, Tunisia, and Syria, liberal professionals have been quite active in economic reform, the depth of economic liberalization is not the determining factor in the political activities of these associations. In many of the states of the Persian Gulf as well, where economic development goals have been reoriented because of falling oil prices, but structural adjustment programs have not been as thorough as in the non–oil producing states, business groups have stepped into the political arena to challenge ruling elites.

In the Gulf monarchies, chambers of commerce have become a meeting place for merchants and traders to discuss issues relating to government policy. Kuwait stands out as one of the more prominent examples. In the May 1992 election to the Kuwait Chamber of Commerce, a group of candidates led by Khālid al-Mazrūq challenged the authority of the chamber that had been traditionally led by ʿAbd al-ʿAzīz al-Ṣaqr, the leader of a prominent merchant family that helped the Ṣabāḥ family establish Kuwait. Though the al-Ṣaqr candidates won twenty-three of the twenty-four seats within the chamber, the event illustrated that political groups will contest the traditional power sharing arrangements when permitted by the state.[19]

## LABOR UNIONS

Labor unions have not been particularly strong in most Middle East and North African countries. One factor complicating the formation of labor unions is that many of the inhabitants of this part of the world have nomadic rather than urban roots. Still, in Morocco, Algeria, Tunisia, Egypt, Turkey, and Bahrain, labor unions do exist and have had an impact on domestic political processes. In countries like Iran and Iraq, there is almost no union activity; the labor unions that do exist hardly function as active forces in political life. And in Saudi Arabia and Oman, trade union organizations are simply nonexistent.[20]

Jordan provides a good example of the difficulties many states in the area experience when attempting to form workers' groups. Labor unions have never been particularly strong in Jordan as a result of the nomadic

[19] See F. Gregory Gause III, *Oil Monarchies: Domestic and Security Challenges in the Arab Gulf States* (New York: Council on Foreign Relations, 1994), 93–4.

[20] Bill and Springborg, *Politics*, 87.

and pastoral roots of the economy. When the Emirate of Transjordan was formed in 1923, 46 percent of the population was Bedouin. By 1946, that figure had dropped to 22 percent as a result of land registration and a policy of sedentarization by Amir Abdallah. Additionally, seasonal migration among the neighboring Arab countries, especially British-Mandate Palestine, made it difficult to establish a permanent labor force. Moreover, most of the Bedouin who were settled became farmers and not manufacturers, which would have lent itself more to union organizing. Nonetheless, some attempts to form labor unions did succeed. The most prominent of these was in the second half of the 1930s among taxi drivers and in the 1940s within the Iraqi Petroleum Company.[21]

The 1948–9 Arab-Israeli war and subsequent Jordanian annexation of the West Bank did increase labor activity. The West Bank's more urbanized population had a much longer tradition of manufacturing and labor organizing, for British-Mandate Palestine had a flourishing middle class and a substantial labor force while there was no such tradition in Transjordan. Most of the unions in Jordan were formed in the 1950s. The National Alliance (*al-Tajammuʿ al-Waṭanī*) was one of the first to include labor unions, Baʿthists, and communists. It became the Professional Alliance (*al-Tajammuʿ al-Miḥnī*) in the 1970s, but maintained close contacts with the state. Whereas there were seventeen labor "strikes" on the East Bank in 1969, they increased considerably by 1970–1 as a result of the Black September civil war. From 1971 to 1977, no coordinated trade or professional unions were allowed. However, after Anwar Sadat's trip to Israel in 1977, the Council of Professional Unions (*Majlis al-Niqābāt al-Miḥniyya*) was formed even though its activities were quite limited. This group visited the prime minister's office twice after the riots at Yarmouk University in May 1986.[22]

There were more strikes in Jordan in the 1980s, but state control of the economy still limited labor activity. The Ministry of Labor was created in 1975, and all unions were required to register with the government. Prior to that, the Intelligence Services (*al-Mukhābarāt*) kept a close watch over all unions. Because the private sector was so small and much of the guest worker population performed the jobs where unions

21 See Hanī Ḥūrānī, *Muḥāwalāt al-Tanẓīm al-ʿUmmālī fī Sharq al-Urdunn: 1926–1948* (Attempts at labor organizing in Transjordan: 1926–1948) (Amman: Markaz al-Dirāsāt al-Jadīda li-al-Urdunn, 1993), 200–23 and 92–3.

22 See Laurie A. Brand, *Palestinians in the Arab World: Institution Building and the Search for a State* (New York: Columbia University Press, 1988), 154 and 179; also Hanī Ḥūrānī, *al-Ḥarakāt al-ʿUmmāliyya al-Urdunniyya: 1948–1988* (Jordanian labor movements: 1948–1988) (Amman: Markaz al-Dirāsāt al-Jadīda li-al-Urdunn, 1989), 28–9.

traditionally organized, labor unions have been ineffective at making their demands heard and met. Politically, they have the support of many of the leftist parties, but that does not guarantee political gains. The Petra Bank strike has been mentioned. Another strike took place at al-Bashīr Hospital to protest the poor quality of food.[23] Health workers also staged a token strike in March 1992. General practitioners and specialists employed by the Ministry of Health complained of work overload, low pay, and few incentives. The National Society for Consumer Protection took up their cause and demanded that drug prices set by the Ministry of Health be respected by all wholesalers and pharmacies.

Of all the countries of the Arab world, Egypt continues to have the most vibrant labor activity. When the Open-Door Economic Policy (*Infitāḥ*) was adopted by the Egyptian government in the mid-1970s, the Egyptian Trade Union Federation (ETUF) argued that such a policy should serve development needs and preserve the public sector. Marsha Pripstein Posusney has outlined a number of examples where the ETUF opposed the sale of public sector companies to the private sector, including the United Wholesale Textile Trading Company.[24] Subsidies were also an important issue for the labor federation. ETUF supported maintaining subsidies on such staples as bread and sugar; and when subsidies were cut in January 1977, riots immediately broke out. As the crackdown on leftist elements intensified, the activity of private sector business associations became more prominent. This was particularly the case with the General Union of Hotel and Tourist Workers.

In sum, labor has been active and often effective in organizing to protect its interests and to challenge prevailing notions of economic policy and structural adjustment, but has not been as effective in penetrating the political arena to challenge ruling elites.

## THE POLITICS OF LIBERAL PROFESSIONALS

Since political parties have never been particularly strong in most Arab states, other vehicles of representation have been used to circumvent the political process. In Jordan from 1957 to 1989 and Libya since independence, formal political party life was dormant; in the single-party regimes of Algeria, Syria, or Tunisia, it was dominated by the govern-

23 See Ghadeer Taher, "Regular Platefuls and 'Food Strike' at Hospital," *Jordan Times*, 5 February 1990, 3.

24 See Marsha Pripstein Posusney, "Labor as an Obstacle to Privatization: The Case of Egypt," in *Privatization*, 83 and 85–9.

ment party. When parties have been allowed to play a more active role, tribal or religious infighting has broken out, or the parties were erected as mere appendages of the state. Nonetheless, the professional middle class has found other, less traditional, ways to practice politics.

Political activity among the business community is not new to Jordan and has grown since the onset of the country's economic crisis in the mid-1980s. The government of Aḥmad ʿUbaydat (1984–5) addressed declining foreign aid and remittances, maintained the spending of previous governments, and covered shortages in revenue by borrowing from international lending agencies and increasing domestic taxation; it also guaranteed loans to companies and raised prices by artificially supporting production in addition to making it more difficult to license new companies and encouraging the growth of the private sector through tax exemptions and incentives. All this resulted in the state being deprived of much needed revenue and these moves being opposed by Jordan's financial and commercial bourgeoisies.[25] Still, ʿUbaydat's policies now stand out as the forerunners of the policies instituted by Jordanian governments in the 1990s.

Business associations certainly played a role as Jordan moved toward closer economic coordination with Iraq, which culminated in the establishment of the Arab Cooperation Council in February 1989.[26] Though the decision to side with Iraq during the 1980s was influenced by a mixture of strategic, political, and economic factors, there was no doubt that Amman's business community would stand to benefit through increased trade. This became one of the cornerstones of the policies toward the government of the Amman Chamber of Commerce and the Amman Chamber of Industries.

Iraq became a natural market for Jordanian industry, especially at the end of the Iran-Iraq war. Beneficiaries from the rebuilding of Iraq included agricultural groups, fertilizer and cement companies, the pharmaceutical industry, and the banking sector in Jordan. Coalitions of private and semi-private Jordanian industries with ties to Iraq over the previous decade saw a chance to increase their exporting capacity. All of

[25] See Laurie Brand, "Economic and Political Liberalization in a Rentier Economy: The Case of the Hashemite Kingdom of Jordan," in *Privatization*, 171–2, who also observes that ʿUbaydat's proposals implied a strengthening of the state bourgeoisie when the financial and commercial bourgeoisie disliked government competition; also Hanī Ḥūrānī, *Azmat al-Iqtiṣād al-Urdunnī* (The Jordanian economic crisis) (Amman: Markaz al-Dirāsāt al-Jadīda li-al-Urdunn, 1989), 121.

[26] For a discussion of this topic, see Laurie Brand "Economics and Shifting Alliances: Jordan's Relations with Syria and Iraq, 1975–1981," *International Journal of Middle East Studies* 26, no. 3 (August 1994): 393–413.

these industries and groups were ostensibly intent upon promoting Jordan's manufacturing and trade sectors. And since many of those industries were Palestinian dominated, this undertaking helped to smooth over social divisions between Palestinians and East Bank Jordanians. However, riots broke out in the southern city of Maʿan in April 1989 as a result of the imposition of an IMF-backed austerity program. Known as the squalls of April (*habbāt nīsān*), the riots were centered in the country's normally supportive Bedouin population and transformed liberal professionals into a more politicized entity.

The disturbances led a group of notables from the southern city of Kerak to petition the government for Prime Minister al-Rifāʿī's resignation, changing the country's electoral laws away from ethnic and confessional lines, punishing officials guilty of corruption, ending austerity measures, and bringing about greater democratization.[27] The latter demands came mainly from intellectuals and professional associations like those formed by doctors, lawyers, and engineers. Because of a ban on the activities of political parties, they became one of the more effective vehicles through which interest articulation and interest aggregation took place. Believing that the king's credibility would be shaken if reforms did not take place, these associations assumed a leading political role during the parliamentary election of 1989.

Underground leaflets were distributed from elements of the banned Jordanian Communist Party, the Jordan branch of the Popular Front for the Liberation of Palestine, unions, and influential tribes like the Banī Sakhr. The king met with tribes and associations,[28] and candidates' views were expressed through the country's three major Arabic dailies. ʿAbd Allāh al-Malkī and Fahd al-Fānik, economic analysts for the newspaper, *al-Ra'y* (Opinion), wrote articles on ways to cut the country's budget deficit. Munā Munīr Shuqayr, a prominent pan-Arabist writing for *al-Dustūr* (The Constitution), appeared on its pages comparing Jordan's democratic experiment to other democratic experiments in the Arab world.[29] And during and after the election, one section of *al-Ra'y* entitled *Hiwār* (Dialogue) presented a number of diverse points of view ranging from extreme Islamist to royalist to leftist. Many of the more

[27] A similar petition was issued by a number of the leaders of Salt, the Ottoman capital of Transjordan; see Abla Amawi, "Democracy Dilemmas in Jordan," *Middle East Report*, no. 174, January–February 1992, 27.

[28] See Kamel Abu Jaber, "The 1989 Jordanian Parliamentary Elections," *Orient* 31, no. 1 (March 1990): 69–70.

[29] See, for example, her article, "*Abʿād al-Tajriba al-Jadīda wa Dalālatuhā*" (The Dimensions of the new experiment and its meaning), *al-Dustūr*, 9 January 1990, 7.

than six hundred candidates for the 1989 election presented their views on various issues in these op-ed pieces. So, in the absence of formal political parties, a wide range of political views were expressed through a variety of organizations.

Since political rallies were not allowed, meetings were held in clubs, professional centers, and private homes, thus raising the profile of many of these liberal professionals. Into 1990, these professional groupings worked to lift political restrictions like the anticommunist law of 1953 and to eliminate restrictions on obtaining passports such as the requirement for a clearance from the state intelligence service.[30] In addition, the Public Freedoms Committee, consisting of twelve professional groups, was formed and proceeded to lobby the government to grant amnesty to fifty-five prominent political prisoners at the beginning of 1990.[31]

The post-1989 period in Jordan also witnessed increased activity among liberal professionals concerning social and foreign policy. Legislation sponsored in parliament by the Muslim Brotherhood to ban male hairdressers from working on women's hair met stiff resistance by the Hairdresser's Union. The union immediately formed a delegation to ask Minister of Interior Salīm Maṣāʿida for "clarification" on the scope of the legislation. The ban was implemented in the northern town of Irbid but was rescinded by the Ministry of the Interior a few days later.[32] In May 1990, the Council of Jordanian Professional Associations helped to organize a peace march to the Allenby Bridge in which five thousand people participated. Nurses have also formed their own group to make the plight of their profession more public, and ʿAbd Allāh Nuṣūr, the Minister of Industry and Trade in 1992, urged company executives, bankers, government officials, and economists to press their demands on any economic issue by lobbying parliament. Finally, in June 1993, the Amman Chamber of Industry urged the government to set wages for Jordanian workers.[33]

[30] See Laurie A. Brand, "Liberalization and Changing Political Coalitions: The Bases of Jordan's 1990–1991 Gulf Crisis Policy," *Jerusalem Journal of International Relations* 13, no. 4 (March 1991): 19 and 21.

[31] See Nermeen Murad, "Amnesty Sought for All Political Prisoners," *Jordan Times*, 20 February 1990, 3.

[32] See Ghadeer Taher, "Women Move to Block Male Hairdresser Ban," *Jordan Times*, 8 May 1990, 1, and Mariam M. Shahin, "Hairdressers Elect Panel in Recent Turnout," *Jordan Times*, 4 June 1990, 3.

[33] See Mariam M. Shahin, "Unionists Plan March," *Jordan Times*, 12–13 April 1990, 3, and Samir Shafiq, "Minister Tells Jordanian Businessmen to Press Demands," *Jordan Times*, 5 September 1992, 7; see also *The Star*, 25–31 January 1990, 3, and *Jordan Times*, 17–18 June 1993, 3.

The event to electrify liberal professionals and Islamic groups within the kingdom, however, was the Gulf War. Since the crisis affected all levels of Jordanian society, liberal professionals, especially lawyers and engineers, were the groups through which many of the rallies and demonstrations against U.S. policy organized. In August 1990, the Jordan National Front was formed among communists, Islamists, Arab nationalists, and the various traditional parties to protest the U.S. military build-up in Saudi Arabia. A month earlier, the Jordan Arab Nationalist Democratic Alliance was formed among Marxists, Arab nationalists, and independent leftists.[34]

Following the elections, the king appointed a sixty-member royal commission, chaired by former prime minister and security chief Aḥmad ʿUbaydat, to work out a political formula to incorporate political parties into the governing of the country.[35] In January 1991, the royal commission handed the king a "National Charter," which outlined, *inter alia*, the role of political parties in Jordan and the basic principles of Jordan's domestic and foreign policies. While the National Charter in no way supersedes the 1952 constitution, it does lay out the general parameters for the participation of parties in political life. Nonetheless, it is deliberately vague about what political parties can and cannot do, merely granting the executive branch power to intervene in the electoral process if the king deems it necessary.

In other countries, consultative assemblies have been used in place of formal parliamentary structures. In Bahrain, the actual give and take of political life has been carried out through a complex network of clubs (*nawādin*) and societies (*jamʿiyyāt*). Though ostensibly organized for recreational and social purposes, many of these networks are quite political. The Arab Club is composed of over 250 Bahrainis who have pushed for more democratic goals, and the University Graduates' Club consists of more college-educated intellectuals from both upper and middle classes.[36] In other countries of the Persian Gulf, the same process has taken place, but in varying degrees. The Kuwaiti institution of the open house or consultative council (*diwān*) has been an important institution

[34] See Laurie Brand, "Liberalization," 9 and 33.

[35] The people assigned to the commission included royalists, Islamists, mainstream governmental leaders, leftists, industrialists, and the heads of most of the major professional organizations including the Amman Chamber of Industry and the Jordan Bar Associations; see *Jordan Times*, 10 April 1990, 1 and 5.

[36] See Bill and Springborg, *Politics*, 94, who draw on Emile Nakhleh, *Bahrain: Political Development in a Modernizing Society* (Lexington, Mass.: Lexington Books, 1976), 41, for this information.

through which liberal professionals have participated in political life. When parliament was suspended by the Amir in 1986, thirty members of the parliament met regularly; in 1989, they initiated a petition drive calling for a restoration of constitutional rule. Thirty thousand Kuwaitis signed the petition. And since the ousting of the Iraqi army from Kuwait, the consultative council movement has become more diverse, with elements of the Sunni Muslim Brotherhood, the Sunni Salafi movement, and Shiite Islamists all being represented.[37]

In Saudi Arabia, councils like these have played a lesser role. In the wake of the U.S. military build-up in the Persian Gulf, King Fahd announced in November 1990 that he was planning to form a consultative assembly (*majlis al-shūrā*) for Saudi citizens to present their political demands in a more organized fashion. However, the Saudi royal family has been slow in following through on its promise to implement more liberal measures. Similar movements to establish quasi-parliamentary bodies in the wake of Desert Storm and Desert Shield have met with limited success in Qatar and Bahrain, and no such movement has taken root in the UAE or Oman.

Many of these assemblies are hand-picked by the state's leaders as was the case in Jordan's National Consultative Council from 1978 to 1982 and in Saudi Arabia's proposed consultative assembly. Nonetheless, the appearance of such assemblies among the liberal professional class indicates that there is no bias against increased pluralism in the Arab world.

One criticism of this type of consultative rule is that members are simply co-opted. Yet, even if that is sometimes the case, liberal professionals have found different venues to express their political views. In Jordan, three of the principal think tanks include the Amman World Affairs Council (*Majlis Shu'ūn ʿAmmān Dawliyya*), the Center for Strategic Studies (*Markaz al-Dirāsāt al-Istrātījiyya*), and the Center for New Studies on Jordan (*Markaz al-Dirāsāt al-Jadīda li-al-Urdunn*). These have served as an alternative to the more accepted patterns of participation and expression.

The Amman World Affairs Council, as the name suggests, is concerned primarily with foreign affairs. The group brings together businessmen and government officials, but they are mainly from the established families of Jordan. Its publication, *al-Nadwa* (The Study group), basically reflects the king's views on foreign policy. The council also provided a forum for a speech by the founder of the Central Bank

[37] See Gause, *Oil Monarchies*, 92.

of Jordan, Khalīl al-Salām, to discuss the economic and financial crisis facing Jordan in 1987. Two years later, commentators continued to cite his speech for its penetrating remarks concerning unprofitable projects such as the South Cement Company, the Plaza Hotel, and the Jordan Fertilizer Industries Company.[38] The Arab Thought Forum, also based in Amman, is another mainstream think tank with a much more regional orientation. While it, too, receives a great deal of government money, it has been one of the leading academic institutions of the Arab world with respect to hosting conferences on issues such as democratization and human rights.

The Center for Strategic Studies is attached to the University of Jordan and designed to be an independent intellectual forum providing information to citizens on economic and foreign affairs. However, it has avoided more frank discussions of the country's democratization process. Exemplary of its role in political life is a conference it organized on Jordan's economy in June 1993 that brought together a wide array of government officials, businessmen, and academics to discuss the prospects for Jordan's economy in light of its relationship with the IMF and World Bank, the effects of the Gulf War, and the Arab-Israeli peace process. In many of the papers that were presented, examples of government red tape, bureaucratic infighting, irrational export procedures, and lack of government support for promoting exports were highlighted. Additionally, over a three-day period debates ensued on how to proceed with the privatization of the economy and whether to cut subsidies or sell off government shares of the state-owned enterprises.

The Center for New Studies on Jordan provides leftist interpretations of Jordanian history, politics, and economics. The Center's director, Hanī Ḥūrānī, was editor-in-chief of *al-Urdunn al-Jadīd* (The New Jordan), which he originally published in Cyprus, until he was allowed to return to Jordan after having resided in Syria for almost twenty years.[39] Of the

[38] See Waleed Sadi, "An Early Warning System Called Khalil Salem," *Jordan Times*, 28–29 September 1989, 4.

[39] The center has published a series of books and monographs that gives new interpretations of Jordanian history, politics, and economics, some of which have already been cited: *Azmat al-Iqtiṣād al-Urdunni, al-Ḥarakāt al-ʿUmmāliyya al-Urduniyya: 1948–1988, Muḥāwalāt al-Tanẓīm al-ʿUmmālī fī Sharq al-Urdunn: 1926–1948*. Others include: *Ta'rīkh al-Ḥayā al-Niyābiyya fī al-Urdunn* (The History of parliamentary life in Jordan) (Amman: 1989) and *Ḥizb Jabha al-ʿAmal al-Islāmī* (The Islamic Action Front Party) (Amman: 1993). Hanī Ḥūrānī's first major work on Jordan, *al-Tarkīb al-Iqtiṣādī al-Ijtimāʿī li-Sharq al-Urdunn (1921–1950)* (The Socioeconomic Structure of Trans-Jordan, 1921–1950) (Beirut: Palestine Liberation Organization Research Center, August 1978), was long banned but is now available in limited circulation.

three think tanks, this last one is the most nontraditional. Its mere presence in Jordan indicates a much more tolerant political atmosphere in the country.

Newspapers have also become quite important. While Jordan's three main dailies—*al-Ra'y*, *al-Dustūr*, and *Ṣawt al-Sha'b* (Voice of the populace)—continue to have substantial government ownership—40 percent, 35 percent, and 75 percent respectively—other papers have begun to appear. In the business sector, *al-Aswāq* (Markets) and *Akhar al-Khabar* (Latest news) have published numerous articles on unemployment and investment in Jordan; two weekly papers, *al-Bilād* (The Towns) and *Shīhān* (Falcon), have published articles concerning homosexuality and prostitution.[40]

Various political cartoons that have appeared in all three daily newspapers provide a more subtle barometer of political expression. One appeared in the January 3, 1990, edition of *al-Ra'y* featuring a map of Jordan without the West Bank. Two months later, the same paper published a cartoon depicting a hand with a flashlight shining on two rats labelled *al-fasād* (corruption) over the caption *al-maṣlaḥa al-waṭaniyya* (the national interest). The majority of the corruption cases have been brought against former government ministers. A decade earlier, such cartoons would have been banned; their existence in Jordan's more politicized atmosphere indicates that a certain autonomy in the realm of expression has taken hold.[41] In Egypt, the weekly *al-Ahrām al-Iqtiṣādī* (Al-Ahrām Economics) has been quite vocal in criticizing prevailing government economic policy; in pre-1990 Kuwait, the daily, *al-Qabas* (Firebrand), presented a host of diverse views on political and economic trends in the Arab world.

Even though political parties have recently been allowed to function in places like Jordan and the political atmosphere in many of the Arab oil monarchies has become more open, professional associations are still more directly structured to address political concerns. The Jordan Banking and Insurance Employees Association has approximately six thousand members. In many of these organizations, such as the Jordan Writers Association, elections have occurred on a regular basis. In the

[40] Ben Wedeman, "New Tabloids Shaking Up Staid Jordanian Press," *Middle East Insight* 10, no. 1 (November–December 1993): 10–11.

[41] For the two cartoons, see *al-Ra'y*, 3 January 1990, 6, and 24 March 1990, 21; for an analysis of the political content of cartoons in the Arab world, see Haim Shaked, "A Stereotype Illustrated: An Egyptian Cartoonist's Perception of the United States," in *The Middle East and the United States: Perceptions and Policies*, ed. Haim Shaked and Itamar Rabinovich (New Brunswick: Transaction Inc., 1980), 301–46.

Jordan Engineers Association, Pan-Arabs and leftists captured eight of the nine seats; and in the General Shippers and Dock Workers Association, leftists and Islamists split the vote.[42] These types of associations have circumvented the normal vehicles of interest articulation and interest aggregation in both the oil-rich and the non–oil producing countries of the Arab states.

What role do kinship and ethnicity play? Are these associations simply places where certain clans, cliques, and coteries immerse themselves in the political issues of the day? To illustrate how associational life has changed, it is necessary to compare political life in the nineteenth and twentieth centuries.

## KINSHIP, ETHNICITY, SOLIDARITY

Family and ethnicity continue to be important, but not necessarily determining, elements in patterns of political interaction. Informal groupings based on the year of graduation from university (*duf*ʿ*a*) or on having graduated from the same faculty within a particular university (*shilla*) continue to penetrate much of the associational life of liberal professionals. Though rational action based on formal or informal group solidarity has not taken hold as yet and some of the organizations discussed thus far seem to carry on traditional patterns of Arab political life, there is increasing evidence that institutional solidarity rooted in rational action is replacing old-boy network politics.

In Egypt, Clement Henry Moore's study of Egyptian engineers found that, as a group, they were not immune from the internal infighting of other syndicates. Though Nasser appointed a disproportionate number of engineers to posts at the expense of lawyers and the Free Officers into the 1960s, engineers did not become the vanguard of a new technocratic class interested in achieving rational development goals. Ethnicity and kinship continued to matter, and Moore pointed to declining financial resources as one of the key reasons why engineers as a whole did not become a dynamic, upwardly mobile, middle class.[43]

In Jordan, prominent Palestinian families continue to dominate the commercial and financial bourgeoisie of the private sector. And many of

[42] See Mariam M. Shahin, "Progressive Members Take Over Engineers Council," *Jordan Times*, 26 February 1990, 1 and 3, and Lamis K. Andoni, "Leftists Forced to Settle for Partial Control of Dock Workers' Union," *Jordan Times*, 7 April 1990, 3.

[43] Clement Henry Moore, *Images of Development: Egyptian Engineers in Search of Industry* (Cambridge, Mass.: MIT Press, 1980), 166 and 210.

the new political parties established since the country's introduction of limited pluralism are tribally based. Representation in Jordan's 1993 parliament is heavily skewed toward the Bedouin tribes of the south, and the family as a structural unit continues to be important. Though Zayd al-Rifāʿī was forced to resign as prime minister in April 1989, after the riots in the south of the country, his family continues to play an important role in the decision-making structure of the country. His long friendship with the late King Hussein still guarantees him access to the corridors of power in Jordan. Likewise, the powerful al-Tal family from the northern town of Irbid enjoys great power in the country. This same pattern is found in many other Arab countries.

The most prominent example of a family with extensive links to different regimes is the Marʿī family in Egypt. Through careful marriage arrangements, it extended its kinship bonds into the Sadat family.[44] Morocco has been called the kingdom of cousins, and in modern day Iraq much of the analysis of the internal decision-making structure continues to revolve around Saddam Hussein's Takriti clan. The same type of ethnic cleavages applies to the ruling Alawi clan in Syria. Even successful revolutionary movements are not immune from kinship bonds. One of Ayatollah Khomeini's daughters married the influential Ayatollah Eshraqi, and Khomeini's son Ahmad has been an important middle man in Iranian politics ever since his return to Iran in 1979.[45] And in the monarchies of the Persian Gulf, the closed decision-making circles continue to be dominated by the royal families of those countries. In sum, examples throughout the Arab world demonstrate that kinship and ethnicity are at the roots of patrimonial politics.

Kinship and ethnicity—what sometimes appears simply as tribalism—have been interpreted as obstacles to more meaningful definitions of citizenship or associational solidarity. The general process of economic retrenchment taking hold in the Arab world, however, has transformed the way kinship and ethnicity play out. Not to be viewed as competing explanations of the depth of citizenship nor as precluding participation in associational or civil life, kinship and ethnicity are part of such life. In the Middle East at the start of the twenty-first century, they are less competing than complementary explanations for citizenship.[46] Because

44 For a longer discussion, see Robert Springborg, *Family, Power, and Politics in Egypt* (Philadelphia: University of Pennsylvania Press, 1982).

45 See Bill and Springborg, *Politics*, 102 and 104.

46 See Linda L. Layne, "Tribesmen as Citizens: Primordial Ties and Democracy in Rural Jordan," in *Elections in the Middle East: Implications of Recent Trends*, ed. Linda L. Layne (Boulder: Westview Press, 1987), 135.

the process of economic retrenchment that has gripped the Arab world has catapulted many of these liberal professionals to the forefront of the debate concerning economic restructuring, it is only logical that they will carry their kinship and ethnic biases with them. Structural adjustment programs encompass a wide array of policy instruments. Depending on the type of economic policy adopted, different domestic groups can either benefit or lose.

In Jordan, the state economic bureaucracy maintains control over commercial affairs; overlapping functions of the public and private sectors make adopting new policies less likely, since the major factor determining the adoption of a particular economic policy is maintaining political control over it, not efficiency. Some officials have pointed to corruption as the largest impediment to privatization efforts, while many western aid workers have highlighted cultural factors that make the private sector less willing to assume more responsibility.[47]

Some East Bankers fear an exodus of capital from Palestinians in Jordan to the West Bank and Gaza with the signing of the peace accord between Jordan and Israel. Jawad ʿAnnānī, assistant to the prime minister and former minister of labor, industry and trade, queried: "Is the Jordan River going to be a divide or a point of contact?"[48] In Egypt, traditional government ministries have been unable to secure many of Egypt's development objectives. As a result, extra-state actors have taken on this role. Private volunteer organizations and rural-based groups have been active in recent years in both rural and urban sectors of the economy. Charitable organizations (*jamʿiyyāt khayriyya*) that employ health-care professionals, teachers, and clerical workers have spearheaded this approach in the middle-class suburbs of Cairo. Additionally, Islamic investment companies beyond the reach of the government have given their customers a better return on investment than the official banks.[49]

[47] Private businessmen whom I interviewed in Jordan in June 1993 believed corruption to be one of the key reasons for the government's sluggish moves toward implementing privatization policies. Conversely, whereas one western aid worker interviewed at the same time claimed that privatization had failed to occur in Jordan because "people don't want to do it," another maintained that such a failure was not due to bias against export by the private sector but simply that "people just don't understand it."

[48] See Peter Waldman, "Peace Accord between PLO, Israel Stirs Economic Worries in Jordan," *Wall Street Journal*, 25 October 1993, A17.

[49] See Denis J. Sullivan, "Extra-state Actors and Privatization in Egypt," in *Privatization*, 24–5, 35–6, and 40. The village of Ezbet Zein south of Cairo formed a Community Development Association that mobilized financial resources; and the Sayyida Zeinab Hospital, connected administratively to the Sayyida Zeinab mosque, extends medical services to the poorer areas of Cairo as does the Muṣṭafā Maḥmūd Society, which functions partly as a health center and partly as a mosque.

In 1988, there were over one hundred of these investment companies extending better credit to Muslims and Christians alike. And during Cairo's September 1992 earthquake, many of them provided much needed medical and financial services to quake victims.

Indeed, liberal professionals are supposed to act as intermediaries between the state and society. However, being a diverse group, they are not agreed on what type of economic reform should be implemented. According to a number of businessmen, the factors working against the implementation of an effective privatization policy include the psychology of large parts of the business community, a lack of desire for the responsibility of the free market, tribal law, cultural characteristics, and corruption.[50] By this argument, kinship and ethnicity will be likely to play an important role in the formulation of professionals' views on policy.

Solidarity can be seen as playing a more powerful role in the contemporary politics of these groups. When interviewed, members of the Amman Chamber of Industry, the Amman Chamber of Commerce, and members of the Physicians' Association all voiced similar complaints about poor working conditions, lack of government help, and policies favoring imports over exports. While many of these associations voiced support for more privatization, there was no agreed upon definition of what the term means; and no political party has spelled out a detailed plan concerning economic adjustment beyond vague policy statements. Privatization can mean selling off government-owned assets in certain companies, which most support in principle; cutting government subsidies, which most support in general, but resist in their own case; and reducing government control over the economy. The problem for these business associations is that the type of economic reform and structural adjustment is far from settled. As long as the agenda remains unclear, these groups will find it difficult to lobby or articulate their interests. Under such conditions, ethnicity and kinship will continue to be important elements in any type of associational solidarity. More important, rather than constituting obstacles to citizenship and associational solidarity, kinship and ethnic factors help liberal professionals smooth over

[50] These assessments were gathered from personal interviews with ʿAlī Dajāni, former head of the Jerusalem Chamber of Commerce and the Amman Chamber of Industry, and Adīb Ḥaddād, former director of research at the Central Bank of Jordan and director of the Institute for Banking Studies on 26 June 1993; Ṭalal al-Saʿdī, director-General of the Arab Mining Company and board member of the Arab Potash Company on 27 June 1993; Riyāḍ al-Khūrī, director, Middle East Business Associates, Ltd. on 29 June 1993; and, on 28 June 1993, with a western aid consultant who prefers to remain anonymous.

difficulties when they cannot otherwise agree on a clear set of political and economic goals.

## CONCLUSION

During the 1980s, "bringing the state back in" was designed to open David Easton's "Black Box" and place the state at the center of the scientific analysis of politics. With the collapse of the communist states of Eastern Europe and the fall of the Soviet Union, social forces and influential nongovernmental institutions have begun to join the state as loci of political behavior. Liberal democracy and market capitalism, it has been argued, have triumphed in the long struggle between East and West.[51]

Traditionally, much of the analysis of the politics of the Middle East and North Africa has relied upon the two pillars of the state and Islam to provide explanations of political behavior within Arab society.[52] Recently, the study of Middle Eastern and North African political systems has turned to the growth of nongovernmental organizations and institutions outside the purview of the state and beyond the constraint of religion. New methods of political articulation and aggregation are circumventing the established paths for expressing interests, demands, values, and participation, with liberal professionals taking on an increasingly important role. Though conclusions are preliminary, certain trends are emerging.

Autonomy for liberal professionals will likely be most apparent in the area of expression. Loosening constraints on the role of the press and allowing alternative political points of view will not cost the state much in the short term. However, certain subjects continue to be off limits. In Jordan and Morocco, criticism of past governments is accepted, but not of the king or royal family.[53] In the monarchies of the Persian Gulf,

[51] See Peter B. Evans, Dietrich Rueschemeyer, and Theda Skocpol, eds., *Bringing the State Back In* (Cambridge: Cambridge University Press, 1985); Adam Przeworski, *Democracy and Market: Political and Economic Change in Eastern Europe and Latin America* (Cambridge: Cambridge University Press, 1991); and Francis Fukuyama, *The End of History and the Last Man* (New York: The Free Press, 1992).

[52] For a review of that literature, see Lisa Anderson, "The State in the Middle East and North Africa," *Comparative Politics* 20, no. 1 (October 1987): 1–18.

[53] For example, an article written by Rāmī Khūrī in the *Jordan Times* of September 1992 suggesting that King Hussein step down in order to prepare Jordan for a successor appeared in the morning edition, but had been taken out by the evening edition. My own attempts to retrieve the article at the *Jordan Times* office were unsuccessful, and in June 1993 one editor conceded that mistakes had been made when publishing the original article.

criticism of the ruling families is either severely restricted—as in Saudi Arabia—or dealt with indirectly—as in Kuwait and Bahrain. In Syria and Tunisia, direct criticism of the president is also forbidden. The ability of liberal professionals to alter policy in any significant manner will most likely be evolutionary rather than revolutionary.

Liberal professionals certainly possess the knowledge to influence policy and affect the direction in which countries are heading. Much of their business and activities, however, remains caught up in the state structure of the Middle East. Thus, the state continues to dominate the scene, but that does not mean pluralist tendencies are not emerging. Incremental movement toward economic and political liberalization is evident in Jordan, Egypt, Morocco, Tunisia, and Syria, as well as in the monarchies of the Persian Gulf. It is still far from clear what effect these changes will have on any particular country's overall domestic and foreign policies.

Nonetheless, liberal professionals have grassroots structures—such as labor unions, chambers of commerce, and professional associations—already in place and poised to play an expanded role in society. That these associations have been around a lot longer than some of the more established political parties places them at an advantage regarding interest articulation and interest aggregation.

In general, however, the state has not left the political stage; nor is tribal law about to be replaced by a modified English common law or Napoleonic code. As Augustus Norton has argued, civil society will not topple regimes; but it is a first step toward establishing a more equitable relationship between the state and the citizens. The growth of a vibrant civil society still depends on the representation of all the members of society and not simply upon their becoming pluralized.[54]

During the 1960s, when Samuel Huntington wrote of political institutionalization as a method for addressing change in the developing world, political parties were the key agents of representation. In the Middle East and North Africa, the institutionalization of the state's methods of governance[55] is now being brought into question. During the 1990s, trade associations, business groups, and labor unions have

[54] See Augustus Richard Norton, "The Future of Civil Society in the Middle East," *Middle East Journal* 47, no. 2 (Spring 1993): 209, and Raymond Hinnebusch, "State and Civil Society," 257.

[55] See Samuel P. Huntington, *Political Order in Changing Societies* (New Haven: Yale University Press, 1968); and for a discussion of state governance becoming institutionalized with respect to Algeria, see John P. Entelis, *Algeria: The Revolution Institutionalized* (Boulder: Westview Press, 1986).

become institutionalized in a way they never were before. The state-society dichotomy continues to lean heavily in favor of the state, but the negotiation of a new "social contract" is proceeding, especially in the rentier economies of Jordan, Tunisia, Syria, and Egypt, where the financial capital that drove these economies for so long is quickly drying up.[56] Because the more traditional methods of governance and representation are being transformed, the ability of Arab states to adapt and address that change will be the state's biggest challenge in coming years.

In conclusion, the politics of the Middle East has too often been explained in terms of the state or Islam. Politics in the Arab world is a much more complex phenomenon than is indicated by simple reliance upon those two mutually reinforcing explanations. Studying the professional middle class of bureaucrats and entrepreneurs can help explain what Lucian Pye termed the "crisis of authoritarianism," in which the developing countries and the countries of Eastern Europe are challenging traditional methods of rule and control through the pluralistic institutions of civil society.[57] A better way to approach the implications of that crisis is to place the "middle" back into the equation of Middle East politics.[58]

[56] See Giaccomo Luciani and Hassan Beblawi, eds., *The Arab Rentier State* (London: Croom Helme, 1987).

[57] See Lucian W. Pye, "Political Science and the Crisis of Authoritarianism," *American Political Science Review* 84, no. 1 (March 1990): 3–19.

[58] With many thanks to Jon Anderson of the Catholic University of America's anthropology department for this felicitous formulation.

# 9

# Daniel Lerner Revisited: The Audio-Visual Media and Its Reception: Two North African Cases

JEAN LECA, MERIEM VERGÈS, AND MOUNIA BENNANI-CHRAIBI

## INTRODUCTION

The impact of technological change on society is not a subject to be approached in a homogeneous manner. As A. B. Zahlan has done in this volume, technology can be examined in order to inquire about the way it affects the means of production appropriated by social institutions. Similarly, the consumption of high-tech products (e.g., arms and electronic surveillance equipment) can be analyzed; even the "institutional" technology brought into being by the machinery of the state and its effects can be the focus of study.[1] This chapter is limited to the consideration of the effect one type of technology—namely, television—has on a particular kind of production, that of opinions and culture. The role of technology here is special: it does not so much contribute to producing culture as to diffusing products whose consumption leads to a reworked and autonomous production of the produced messages by those receiving them. In other words, whereas Zahlan concentrated on the producers of technology or, so to speak, on the broadcasters of cultural messages (physicians, veterinarians, hygienists, engineers, weavers and cloth manufacturers, and so forth), we will focus our attention here on the consumers or receivers of those messages.

Despite this difference of focus and approach, our conclusions agree with those of Zahlan on one point, namely, that technology should never be analyzed separately from the social and institutional conditions in which it is used. Whether in the form of new pesticides on a farm, a new operating theater in a hospital, a new computer in an office,

[1] See Bertrand Badie, *L'État importé* (The Imported state) (Paris: Fayard, 1993), and Timothy Mitchell, "The Limits of the State: Beyond Statist Approaches and Their Critics," *American Political Science Review* 85 (1991): 77–96.

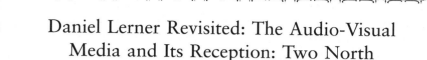

or a satellite dish in an apartment, technology is an interactive social process that does not produce identical, one-way changes. Among those who have tried to make sociological sense of the new communications techniques in the Middle East, Daniel Lerner has left the most remarkable imprint. It is therefore legitimate for us to revisit his analysis.

Although communication theory has burgeoned since Lasswell and Lerner,[2] aspiring now to a level of sophistication its founders never dreamed of, it is useful to re-examine it in the light of some empirical surveys recently carried out under the auspices of the Institute of Political Studies in Paris.[3] There are two advantages to such an undertaking. First, in the social sciences, reassessment is the closest equivalent to a rigorously organized experiment for testing a theory. It is especially called for if the theory in question has been practically abandoned on the grounds that it has failed to pass the test of time, as though viewing a particular historical period—namely, the late 1990s—in a particular way suffices for refuting the way in which an entirely different historical period—namely, the end of the 1950s—was viewed. But could the "modernizers" of the 1990s not be wrong? After all, their only advantage is to have forty years of historical perspective over the former—an advantage that must be weighed against their being, as it were, forty years younger. Second, such a reassessment thereby offers an opportunity to verify whether so-called forgotten theories (who, after all, cites Lerner or McClelland today?) may not still provide accurate and valuable insights, at least in bits and pieces.

Since the empirical material used in the exposition that follows was not collected with the specific goal of testing Lerner's theory, it might be a good idea to give a candid, albeit partial, answer to the question posed by the editors of this volume—what do we know, roughly or in detail, of how young generations of North Africans have been affected as a result of their exposure to the audiovisual media?—and to move back

[2] See Harold D. Lasswell, "The Structure and Function of Communications in Society," in *The Communication of Ideas*, ed. L. Bryson (New York: Institute of Religion and Social Studies, 1948), and Daniel Lerner, "Towards a Communication Theory of Modernization," in *Communications and Political Development*, ed. L. Pye (Princeton: Princeton University Press, 1963). For the Middle East, it is of course necessary to consult Lerner's *The Passing of Traditional Society: Modernizing the Middle East* (New York: The Free Press, 1958).

[3] See Mounia Bennani-Chraibi, *Soumis et rebels: Les jeunes au maroc* (Paris: CNRS, 1994); and Meriem Vergès, "La Casbah d'Alger: Chronique de la survie dans un quartier en sursis" (The Algerian Casbah: A chronicle of survival in a deferred quarter), in *Mélanges offerts à Rémy Leveau*, ed. Gilles Kepel (Paris: Presses de la Fondation Nationale des Sciences Politiques, 1994).

from there to a reassessment of Lerner's inquiries. Indeed, this seems preferable to what would be the more usual academic procedure, namely, beginning with a systematic account of his inquiries. We do not, therefore, intend simply to juxtapose facts to a theory, but rather to juxtapose interpretations of data produced and constructed in the 1990s to a similar operation carried out in the 1950s at a more ambitious and general level. The data, their production, and their context being completely different,[4] we ask the reader to be patient and to defer passing judgment on the usefulness of this comparison until the end of the chapter.

## THE ENIGMA OF RECEIVERS

There are a number of serious surveys about broadcasters and the evolution of the broadcast system.[5] The market shows that the situation in the Arab world is not so different from what can be seen elsewhere in the Third World: news remains extremely national, that is to say, controlled by the state; the rest is to a great extent imported, much to the displeasure of potential native producers. Satellite channels give those who know the broadcasters' language access to foreign news (but, at least on the radio, there are also broadcasts in Arabic). It is difficult to estimate the audience of this transnational hodgepodge in which CNN, Italian Radio-TV, Télé Monte-Carlo, M6, France 2, and TV5 are all mixed up. François Chevaldonné believes he can distinguish three types of receivers divided according to upper, middle, and lower classes:

[4] The areas differ not only in time but also in geographical location. In 1950, Lerner prudently avoided North Africa and the Algerian revolution, distributing his huge 115-item questionnaire in seven countries: Turkey, Lebanon, Jordan, Egypt, Syria, Iran, and Greece (this last one as a pretest).

[5] See, for example, Douglas Boyd, *Broadcasting in the Arab World* (Philadelphia: Temple University Press, 1982), and François Chevaldonné, ed., "Les Médias dans le monde arabe" (The Media in the Arab world), *Revue de l'Occident Musulman et de la Méditerranée* (1989/1). The latter considers radio ownership in Morocco and Algeria to be similar to that of Europe (nearly 95 percent) and evaluates TV ownership in Morocco at 40–50 percent (of households?) and in Algeria at 55–60 percent. For studies about receivers, see Susan Ossman, *Moving Pictures: Mass Images and Society in Morocco*, Ph.D. diss., University of California at Berkeley, 1991. For the way the successful "Dallas" program was promoted, see Joëlle Stolz, "Les Algériens regardent Dallas" (Algerians watch Dallas), in *Les Nouvelles Chaînes* (Paris: PUF and IUED, 1983). Compare this to a much more systematic study about Japan and Israel (including Israeli Arabs, but not the Arabs of the occupied territories): Tamar Liebes and Elihu Katz, *The Export of Meaning: Cross Cultural Readings of Dallas* (Oxford: Oxford University Press, 1990).

The wealthiest users have a large choice—video cassettes, satellite TV, pay channels; the more modest levels of the middle classes as well as a fringe of the working class, severely hit by the economic crisis, depend mainly on public television programs which have images as poor as their content; finally, the others who, depending on the country, represent between one-third and four-fifths of the populace, continue to have access only to fragments of messages snatched fleetingly in shops or in neighbors' homes—better than nothing, but, like their life, "full of gaps."[6]

This rough three-fold division, which we shall provisionally adopt, implies a certain conjecture about the reactions of the receivers. The first category, the "consumers," seems to be integrated into the world market and its tastes and thereby to be estranged from the values of the common people; the second is confined and subjected to watching mediocre propaganda it no longer believes in; the third resembles "mass society" where the objects produced by the news are increasingly foreign to the experience the receiver has of objects "close" to him—all of which increases his feeling of alienation, diminishes his sense of reality and responsibility, and tempts him to react directly without the mediation of any institutional relations that might permit dialogue and provide an idea of possible action.[7] Mass apathy and its inevitable other face, mass violence, are not far off, for the communication system has broken all ties with local and personal forms of communication, and there are fewer social positions from which major structural connections between different activities can be perceived as well as fewer people who can attain such points of view.[8]

The young people of the Algiers Casbah studied by Meriem Vergès offer a good opportunity to verify the accuracy of conjectures concerning the third category of receivers.[9] This quarter is of very important symbolic and historical significance. In the 1950s it was a place of refuge for the nationalists and in 1956–7, the center of the battle of Algiers. As of 1985, the first armed group, that of Mustapha Bouyali, now in hindsight deemed an Islamist, hid there before taking to the countryside. It is also probably the poorest quarter of the capital and has been excluded

[6] François Chevaldonné, "Peut-on encore parler de la radio et de la télévision 'nationales'?" (Can we still speak of 'national' radio and television?), in Camille and Yves Lacoste, eds., *L'État du Maghreb* (The State of North Africa) (Paris: La Découverte, 1991), 413.

[7] See William Kornhauser, *The Politics of Mass Society* (New York: The Free Press, 1959).

[8] See Karl Mannheim, *Man and Society in an Age of Reconstruction* (London: Kegan Paul, 1949), 59, as quoted in Kornhauser, *Politics*, 94.

[9] Unless otherwise noted, all of the following quotations are from Meriem Vergès, "La Casbah d'Alger." Vergès conducted these interviews herself in the Algerian Arabic dialect and then translated them.

from all urban renewal projects for the past fifty years. According to official statistics, 70,000 people live there in 1,700 houses, some of which are almost completely in ruins and extremely unhealthy. Trash is rarely collected. Electricity and water are frequently cut off. With the exception of one sports terrain, there are no "modern" recreation areas (cinemas and youth clubs or cultural centers). The Casbah is also the one area where local identity has, for a long time, been curiously contradictory. At the time of independence, a large influx of people from the countryside moved into it, while other Casbah residents moved out to other quarters claiming the empty houses left by departing Europeans. Until the end of the 1970s, it constituted a local microscene in which various forms of friendly sociability and of leisure activities took place: people whiled away time in Moorish cafes, organized sports events through local committees, or participated in committees for festivals or for popular (*shaʿbī*) music.

The young people (ranging in age from eighteen to thirty-five) interviewed by Meriem Vergès, especially the older ones, insist on this lost age of civic conviviality—"a period where there was a harmonious way of life (*sīra*) particular to each district." Thus, an employee of a state company who is old enough to remember (or to demonstrate great nostalgic imaginative hindsight) recalls

> this marvelous (*maḥbūl*) quarter. The other quarters rarely beat us in soccer. We were the best in the local championships. The best! Really, the best! . . . At weddings, Aymar al-Zahi (a well-known popular singer) said that in his whole career he had never seen a quarter like ours. People from the outside, brought in by friends, adored our quarter. They stayed here for years. They became used to our way of life and married our girls. It was a warm, hearty life. We saw each other, we messed around together. We had our problems, the problems of Algeria; but the ties between us were strong.

Among residents, the "children of the quarter," instances of mutual aid are often evoked; and such practices are to a certain extent linked to the advice given by the prophet to respect one's neighbor.

In the 1980s, this picture deteriorated to such an extent that it became completely reversed.[10] An unemployed twenty-five year old deplores the state of things:

[10] Starting in 1992–3, the quarter's remarkable identity has once again come into an important role. Now it helps preserve against the generalized suspicion and uncertainty that appeared with the outbreak of armed conflict between the authorities and the Islamist groups following the suspension of the electoral process and the ousting of Chadli Benjedid. "We thrive on suspicion," says a thirty-three-year-old shopkeeper. "We are no longer 100 percent sure of the good faith of the people from the mosque." "In this

There is no more compassion (*raḥma*), not even among neighbors. Today everyone's mindset has changed—the children of the quarter, the neighbors, everybody. Each one is affected only by what happens to himself; there is no longer any trust. Young people have become ruthless; they are bitter. Before, we really lived, and even though we didn't have much, we lived well (*anṭiq*). Now, there is no life in the quarter.

Emphasis is put on "the simultaneous disappearance of sincerity (*ḥusn al-niyya*), of politeness, and of everything having to do with harmonious social relations, all of which have now been replaced by vice (*naqṣ*)." This implies a systematic calculation that each individual makes for his own sake, self-censorship, and thus individual isolation. The existential unrest that ensues is expressed by the term *dégotage* (this from the disgust or distaste—the *dégout*—arising from the feeling of no longer being able to find oneself.)

The various stages of the lifecycle no longer have an objective sense because of the uncertainty about the future, sexual frustration, and the housing crisis that prevents young people from starting families or, indeed, from even more precocious initiatives. All this creates an atmosphere evocative of that found in Chekhov's plays—that of a period passing away without our being aware of it until it is too late, yet finding it bear down like a prison while living in it. As a thirty-year-old hair dresser puts it:

When you assess the situation, you remember nothing. You realize that you did nothing and that you possess nothing. It's unbelievable. Where am I living? What am I doing? What did I do to deserve this? Elsewhere, at our age, people start a career. But with us, our heads are empty. It's better not to ask yourself questions; if you do, you go crazy.[11]

climate of distrust, it is no longer sufficient to be an *akh* (a Muslim brother)," comments Meriem Vergès; "nowadays in order to be accepted in the Casbah, one must also be a 'son of the quarter,' someone whose family and individual background is known to everyone."

[11] Nonetheless, in Chekhov, these kinds of remarks are made by the privileged—that is, those with income from investments, daughters of generals, landed gentry, doctors, officers—even though they are all in a kind of social decline, but never by peasants, workers, or the unemployed. Except for servants, these lower classes are absent from his theater. Now this says a great deal about the intellectualization of the Algerian social world: the unemployed, the hairdressers, the small-time smugglers, the political science graduates who have become grocers are all as able to understand things intellectually as any of Chekhov's characters, even though their standard of living is much lower. This may be the reason they can become enraged and very "religious" after having resorted to drugs, whereas Chekhov's characters, apparently alien to all religion (the world of Dostoievski or even of Tolstoy is another world), quietly succumb (some through alcohol) or commit suicide after, for some, a brief period of pathetic revolt.

"We live," says a twenty-six-year-old political science graduate, who is a grocer, "in a difficult and disturbing setting. The Casbah is a tough quarter, prey to all the everyday tensions—lies, malicious gossip, disrespect, and delinquency."

The deterioration of this world to a condition resembling the Hobbesian state of nature is attributed to the absence of order, to the absence of the sacred things (*al-ḥurum*).[12] But this order cannot—yet? or ever again?—be thought of as the statist Leviathan, as was the case with Tunisian President Boumedienne's rhetoric that is now beginning to gain a mythical status among the nostalgic generations: Islam, its law, and its rituals take its place. Against, or in addition to, the drug of the poor—"the party of marijuana" (*ḥizb al-zetla*)[13]—there is Islam and the party of the mosque (*ḥizb al-jāmiʿ*): "Islam is a medicine." (Marx, who said religion was the "opium of the masses," must be shivering with delight in his Highgate grave.) "In the ideal situation, there would be many '*Alilus*'."[14] In place of the family—where no one any longer speaks to one another—and of the psychologist—who gives no advice, offers no shoulder to lean on, and is content to say "don't think too much"[15]—there is Islam and its response: the unity of the people such that "everyone should defend the same cause," as a twenty-four-year-old employee

12 "We are not a people but a blind mob (*ghāshī*): everyone is against everyone else."

13 Now, in addition to marijuana and zombretto (a mixture of methyl alcohol and lemonade), anti-epileptic and anti–Parkinson's disease tranquilizers (*kashit*, i.e., cachettes) are taken. A survey carried out in 1990 by the National Institute of Public Health revealed that, in a sample of 639 subjects, 33 percent of the boys and 18 percent of the girls "regularly" took psychotropic products; see D. Hannoun, R. Selhab, and M. Yahi, "Enquête sur la consommation des psychotropes chez les jeunes de 15 à 24 ans dans la Wilaya d'Alger" (A Survey of the consumption of psychotropes among young people between 15 and 24 years old in the province of Algiers), *Relevé Épidémiologique Mensuel* 1 (November 1990), cited in Vergès, "La Casbah."

14 This is the nickname for Ali Benhadj, the most influential preacher of the Islamic Salvation Front, who has been in prison since January 1992.

15 The psychologist's remark, reported in this manner, may only be an admission of helplessness when confronted with an illness whose social roots are beyond his reach—Frantz Fanon's reaction to this can be guessed—but it is also an invitation to "make the best" of a situation that cannot be changed by mere thoughts: the problem is that his patient *cannot prevent himself* from thinking, that is, from having an opinion because, as Daniel Lerner so astutely noticed in 1958, "psychic participation through opinion is spreading before genuine political and economic participation," Lerner, *The Passing*, 396. This opinion concerns the self and the society in an indivisible manner: the requirements of its expression are not only the result of a "curiously ahistorical process of social change," but almost, on the contrary, that of a process of social mobilization where meaning is required as soon as neither the modes of understanding coming from customary conventions nor those provided by the state are suitable. Meriem Vergès notes that none of the persons she interviewd belonged to the formal structures set up by the Algerian authorities since Independence (party, labor union, or youth organization).

of a state company put it, thereby reaffirming—probably fully aware of what he was saying—the unity of the Arab, Muslim, and Algerian nation (*umma*) and—perhaps without knowing it—also reiterating the nationalist and anti-pluralist ideology that was constantly evoked, from 1962 to 1988, by the powers that are so despised today. Against the over-crowding and increasing anonymity of the Casbah quarter and its perversion (*fasād*) stands Islam, with its systematic, controlled, and uniform occupation of the streets plus the warm and congenial feeling of identification it affords people who are not from the same quarter.

The coming together of believers from the various quarters of Algiers was heart-warming. Often when we came out of the mosque, the neighbors prepared a special serving of tea and cakes. It was magnificent,

says a twenty-six-year-old sociology graduate, who is out of work and therefore totally captivated by a worldview he now takes for granted, seeming to have forgotten the distance his academic knowledge was supposed to have afforded him.

This attitude made it easy for the Islamic Salvation Front (FIS) to infiltrate the public space during the period of free demonstrations following the adoption of the 1989 Constitution. It also helps explain the Islamist victory in the 1990 elections and, above all, the strength of the Islamists during the 1991 preparations for legislative elections. During the general strike of 24–25 May 1991, several thousand militants of the FIS occupied or inhabited two public squares in Algiers, one situated just below the Casbah (Martyrs Square).[16] "Algiers took on the appearance of a camp site: the demonstrators prayed, cooked, stayed up, and slept there." A vast movement of civil disobedience filled public spaces with its sounds and images: "Islamic clothing—the *qamīṣ* and *ḥijāb*—was ever present, as were the loud speakers installed for the call to prayer."

The receivers of radio and television messages interviewed by Meriem Vergès are therefore not merely passive, like empty receptacles taking in pictures and information just as it is broadcast.[17] These receivers have already been subjected to, and predisposed by, other impressions that

[16] Smäil Hadj-Ali, "Ville et violences à travers la grève du F.I.S.: L'Occupation de la ville d'Alger (mai-juin 1991) (Town and violence as seen through the F.I.S. Strike: The Occupation of Algiers) (May–June 1991), *Revue du CERES*, Tunis (November 1991).

[17] This theory did, however, appear plausible to H. Lasswell and N. Lietes, *The Language of Politics: Studies in Quantitive Semantics* (New York: Stewart, 1949). However, Liebes and Katz in *The Export of Meaning* showed that each group makes interactive interpretations and moral assessments according to its own logic. For similar observations with respect to Morocco, see Hannah Davis, "American Magic in a Moroccan Town," *Middle East Report* (July–August 1989); and Susan Ossman, *Moving Pictures*.

touch them more profoundly insofar as they are not images they have more or less attentively observed in the company of other viewers or with a brother or two, hidden under a sheet or blanket so as not to disturb those sleeping in the same room (or so as to look at foreign magazines or watch the soft-porn films shown by M6 and picked up in Algiers), but are real experiences derived from actual, physical participation in mass demonstrations, experiences evocative of Jean-Paul Sartre's "group in fusion,"[18] one of whose functions is to affirm solidarity "when they must confront the aggressiveness of the social milieu illustrated by the notion of perversion of the quarter."

Yet even this picture is too simple. This receiver is also someone who "has been around," who has firsthand knowledge of places such as Morocco, Egypt, France, Barcelona (the destination of choice for all the petty smugglers of the underground economy), and even Austria. He has only one desire, one dream, from which the Islamic experience completely disappears: "to have material means, to live alone, or else to go away and emigrate anywhere," in order to find a country "where one can live," where "each person can live his own life with no one bothering any one else." This is the way a twenty-four-year-old employee of a state company describes the French way of life. Of Austria (where he "earned a living" distributing publicity leaflets), a twenty-five-year-old who never had any schooling and now lives off odd jobs and petty smuggling says: "There, there is real social justice, everyone gets what he deserves. . . . People say 'Good Morning,' and if they were not unbelievers (*kuffār*), they are the ones who would go to paradise." In the meantime, they are the ones who inhabit a terrestrial paradise. Thus television is interpreted in terms of this fundamental mindset that "the antenna shows us paradise, while we dwell in Hell."

In this sense, television diffuses the image of a group whose benefits the receiver would like to share, an image diametrically opposed to the group (or nongroup) to which he really belongs. Does this classic opposition between the group one belongs to and the group one refers to that Lerner so astutely observed with respect to Iran become a good predictor of political extremism and the emergence of a counter-elite when the horizons of the reference group are thus extended beyond the local culture and combined with alienation from the existing social institutions?[19] To be sure, yet this interpretation is not entirely satisfactory.

[18] See Jean-Paul Sartre, *Critique de la raison dialectique* (Critique of dialectical reason) (Paris: Gallimard, 1969).

[19] Lerner, *Passing*, 370ff.

Lerner's thesis seems a little too obvious, and something essential seems to be missing from the analysis. What is more, the thesis cannot so simply be applied to other places. Lerner detected "a classic posture of the political agitator" among the members of his population which was rich in "potential leaders." Our population in Algeria, on the other hand, is far richer in followers skeptical about their own capacity to communicate and agitate.

The key to understanding this difference may lie in the fact that Lerner found Iranian extremists of either the right or left speaking of religious values far less than the moderates and politicians.[20] In Algeria, the situation would seem to be completely reversed, at least if the three-part classification of Western surveys (Left—not political—Right) were to apply in any fashion to the Casbah of 1993. It seems, rather, that the youth of the Casbah have settled on one problem and provided two responses, and this has given rise to two contradictory reference groups. The problem is the lack of control people have over their own lives. They experience material frustration along with the sense of psychological and moral dispossession, and these are manifested in an acute feeling of distress over not being able to find anyone to speak to or even anyone willing to speak.[21] The two solutions are as follows: first, consumer individualism in a world where societies are governed by law, where the abuse of power (*al-hajra*) does not exist and where everyone has equal opportunities; second, cultural holism in a world of Muslim moral order where the abuse of power has also disappeared because everyone is kept in his place by Islam's ritual practices (*al-iltizām*), social benefits, and various services—such as giving charity to the needy, visiting the sick in hospitals, and helping with funerals. All this helps to create a solidarity, a brotherhood not of blood but of religion, that allows the follower to recognize his "true brother" (*al-akh al-ḥaqīqī*)—the one "educated by the mosque . . . in Islamic principles (*mabādi'*)."

The first of these two worlds is the one constantly portrayed on Western television. In it, life's opportunities are available to everyone. Yet, it is also the world of unbelievers where people are shunted aside. Thus in this world one must have a high capacity for patience, for adapting, for being resourceful; the reverse side of all this (its corruption in Aristotelian terms) is cynicism and recourse to manipulating and

[20] This was his observation with respect to the Iran of 1954; although nothing warrants calling its empirical validity into question, it certainly sounds strange to those familiar with the Iran of 1979.

[21] "The failure of fathers" is a theme of Algerian psychiatry that can only be touched on here.

networking. In short, it is a world that operates on the basis of instrumental rationality entirely divorced from any reasoning about moral values.

The second world, constantly re-experienced inside the mosque—a true center where no one is marginal—is one where values are expressed, where putting these values into effect is an end in itself. But as this world does not provide (or "not yet," as the hardened militants would say) any prospect of meeting the demands for autonomy and material well-being, it requires a high degree of ideological commitment to the "cause" that must constantly be sustained by the personnel of the mosque. Such reinforcement is needed because "we are weak; ritual observance is the means to strengthen our faith," says a twenty-six-year-old employee of the private sector. The reverse side or "corruption" of this commitment is the fanatical emphasis on purification, according to which, outside the world of one's religious brothers there are only enemies to be destroyed. This fanaticism can easily be instrumentalized and lead to hostage taking or assassinating particular groups of people such as psychiatrists, intellectuals, or foreigners.

People deal with the existence of these two worlds in many ways, ranging from those who are only a "clandestine brother in Europe" to those who are willing to proclaim themselves an "official brother open to dialogue." Somewhere between these extremes falls the classic "Islamic petty smuggler." And of course there are those who are "versatile" and oscillate between marijuana and the mosque: "a little here, a little there, depending on my psychological state," says that employee of a state company who appreciates the French way of life.

At this point, we cannot press our analysis deeper. It requires such subtlety and comprehensive familiarity with the subject as to be beyond our capacity. Nevertheless, it ought to be emphasized that one should not think of the reception of "audio-visual information" as producing "effects" but rather as being appropriated into a complex, even a contradictory, world of meaning (or of absurdity) formed from the receiver's other experiences. What television "shows"—that is, the way it is reconstructed by the receiver—is a world in which those who will go to Hell, the unbelievers, live in a "paradise" made up of both legitimate fruits (social justice; the possibility of personal autonomy, however marginal; even a minimum standard of politeness, such as that of the Austrians who always say "Good Morning") and illegitimate fruits, spiced with the appeal of the forbidden (freedom to have sexual encounters, compared to which reading "body-building" magazines is only a pale substitute).[22] It is a world of attraction and repulsion, of moral legitimacy and illegitimacy; a world that excludes those who want to enter it from the outside and are constantly trying to force open the door, while at the same time it stimulates and incorporates their desires—the ones they admit as well as those they do not.

This constant hesitation often leads to the interpretation of political information in terms of the aggression of the rich against the poor—e.g., the United States against Iraq, the Europeans against the Muslim Bosnians, the Vatican admitting its Crusader spirit in its recognition of Israel, and, on the domestic front, the government against the people. The world "presented" on the screen is comprehensible only from the perspective of the "experienced" world, where those to whom paradise has been promised—first, the paradise of the national state and socialism, then the paradise of the true believers—live in Hell and ask themselves what they have done to deserve it. When one lives in (what is perceived as) misery while the unbelievers prosper, it actually becomes more difficult to embrace Ibn Badis' sentence: "The one who does not live according to God's law is not among the prosperous, even if he finds himself very well off in the here and now." To the contrary, if the prosperous cannot become pious, they must stop being prosperous and the pious poor should become prosperous. The theme of the "disinherited" often employed by the Lebanese Shiite Hizbollah[23] is not explicitly

[22] It is important to mention the fact that the image of the liberated working woman popularized by the media was not seen as positive by those interviewed—all male, but considered "young" by Meriem Vergès. It is as if the absence of girls from the public space—and therefore from the space in which the interviews took place—was so obvious in a working class district that it became natural: deprived of a public space (they can frequent the mosque, just as they can be part of the mob in demonstrations—but nothing indicates that the stipulation set down by Ibn Badis, having the prior permission from the male responsible for them, is forgotten), they are also deprived of speech. That the young men accepted to speak to a young, obviously "Westernized" woman is not a slight difference. It is as a forbidden fruit *and* symbol of what Malek Bennabi in his time called "the degrading atmosphere that made her masculine and that emasculated man" (Malek Bennabi, *Vocation de l'Islam* [Vocation of Islam] [Paris: Le Seuil, 1954]), that is, of the decadence of Western society, that many female figures are typified. This conjecture is all the more plausible given that the attitudes explored by Meriem Vergès are in no way the simple continuation of "traditional" attitudes transmitted intact within homogeneous milieus but, quite the contrary, the result of resentment in a mass society that is practically anomic but always deeply nationalist and in search of an institutional and moral renascence. See the discerning essay by Hocine Benkheira, "Machisme, nationalisme et religion" (Machismo, nationalism, and religion), *Peuples Méditerranéens* 52–53 (July–December 1990): 127–44. The return of the "Badisian" religious scholars (*'ulamā'*), who are more extreme than the Islamic Front, can be understood only in this context of reaction to "disorder" and "injustice."

[23] See Olivier Carré, "Quelques mots-clés de Mohammad Husayn Fadlallah" (Some of Muḥammad Ḥusayn Faḍl Allāh's Keywords), *Revue Française de Science Politique* 37 (August 1987).

present (it is never used), yet its meaning resonates in the sentiments expressed by the inhabitants of the "liberated districts" (another Lebanese analogy) as well as by the denizens of the Casbah.

## "SCHIZOPHRENIC" OR "JURY-RIGGER"? THE IDEALIZATION AND DIABOLIZATION OF MESSAGES[24]

Between 1989 and 1991, Mounia Bennani-Chraibi also surveyed young people between sixteen and thirty years old. Carrying out her survey in Morocco, Bennani-Chraibi excluded married people from her sample, but expanded it to include women, youth from diverse social strata, and from different regions: Tangiers, Tetouan, Nador, Oujda, Marrakech, Agadir, Fez, Rabat-Salé, and Casablanca. All the subjects of the survey had extensive exposure to the television media. At the end of 1988, 89 percent of the households in urban areas possessed a television set. Television might be watched at any hour and in the company of neighbors who do not have a set. The two daily newspapers, one representing the views of the Independence Party and the other those of the Socialist Union of Popular Forces, devote one page a week to television. The Moroccan radio-television network competes with Spanish TV in the North and with TV5 in Marrakech, Agadir, Fez, and Casablanca.[25] Since 1989, it has also had to compete with the coded, private channel 2M International and, since 1990, with the Arabic channel MBC. Further competition comes from videocassettes; indeed, 20 percent of Moroccan households possess a VCR, and 80 percent of the fifteen to eighteen age group and 73 percent of the twenty to twenty-nine age group watch video.

The Moroccan sample presents certain analogies with the Algerian sample, though the lives it portrays are more diversified, less confined, and relatively less frustrated:

[24] Mounia Bennani-Chraibi (*Les Représentations*, 11) borrowed this term from Mohamed Tozy who applied it to the large mass of students he studied at the University of Casablanca who consider themselves mid-way between the "Islamists" and the "atheists"; see Mohamed Tozy, *Champ et contre-champ politico-religieux au Maroc* (The Political-religious field and its converse in Morocco), doctoral diss., University of Aix-Marseille, 1984.

[25] State control is exercised nevertheless in a simple and radical fashion: the re-transmitter of TV5 does not work on Saturday nights, the day when the soft-porn program "Sexy folies" is shown. TV5 has a young and active Moroccan audience: two-thirds of the correspondence received by TV5 from "the new audience territories" (Spain, Portugal, Greece, Turkey, Poland, Hungary, Algeria, and Morocco) is from Morocco; 65 percent of the correspondents are under twenty-five, and 75 percent are men; see Bennani-Chraibi, *Les Représentations*, 64, 102–13. Unless otherwise indicated, all of the quotations are from Bennani-Chraibi's dissertation.

> The first job, marriage, leaving home all occur later and later. . . . The average age of young graduates in search of their first job is twenty-eight, and the vast majority of them are not married and continue to live with their parents. . . . This delay in entering adult life [contributes to] a "symbolical being shunted aside" and thus ratifies the exclusion of two-thirds of the population.[26]

There are, of course, differences between the two samples: Moroccans of the same "professional" level have less schooling than Algerians because of the lower level of literacy and lower educational standards, though this difference is more pronounced in towns, where the survey was conducted, than in rural areas; Moroccans have traveled less outside the country, but they speak much more often of the foreigners who come to Morocco for various reasons—tourists, above all. (In this respect, the Arabs of the Gulf are looked upon most unfavorably: they attack Moroccan honor through its "girls," do what is forbidden [*munkar*]—so that they are sometimes called "pigs" [*khanāzīr*]—and are unjust "nouveaux riches" without any cultural heritage.) The autonomy of women seems greater in Morocco, since it is not forbidden for them to watch soft-porn films, though only in a single-sex setting (men watching with men and women with women).[27] This difference is not due to a bias in the Algerian sample—namely, the absence of upper class women—for the Moroccan women surveyed do not come from the upper classes either.

While the Moroccans are, at least for the moment, less harried by events, they nevertheless express the same sort of eclectic construction of what is going on as their Algerian counterparts. They do so, however, in a more relaxed way. The messages they watch are in no way good predictors of what they think: "bi-polar sets—Westernized as opposed to Arabic-speaking, educated as opposed to illiterate, male as opposed to female—do not adequately encompass the diversity of practices; it is true that those who have a bi-cultural social and educational background and those who are turned towards what is elsewhere watch mostly Western productions." But their dominant characteristic remains their elasticity, which makes them consumers of *à la carte* images rather than those from the fixed price menu; and from the greediest to the poorest, they consume "everything they can lay their hands on." The common "hard core" in nearly all their perceptions is a spontaneously unfavor-

[26] See Bennani-Chraibi, *Les Représentations*, 27. The expression a "symbolical being shunted aside" comes from Pierre Bourdieu, "La jeunesse n'est qu'un mot" (Youth is only a word), in *Questions de sociologie* (Paris: Éditions de Minuit, 1984).

[27] See Hannah Davis, "Des femmes morocaines et 'La chaleur de Saint Tropez' " (On Moroccan women and "The Heat of Saint Tropez"), *Cahiers de l'Orient* 20, no. 4 (1990).

able judgment, even a prejudgment, with respect to the national radio-television network that they frequently accuse of being foreign or penetrated by foreigners and foreign programs. The same reproach is not made of the television programming that really is foreign, though these—like the national channel—are accused of being unsuitable or of broadcasting messages "contrary to Moroccan values" and "bad for society." These messages seem to conflict more with the image each person has of what should be watched in a group than with the image each has of himself: "We are in an Islamic country," says an unemployed man from Nador, who is nevertheless "very positively inclined towards what goes on elsewhere . . . we, the young, are aware: sitting next to our families, we see films in foreign languages; there are gestures . . . that seems shameful to us."

It is commonplace that the way people receive a message differs according to the group in which they find themselves, and the judgment they make about the message depends on the norms attributed to, or imposed by, the group. "Watching television, a highly social activity, becomes an occasion to negotiate norms and reference points." This makes it "a place where images of the self and of the other are fabricated," this "other" sometimes being the other shown on television and sometimes the other watching it with you. What is less commonplace, however, is the extent to which the receivers are conscious of the co-existence of looser and stricter norms, applicable in a differentiated way to the same product according to the context in which it is received. This awareness of the game, more than the game itself, allows us to speak of a process of individualization by which young people negotiate their identities, though they are not necessarily winners in this process.

The reception of the media is therefore subject to "a permanent movement of comparison with oneself and of negotiating one's own norms." Given the presence of the media, tourists, travel, and emigration, this movement is all very natural and leads to the West being perceived as "omnipresent." This in turn prompts each one to define himself in relation to the West through a process of differentiation that reinforces the identity of young Moroccans as members of a national, cultural, and religious community. Some consider this community to have been invaded and threatened by the foreign "other," while others (and often the very same ones) compare their own country unfavorably to the West. Indeed, Moroccan society is perceived as being unjust, unequal, rife with cronyism, undemocratic, subjugated, and lacking in freedom of speech, all of which makes these young people look upon what is happening in the West (in Spain, in the United States, in the USSR before its collapse, and in France) as the opposite of their own situation and therefore "good." It also makes these receivers more interested in what is happening in the West than in the Moroccan political or social scene, which they perceive as excluding the majority from participation and conferring sham powers on political and corporate groups thereby making puppets out of them, and leads to a feeling of alienation that facilitates their identification with a series of other objects.

This identification has something in common with empathy, but empathy of an unusual sort: the "other" remains different, an enemy insofar as he is seen to be unfavorably disposed (to put it in euphemistic terms) toward national and Muslim values—these standing as much for an affirmation of the collective authority of power as of omnipresent moral authenticity).[28] Empathy is made up of two mechanisms: "projection" or crediting the other with some of the subject's positive attributes and "introjection" or crediting the subject with some of the positive attributes of the other.[29] In the Moroccan case, projection credits the other with the attributes the subject would like to have but of which he feels more or less dispossessed.[30] Introjection, therefore, can function only negatively, as a deficit that generates conflicting feelings of attraction and repulsion—a phenomenon we see acted out in the constant desire to talk to foreigners and to ask them to justify themselves for being what they are (that is, for having what they have). The imperfect empathetic identification is thus accompanied by a negative identification (distancing) whereby the subject projects onto others some of his own attributes that he dislikes—his "dark side" or moral shortcomings, his shame. It is not surprising, therefore, that one can affirm one's Islamic (or Islamist) character and identify Islam with democracy (e.g., "democracy is not to permit the sale of alcohol to believers"), while at the same time glorifying the equality of opportunity in the United States and Spain, or the equal revenues in the USSR.

Behind these jury-rigged and syncretic comparisons, there is a pro-

[28] Collective autonomy through the "power" of Saddam Hussein or Muammar Qaddafi is therefore a projection of a desire for individual autonomy. The fact that the power of each one is authoritarian and therefore contrary to individual autonomy is not pertinent here. What is important is "the will for power lived by proxy." See Bennani-Chraibi, *Les Représentations*, 350, and Bruno Étienne, "Recherche héros positif, désespérément" (In desperate search of a positive hero), *Pouvoirs* 62 (1992).

[29] Lerner, *Passing*, 49.

[30] See, for example, the hymn to the "American regime" by a young, nonworking woman from Casablanca in Bennani-Chraibi, *Les Représentations*, 340. Bennani-Chraibi even speaks of "counter-productive" construction and of self-distancing; ibid., 115.

found and often millennial desire for a "different" life, a life of unity, justice, and equality. Alongside the other, the foreigner, presented by the Western media, there appears "another other": the representative of an ideal Islam to which Moroccan society must return in order to escape self-mockery. Thus, we find the two worlds already identified in the Algiers survey equally present in Morocco, but the indications of their presence are more subtle because those who express them are under less stress.[31]

From this, the selection of the number and intensity of messages from—and about—the West follows quite naturally. To be sure, it is quite possible to find among those interviewed by Mounia Bennani-Chraibi two relatively distinct groups: those who idealize the West and those who demonize it.[32] On the one hand, there is appreciation for "the individual who is reconciled with the group and the joys of the fulfilled individual" in this consumer paradise open to all, even those of modest means, where self-control is greater and social control more bearable, civic awareness and solidarity greater (a new theme corresponding to the critique of individualism and the increasing materialism of Moroccan society and thus in keeping with the frustration of the Algerian mass society). Even "true Islam is to be found in Europe." On the other hand, there is rejection of the value systems opposed to "ours," the films about sex, the immodesty, the illicit relationships, the life-style that is ignorant of "our principles and Muslim honor," and the racism. This last theme, racism, is extremely present in the perception of messages, whether produced by the Moroccan press or given particular attention when produced by the foreign media. Its importance shows that, in reality, the frontier between the two groups becomes blurred very quickly. The "idealizers" are realistic enough to notice and underline racism, imperialism (the use of this abstract term is diminishing for the moment), and many other defects; the "demonizers" are rational enough to be envious of the other (even while condemning them) and to try to make abstract choices—choices sometimes different from those they make in concrete circumstances—between what they can borrow directly and what must either be adapted or categorically refused.

The two images are combined in this way: "if the idealization of the West rests on the person thinking about it as both an individual and as a member of a group, its demonization comes about from the person

[31] The proliferation in Morocco of jokes (*nukat*), which used to flourish in Algiers, is evidence of this.

[32] See Bennani-Chraibi, *Les Représentations*, 109–24.

viewing it exclusively from his awareness of belonging to a community."[33] For this reason, if the person who appears to be schizophrenic manages to harmonize both aspects of his social personality, he transforms himself into a "mutant" who "sometimes seeks to distance himself from his group by looking for roots in the West and validating it and at other times to rebuild his relations with his community by distancing himself from what he builds up." This is not all that far removed from what Lerner singled out as the dilemma of nationalist-modernizers: "The articulation of a stable identity is particularly difficult for individuals in the contemporary Middle East, because today the great drama for the area as a whole resides in its quest for a suitable collective identity."[34] Though none of those interviewed by Mounia Bennani-Chraibi was even born when Lerner carried out his research, is there really a great difference between his "transitional" individuals and her "mutants?" Well, yes and no. This brings us to reflect upon the links between the sociological generalizations and historical conjectures coming forth from historical contexts that are two generations apart.

## RETURN TO LERNER

The modernization process begins with new public communication—the diffusion of new ideas and new information which stimulates people to want to behave in new ways. It stimulates the peasant to want to be a freeholding farmer, the farmer's son to want to learn reading so that he can work in the town, the farmer's wife to want to stop bearing children, the farmer's daughter to want to wear a dress and do her hair. In this way new public communication leads directly to new articulation of private interests.

Simultaneously—by analogy with the significant increase of real income that enables both saving and demand to rise simultaneously—new public communication activates new modes of socialization. If new interest-articulation parallels demand, then new socialization parallels saving—the factor that will make possible new investment and, ultimately, the supply of new satisfactions for the new demands. So, while new communication is promoting new articulation of

[33] This collective and communitarian dimension of the second position explains in a sociological way why the very people who demonize Le Pen's National Front regret the absence of a party like the Islamic Salvation Front in Morocco. From the perspective of "abstract" individualism (i.e., of the Cartesian or Kantian individual), members of both parties share the same ideological structure of exclusion; from the perspective of an individual situated in and constituted by a community, they have nothing in common—members of each party have to deny the possibility of coexisting with the others in order to exist (or, what amounts to the same thing, have to think they have the right and the duty to defend themselves against the aggression of the others).

[34] Lerner, *Passing*, 403.

interests among the existing generation, it is also preparing a new generation who will incorporate these interests and go beyond them. The farmer's daughter who wants to show her face is likely to raise a daughter who wants to speak her mind. The farmer's son who wants literacy and a town job is likely to raise a son who wants a diploma and a white collar. Socialization thus produces, ideally, the new man with new ideas in sufficient quality and quantity to stabilize innovation over time.[35]

This long passage sounds somewhat strange today. That is due, in part, to its ethnocentricity all too typical of the pre–Edward Said era when American society was thought to have bestowed upon the world its "model of the most developed modernity."[36] After all, the "modernization" of behavior (the broadening of reference groups through the development of empathy for one's own society and fellow citizens—and not only for "foreign" societies—so that "psychic mobility" might bring everyday problems together into a coherent, participatory life-style and extend the horizons of each individual's knowledge) as an idea to be promoted by rulers in response to the current petitions of the masses and to have positive effects for forming personality as well as society was a notion widespread among nationalist leaders from Nasser to Bourguiba and on to Boumedienne—all of whom are now either discredited or, on the contrary, mythically revered. Moreover, the surveys we have used demonstrate the presence of a perceived need for modernization among all the subjects, none of whom would disagree with Lerner on this point: "The evidence of our survey clearly shows that Middle Easterners have themselves identified poverty and ignorance as their twin curse."[37]

They would, to be sure, discuss more seriously the sentence that precedes it: "The symbols of race and ritual fade into irrelevance when they impede living desires for bread and enlightenment." What is the race in question, they would ask; and why should enlightenment make ritual "fade into irrelevance" when ritual seems to make more sense, even to bring about more understanding, than enlightenment. To all this, the more sophisticated would add, why should a woman have to show her face in order to express an opinion? The sociologist, even if he is not taken in by the polemical nature of these remarks, would say that Daniel Lerner lacked a sense of context. This is easy to say forty years later,

[35] Lerner, "Communication Theory," 348–9.

[36] Ibid., 343. We should not forget, however, that Lerner took great pains to clarify elsewhere: "There is no suggestion here that all Middle Easterners should learn to admire the same things as people in Western society," *Passing*, 405.

[37] Lerner, *Passing*, 405.

when the opposition between tribal or rural tradition and urban or industrial modernity is no longer warranted due to the urban explosion—as is the case in this time of "national disillusionment" with the opposition between modernizing states or nations and traditional backward communities.

Instead, the real question is: Does Lerner's understanding allow us to explain what we have observed in a world that seems to have little in common with the one he studied? Are his apparently obvious blunders (a balanced process of modernization was under way in Lebanon, most extremist leaders in Iran were indifferent to religion, the traditional male-chauvinist culture would be defenseless against the inroads of the mass media, particularly films)[38] due to an erroneous interpretation of the historical context (a reckless conjecture based on generally accurate observations that were then interpreted out of context) or do they reveal a fundamental error in the theory itself?

The structure of Lerner's theory can be summarized in four theses:

1 The essence of modernization lies in the passage from closed societies with limited horizons, stable means of production, hierarchical structures, and weak entrepreneurial spirit to open, individualistic societies with broad horizons, enlarged means of production, entrepreneurial spirit, and social mobility where everyone tries his hand.
2 The media play a crucial role (which raises them nearly to the status of an independent variable) in exposing the masses to new messages and putting them in contact with other worlds, thereby changing their view both of the world and of themselves.
3 Exposure to the media (whether exclusively controlled by the state or coming from outside sources) without any improvement in the satisfaction of personal aspirations produces a disequilibrium between the sense of need and the sense of success. This transforms the "revolution of rising expectations" into a "revolution of rising frustrations."[39] Such "unphased growth" leads to the over-production of transitional individuals equipped with new desires and new skills but lacking access to real opportunities and satisfactions because of the rigidity of the traditional structures.[40]
4 The combination of rising frustrations and the "catastrophe of communications" whereby short-sighted politicians have incited people to "expect everything from politics"—the "insatiable expectations of politics"[41]—without producing a system of social cooperation that

[38] Ibid., 401, 370, 399.
[39] Lerner, "Communication Theory," 330, 344–5.
[40] Lerner, *Passing*, 402–3.
[41] Lerner, "Communication Theory," 350.

> allows them to experience a positive relation between their effort and the reward derived from it leads to aggression or to regression—that is, to fear, greed, and hatred or to apathy and the narcotic of resignation. "Aggression among transitional peoples victimizes others; regression victimizes themselves."[42]

From these four main sociological theses that we have drawn together here, Lerner draws several historical lessons. One concerns the need for "a great rational prophecy" (in Weber's terms) and for a "delegated speaker" or "spokesman," an "innovator in the symbolic realm of the words by which men live."[43] Another concerns the temptation of intellectuals to ride the wave of Islamic self-glorification when xenophobia rises in the public's mind. Not able to call upon a "native" tradition that would protect them from the accusation of having become foreigners in their own countries, intellectuals cannot use the "right of asylum" bestowed on Western intellectuals; they cannot successfully claim that "the appropriate criteria for evaluating modernism are its consequences, not its antecedents." For them, "it is hard . . . to establish the crucial but subtle point that the Western genesis of their modern perspectives is, so to speak, a historical accident; that thought-ways once acquired develop an autonomous status."[44]

We cannot help but be struck by the accuracy of the observations and the coherence of the sociological constructions, if we only read these texts as they are presented: honest, albeit imperfect, efforts to understand and explain social phenomena. Though carried out in the midst of the Cold War and during a time when the imperialist American republic was expanding, Lerner's work nevertheless maintains a reasonable distance from superficial, political apologetics. A dated undertaking, to be sure, perhaps even one that has been passed by—but to what extent and why?

First, the text is dated due to Lerner's remarkable optimism, in spite of everything, about the transcultural validity of modernity. No one recalling the almost unanimous reactions cited in the first two parts of this chapter can be convinced by Lerner's assumption that "the end [i.e., modernization] justifies the means." Modernity retains its appeal as a desirable state (as much an ideal as that of producing a "new man," cited at the beginning of this section). Yet the real consequences of modernization to be observed in these countries—whether we ascribe them to

[42] Ibid., 349–50.

[43] Lerner, *Passing*, 406–7.

[44] Ibid., 408.

authoritarianism, corruption, cultural dependence, or the loss of moral and religious values—are disastrous. Automatically identified with the West by nearly everyone, despite Lerner's sagacious distinctions, modernity is apparently considered good in bits and pieces but not in its rather baroque totality.

Second, it follows that the binary opposition between closed societies and open societies noted in the first of those four sociological theses by which we summarized Lerner's teaching has become less credible: not only does such a bipolarity on the same axis appear dubious from the standpoint of Weberian sociology, but far from being a sociological type (i.e., an ideal-type) the modern becomes for the young North Africans an unattainable ideal that makes their frustrations all the more polarized.

Third, it therefore appears that the second and fourth of those theses are, in fact, teleological, despite the impression they give of solidity and equilibrium. Social evolution, governed by the process of communication, ought to advance in the predicted direction, unless it is poorly directed by demagogic elites who are incapable of controlling the process they have set in motion. Social engineering is not reprehensible in itself, but the strong top-down aspect it has here strangely brings to mind the accusations of governmental negligence, incompetence, and greed voiced by so many of those interviewed by our contemporary researchers.

Finally, rid of their teleological and managerial aspects, Lerner's theses have dated remarkably little as general sociological propositions. This is especially true of the third thesis: it suffices to replace Lerner's "traditional structures" with "bureaucratic structures of state control" or with Hisham Sharabi's "neo-patriarchical" structures to bring it into line with what young North Africans are saying today.[45] Even Islamist movements, notably absent from Lerner's analysis, except as a possible step backwards, can be encompassed within his argument if interpreted as a sort of "apology for frustration."[46] But are these Islamist movements not more than that; does this pathological view that is more or less linked in Lerner's fourth thesis to the notion of the "catastrophe of communications" give a complete picture or address even the essential points of the history of Islamism in these countries?

It is here that we can see Lerner's almost total indifference to depen-

[45] See Hisham Sharabi, *Neo-Patriarchy: A Theory of Distorted Changes in Arab Society* (New York: Oxford University Press, 1988).

[46] See Olivier Roy, *L'échec de l'Islam politique* (The Failure of political Islam) (Paris: Le Seuil, 1992), 92.

dency theories—nearly absent, to be sure, from the thinking of American behavioralists and, moreover, in their infancy during the 1950s. Yet theories about colonialization had already begun to flourish among specialists on Africa, even among those outside the Marxist tradition.[47]

Nationalism, occasionally divorced from its religious base,[48] possesses a dual aspect in Lerner: positive as a promoter of modernization and "nation-building" that initiate a process of social cooperation; and negative as a collective affirmation of one's own group against the other and as a source of demagogy and aggressive, divisive mobilization. But can these two aspects be separated in such a clear-cut way?[49] For this reason, the general politicization deplored by Lerner is not simply an unfortunate innovation caused by demagogic politicians poorly managing the communication revolution; it is also an almost inevitable effect of anti-colonial nationalism and subsequently of national disillusionment. The same holds when aspirations for individual autonomy (the positive aspect) are mixed with the affirmation of collective values more or less reinterpreted by the social imagination in the most diverse—and not necessarily sympathetic—manners. Thus the equality between men and women posited by the modern or post-modern individualist perspective is not the only possible outcome of the weakening of "tradition" due to changes in the social structure, education, and communications.[50] On the contrary, these changes can produce quite opposite aspirations, fruits of a rejection of "wild modernization." A "conservative revolution" can be the outcome, different from the one German ideologues presented under the same name but fulfilling the same social function of reconstituting a collective moral order that is presumed to permit the integration of the personality and the assumption of an antagonistic stance of distinctiveness with respect to the other.

A final, more general, remark must be made. No more than technology, by itself, creates the conditions for its own reproduction (as Zahlan shows in this volume) do "communications" mechanically produce

47 See Georges Balandier, "La situation coloniale: approche théorique" (The Colonial situation: A theoretical approach), *Cahiers internationaux de sociologie* 11 (1951): 44–79, translated in Immanuel Wallerstein, ed., *Social Change: The Colonial Situation* (New York: John Wiley, 1966), 34–61; note also, that Frantz Fanon's *Peaux noires, masques blancs* (Black skins, white masks) was published by Seuil in 1952.

48 And yet, the Moroccan "Berber Dahir" dated from 1930; see Jamil Abu Nasr, "The Salafiyya Movement in Morocco: The Religious Bases of the Moroccan Nationalist Movement," in Wallerstein, *Social Change*, 489–502.

49 Even the late Albert Hourani, whom Lerner often cites in his last chapter, was more subtle and uncertain on this question; see Albert Hourani, *Arab Nationalism in Syria and Lebanon* (London: Oxford University Press, 1946).

50 Lerner, *Passing*, 399.

"communication" in the sense of a better understanding between transmitters and receivers, between different groups of receivers, or between the groups presented on the television screen and the groups watching it. The understanding of a message generally comes about through a multitude of preconceptions being called up by the one who receives it, preconceptions constituted from his full-scale life experiences and the types of social networks they are rooted in. There is no possibility for these preconceptions to be universally shared in a social world made up of divisions, structural inequalities, and antagonisms. Communications therefore have every chance of producing misunderstanding, ambiguity—and thus miscommunication—and, in the eyes of pessimists, of reifying ideas and transforming them into "obsolete ideas." The media are probably neither the globally positive instrument imagined by Daniel Lerner, nor the demons reviled by intellectuals and clerics when they cannot make them serve their own ends. The disappearance or the weakening of authentic communities of thought is quite regrettable, as is "the extension of the reign of opinion (which is, at the same time, the extension of miscommunication), the invitation to perceive the ideas of others as idea-things, the extension of solipsism, and thus the reign of might makes right."[51] To try to understand presupposes seeking to know what is happening in the receiver's mind and in his concrete life so as to make sense of his opinions rather than deducing them from the messages he is presumed to have received as though they were absorbed without interpretation or alteration. In this respect, the problems the sociologist encounters in North Africa are not so different from those he may (mistakenly) believe he has solved in the world of those he lives with, whether in Paris or in Washington.

[51] See Raymond Boudon, "Petite sociologie de l'incommunication" (Concise sociology of miscommunication), *Hermes* (Paris: C.N.R.S) 4 (1989): 65–6.

# 10

# Islam, the State, and Democracy: The Contradictions

I. WILLIAM ZARTMAN

## ON RELIGIOUS AND POLITICAL PLURALISM

Between the stone mountains of a monolithic religious order and a monolithic political order lies the open playing field of religious and political pluralism, where democracy is practiced.[1] Clearly the monolithic state is incompatible with the basic tenets of democracy: pluralistic competition, free debate, and regular electoral accountability. But what about religion? Over and above the specific beliefs of a particular religion, is there any inherent compatibility or incompatibility between religion and democracy? And if the answer is not an absolute yes or no, where is the line between that compatibility and incompatibility?

It should be evident from the outset that there is no essential incompatibility between religion per se (including Islam) and democracy. Indeed, there should be no incompatibility between religion—involving the relationship between the individual and the Creator and the moral conduct that derives from it—and politics—involving participation in a temporal order for the governance and improvement of the human condition. In fact, it is entirely reasonable to maintain that the two spheres of activity have a necessary relation to each other since the person-to-God relationship has implications for the person-to-person relationship that should motivate the individual's participation in the political order, although not, of course, determine the nature of that order itself, out of respect for other individuals' person-to-God relationship. In other words, the logic of the two spheres' coexistence indicates that as long as religion remains a personal guide for oneself, but not a collective

[1] For an excellent discussion of pluralism and Islam, see Yvonne Haddad, *Islam and the Challenge of Pluralism* (Washington, D.C.: Georgetown University CCAS, occasional paper, n.d.).

imposition on others, it is acceptable within the political domain, in the same way that politics is acceptable within the religious domain to the extent that it provides an order for the protection of individual rights but does not impose collective beliefs on the relation (or nonrelation) between God and His creation.

Both religion and politics establish rules for the correct practice of their domains so as to defend their integrity and fend off false prophets, and they tend to agree within each of their domains as to the definition of the activities that the domain covers. The two domains coexist as non-overlapping magisteria.[2] A problem arises when one domain includes in its definition of itself the activities of the other, namely, the God-and-Caesar problem. In the days when it was so formulated, it referred to a self-definition of politics that included religion by making Caesar God. The other face of the problem occurs when religion seeks to subsume and define politics within its doctrine, excluding all others who do not subscribe to the same belief and thereby making God its Caesar.

The first face of the God-and-Caesar problem has often been found in the Muslim world in the postwar era, at least since the 1950s. In the view prevalent over the entire Third World, the state, the highest prize of the nationalist movement, was seen as the locus of political initiative and control and the necessary motor of economic growth and accumulation. In a maximalist extension of Weber's definition of the state as "a human community that [successfully] claims the monopoly of the legitimate use of physical force within a given territory,"[3] state officials claimed the legitimate monopoly of all power, not just force, including the control over people's beliefs as well as over the means of production and distribution. Kwame Nkrumah's neo-scriptural aphorism, "Seek ye first the political kingdom and all other things shall be added unto it," was applied more broadly than to his Ghana alone. This was done as an extension of the nationalist movement, which supposedly represented the nation and rose to throw out the foreign ruler, legitimately claiming all power, wisdom, glory, honor, and might in its name.

The social corollary was seen not only in the state incarnation of nationalism and national ideology, but also in its control over the exercise of religion. In Muslim countries, religion was harnessed as part of the

[2] Many have gotten lost in this subject, which mercifully is beyond the present purview; see, for example, Max Weber, "Religious Rejections of the World and Their Directions: The Political Sphere," in *From Max Weber: Essays in Sociology*, trans. and ed. H. H. Gerth and C. Wright Mills, with an Introduction (Oxford: Oxford University Press, 1958), 333–40. On the two domains coexisting, see Stephen Jay Gould, *Rocks of Ages* (New York: Ballantine, 1999).

[3] See "Politics as a Vocation," in *From Max Weber*, 78.

nationalist message, since it distinguished the Self from the Other across the traditional-modern divide and provided a vehicle for anti-colonial mobilization. After independence in these countries, even in Sunni Muslim countries, religious life was organized under a ministry of Waqfs or Habus or religious affairs, spiritual leaders (imams) were trained and appointed by the ministry, and religious jurists (*ʿulamāʾ*) operated within state organizations, issuing sympathetic decrees (*fatāwā*) in support of state policies.[4] It was against state monopolization of both religious and political expression that independent religious preachers and groups arose in the 1970s and sometimes earlier, contesting state religion and providing the only outlet for political expression beyond state control. Ironically, these groups were often assisted and encouraged by the state in order to counter left-wing opposition groups making inroads among the youth and unemployed. Yet such efforts to solve the God-and-Caesar problem in favor of the state only fueled the problem in reverse.

Thus, the other face of the God-and-Caesar problem appears when religion asserts its dominance over politics. The assertion has long been part of many religions and particularly of Islam, but it was in part the monolithic state's efforts to control religion that incited religious opposition movements to assert religious control over politics in response. In so doing, the claimants put themselves at odds not only with the opposing claims of states, but also with other people in politics who do not see their domain as a subservient part of religion, as well as with co-religionists who do not define the scope of their religion in the same way. This conflict between the two overlapping visions of the competing monoliths is obvious, but the question here is whether the introduction of a particular form of politics—democracy—changes the relationship.

Democracy is a political system in which sovereignty is held by the people, rulers are held periodically accountable to the ruled, minority rights (including the right to become the majority) are protected, and political competition among individuals and ideas is open and unfettered. All these elements are important; it is disingenuous to stop at the first element alone, since it is open to so many ways of implementation that the principle can easily be undone in the detail. The first element, locating (temporal) sovereignty, puts it squarely in conflict with some religious notions of politics; the second, locating accountability, contrasts

[4] See Mohammed Tozy, "Islam and the State," in I. William Zartman and William Mark Habeeb, eds., *Polity and Society in Contemporary North Africa* (Boulder: Westview, 1993).

accountability to the many with its false alternative before the few; the third, protecting minorities, has a checkered history; and the fourth, regarding open competition, raises more conflict but also contains a classic contradiction for democrats.

To most religions, sovereignty belongs to God the creator, who then leaves human beings to act as they are wont, their accomplishment of God's will or not being up to them (and answerable before God at the end). Temporal sovereignty (the adjective being implicit in temporal discourse) lies in human hands, since God's kingdom is not of this world. To those, including fundamentalist Muslims, for whom God's kingdom is of this world, popular assumption of sovereignty is usurpation of God's throne. "Wherever this order [democracy] exists, we do not consider Islam to exist, and wherever Islam exists, there is no room for this order," decreed Abū al-Aʿlā al-Mawdūdī.[5] To say, as he also does, that Islam is real democracy is playing with words.

Absolute as this sounds, and absolute as it would be if a Mawdūdī came to power, it need not be so. If God is actively and temporally sovereign, there is no problem because His will shall be done without our praying so. But if God allows free will, then His followers would be serving Him best by putting forward policies that will answer national questions and win people's votes, thus putting His will to work. Telling people to give up their own free will and to trust the clerics (who have never in history proven themselves to be any more trustworthy without mechanisms of accountability—i.e., democracy—than any other people) is poor religious thinking. Accountability can mean only accountability before the consumers, since any other referent group is not itself accountable; accountability before God (other than at the end) is only self-serving trickery, since it really means accountability before a self-selected but unaccountable group of people. Asking elected officials to stand reelection and risk replacement is the only way to keep a humanly fallible conscience on track. A refusal of democracy in the name of God's sovereignty shows very little trust in the community of believers and little faith in the ability of God to inspire convincing discourse among those who speak for Him. But such logical arguments only point out possibilities; they do not take care of the Mawdūdīs and other fellow believers.

[5] See Abū al-Aʿlā al-Mawdūdī, *al-Islām wa al-Madaniyya al-Ḥadītha* (Islam and modern civilization) (Cairo: Dār al-Anṣār, 1978), 42; as cited in Shukri B. Abed, "Islam and Democracy," in David Garnham and Mark Tessler, eds., *Democracy, War, and Peace in the Middle East* (Bloomington: Indiana University Press, 1995), 123. The quotation is clearer when "Islam" is also understood as "submission to God."

## THE WEEDS AND THE WHEAT

One of the Achilles' heels of democracy is its vulnerability to challengers[6] who would use the opportunity offered by its own rules to annul it. This was a major philosophical challenge posed to democracy during the Cold War era, when democracies had to wrestle with the problem of permitting communist participation when the communist parties clearly indicated their intention of eliminating or narrowly restricting democracy once they came to power. It was resolved by allowing communist participation in situations that precluded them coming to power and by forbidding them in situations where they posed a real threat. This practical solution is hard to justify in logical or philosophical terms with respect to Islam as much as communism. As in the Islamic case, the real challenge came in the gray line between the two, since the policy to be adopted toward the challenge depended on one's prior estimate of the outcome of the contest.

Thus, the rules of democracy prevent the political domain from contesting the religious invasion, forcing democrats to admit the legitimacy of the contest to their rules in the name of those same rules. The dilemma is real because of the basic democratic belief that the weeds and the wheat should be allowed to bloom together (to use a New Testament image) so that their true nature will come out in the harvest.[7] It is an article of democratic faith that the full, free, and open contest of ideas will produce victory for the best of them (at least in the long run) and therefore that the contest is necessary to provide the validation of quality, as well as responsiveness to change and assurance of accountability. The campaign, based on intellectual confrontation, is as important to democracy as the vote itself. But equally important is the assurance of continued confrontations and votes, since democracy is not a short-term guarantee but works only to produce substantive results in the long term and is as much a mechanism of accountability, after incumbency, as it is of selection, before incumbency.

Despite some roots in the ancient world, this article of faith is essen-

[6] The other is that democracy is only a process and does not guarantee substantive results in the short run. Thus, (enlightened) dictatorship may well be the best—if not the best form of—government at any given moment. The problem is that it contains no guarantee of being the best government in the long run, which is democracy's claim.

[7] However, both Alfarabi and Ibn Bajjah also speak of weeds, albeit in opposite senses—Alfarabi as deviant and false material to be uprooted or cured and Ibn Bajjah as deviant but true opinions, also to be uprooted; see Alfarabi, *Political Regime*, and Ibn Bajjah, *Governance of the Solitary*, in Ralph Lerner and Muhsin Mahdi, eds., *Medieval Political Philosophy: A Sourcebook* (Ithaca: Cornell University Press, 1972), 55, 127.

tially modern, because it provides for continual verification and revision. It clashes with another article of faith held by communists, political religionists, and other traditionalists that the best path is already known by some previous and immutable revelation and that good governance is provided by particular substantive, not procedural, formulas. Both are articles of faith, with the difference that one declares that it *ensures* the best policies through external validation whereas the other contends that it *is* the best policy based on internal validation. Once again, it is important to note that the former includes the latter, that is, that democracy has room for dogma to enter the contest and try its hand at both vying for support and plying its policies, under the sole condition that it leave its dogmatic nature at the door and open itself up to accountability and repeated validation.

## OVERLAPPING THE CIRCLES

The above argument begins to point to a condition under which the two approaches can operate together, although it then gives rise to additional objections. Each activity has a logical right to operate within its own domain and to contend for the definition that will govern the domain's activities. Hence politicians control the political domain of public policy and religious actors the religious domain of spiritual belief and democratic competition needs therefore to be conducted under political, not religious, rules and authority. This arrangement is best exemplified by the participation of Islamic parties or candidates in electoral politics in Jordan and Morocco, where democracy is exercised under overarching monarchy, or perhaps in Algeria and Turkey, where it is conducted under an overarching military. But the answer is obviously not universal and satisfying—not really, logically, nor practically.

A first objection, concerning those systems that are no longer monarchies, is the easiest to handle. The modern functional equivalent of the monarch is the constitution, which contains the fundamental rules of order defining the state. Thus, the requirement to act in accordance with a democratic constitution is a valid guarantor of the democratic system and of the control of the political domain by political authorities. It does however require politicians to defend that domain and be guided by the constitution, which was not the case when President Chadli Ben-Jedid recognized religious parties in 1989 in Algeria despite the constitutional ban on religious parties. A looser, political equivalent to the legal obligations of a constitution is the national charter, as used with greater success in Jordan in 1991 than in Tunisia in 1988 to define the political system as noted above in chapter seven.[8]

Ideas of constitutionality are well enough known not to require further discussion, but it must be noted that constitutions (like monarchs) are mutable frameworks and hence subject to the same invasion by forces of constitutional change in a nondemocratic direction as the electoral process itself. This was one of the fears that underlay the annulment of elections in Algeria in 1992. Obviously—so basically as to be definitional—if a democratic system is changed to something else, even democratically, it is no longer democratic.

The second objection is the equivalent of the military custodian's question, *quis definit definitorem* (who defines the definer)? The whole nature of the present problem hangs on the inability of one side to determine the proper domain for the other. The political Islamist's goal is to change the constitution and to take the defining terms for the state into his own hands. If he does this to a democratic state, the state is obviously no longer democratic. The whole problem is that there is no agreement on the rules of the game, including on the legitimacy of those who would define the rules of the game, and that is what the battle is over. There is a certain irresoluble circularity to the debate.

Third, as a result, the more specific form of the problem is posed by the religious politician who plays by the rules of the democratic politicians only to the point of taking over the system, then uses his position to overthrow the system. Former National Security Adviser Anthony Lake warned against creating "a fundamental divide pitting Western liberal democratic traditions against . . . Islamic and other religious traditions," but also against "Islamic extremism" speaking an "age-old cant of hatred, fear and prejudice."[9] The litmus test is clear: those who speak cant, hatred, fear, and prejudice are extremists; so the natural response for those who want to pass the test is to avoid the incriminating speech or muffle the incriminating spokesmen until the democratic contest is won and then revert to the religious definition of the political domain.

But the problem of any democratic exercise, or indeed of any politics, is that the politician may not mean what he says. In reality, our tongues betray us: it is difficult, even for a clever authoritarian, to speak a consistently democratic language and then deny it all later on. Slips in the

[8] See Lisa Anderson, "Political Pacts, Liberalism, and Democracy: The Tunisian National Pact of 1988," *Government and Opposition* 26, no. 2 (1991): 244–60.

[9] *The Washington Post*, 19 May 1994.

message—as the Islamic Salvation Front (FIS) spokesmen in Algeria in the early 1990s can testify—give warning signs, and indeed the danger of a change of heart (or of language) is no greater than that posed by a democratic politician who, once in office, finds authoritarianism attractive.

A fourth objection comes from a different direction.[10] It asserts that the time frame is too short; since democracy guarantees good results only in the long run, it should allow its challengers their time at governing; when they have failed, they will be removed—democratically. Even a suspension of democracy ultimately produces accountability, which is democracy. This is probably the most frequently produced argument from the democratic side for encompassing all religionists in the political domain, and it has integrity. It declares that the fidelity democrats have to their own ideals should not be a function of the lack of fidelity their opponents have to democratic ideals. This is unexceptionable as far as it goes, but its implications remove any meaning specific to the notion of democracy. It ends up saying that all politics are democratic, since in the end the people will rise to call their rulers to account. The histories of Russia and Haiti are vibrant examples, but a testimony to the absurdity of the argument.

In addition to its lack of logic, this objection fails to take into account the cost. The diversely religious polities of Sudan, Iran, Saudi Arabia, and Libya have imposed a definition of politics without accountability on their people, but at great cost to democratic freedoms—and probably at other, even greater costs were it not for the oil cushion in the latter three countries. Since in Algeria the radical Islamic option was rejected in December 1991 by over three-quarters of the voting age population—those who did not vote for the FIS—it is inappropriate to maintain that the Islamist experiment should nonetheless be tried, under the pretext that it can always be reversed at a later date. In fact, it is most unlikely that it could have been reversed at an early date, since a majority in the National Assembly would have been able to challenge the government, retire the army, and change the constitution.

Finally, a related objection is that responsibility moderates, so that the initial conflict between politicians and religionists in defining the political domain will eventually be resolved in the practice of governing;

[10] See Addi Lahouari, "The Algerian Problem," in Charles E. Butterworth and I. William Zartman, eds., *Political Islam: The Annals of the American Academy of Political and Social Science* 522 (November 1992), and Dirk Vandewalle, Testimony to the Africa Subcommittee of the House Foreign Affairs Committee, March 22, 1994.

religionists will see that religion does not provide practical guidelines for resolving political and policy problems and so will turn away from their substantive prescriptions to the procedures of open competition in the search for new ideas and leaders. Again, the history of true believers in charge of the French, Russian, Chinese, and even Algerian revolutions shows both the soundness and the limitations of this judgment. Responsibility does indeed moderate, but only in the long run and, again, at great cost in the meanwhile. It has taken twenty years for the Iranian Revolution to show even a few signs of moderation.

In addition, there is an inherent internal dynamic in religious groups coming to political power that further lengthens the path to moderation. The Islamist movement is inspired by a deep-seated belief in the wrongness—indeed even the infidelity and apostasy—of the previous governments and in the divine command that legitimizes the movement's activity. It cannot fail; God has ordered its members' activity. It dare not fail; a religious movement is even less likely than other political incumbents simply to admit failure and withdraw from power or to call for open elections and a public accounting of programs. To the contrary, historical patterns indicate that militants are likely to sweep aside their moderate members in office and take over power, installing a repressive regime that keeps criticism from surfacing—as Alexander Kerensky in Russia, Mohammed Naguib in Egypt, Mehdi Bazargan in Iran, Suleiman al-Maghribi in Libya, and others can testify. Criticism is the work of the devil, because it is criticism of a divinely ordained regime. In this way, religionists only intensify their rule and even further postpone the moderating effects of responsibility.

Thus, to say that each group should be in charge of its own domain and religionists who do politics should be subject to the rules of the politicians—in this case, the democrats—begs so many questions that it returns the debate to its starting point. Between those who declare that politics should follow religious rules and those who declare it should follow political rules, who is to say who is the authority? And if the people are to make that pronouncement, who is to declare the rules under which that pronouncement is made, that is, whether it shall be done once and for all, or repeatedly? National self-determination, a related matter, is a once-and-for-all pronouncement, to be reversed only by resort to arms and civil war, the ultimate *ratio regis* or *ratio populis*. Is the determination of the political system and its rules any less ultimate as a political question?

## DEFINING DIALOGUE

The subject is of crucial importance today in the Algerian, Sudanese, Egyptian, Tunisian, Afghan, Tajik, Turkish, and other situations, where liberal secular (if not democratic) politicians seek to end various degrees of civil strife by arranging dialogue with moderate religious politicians while extremist terrorists (often no longer with any claim on religion) are demonstrating in the wings. The relations between the terrorists and moderates remain unclear, the moderates' control over the terrorists uncertain, and the extent to which an agreement with the moderates would end the terrorism unassured. For a large part of that spectrum, entry into the political system should pose no problem—to either party. For the rest, three questions need an answer: on what basis can dialogue be grounded? what is negotiable? and what is the outcome of the negotiation, other than a phased surrender of one side?

The basis of answers must be found in the concepts of negotiation, not in the logic of philosophical content. That means a recognition that though the two positions are mutually exclusive at the start, as indicated, some overlap must be established in the process of preliminary dialogue before the search for a common position can begin. Thereafter, any hope for negotiation must be found in the expectation of giving something to get something, trading toward agreement on a less than total position for the end of a painful or otherwise unacceptable status quo. In this encounter, the distribution of shares in the joint political outcome is not based on the compatibility of political or philosophical positions, but rather on the power of each side at the outset and during the course of negotiations, and on the notion of a just solution embodied in the formula for agreement.[11] A negotiated cohabitation of the two groups, therefore, like so much other conflict management, depends on a period of heightened conflict before the chances of total victory for either side can be proven illusory and the negotiated future can come to appear more attractive than the increasingly painful present.

Yet here, too, there is a contradiction. Conflict leads to polarization, yet negotiation depends on the existence of a reconciling center, in parties as in positions. Polarization can reinforce the negotiation option by providing a credible threat if the parties do not come to terms. But its inher-

[11] See Victor Kremenyuk, Gunnar Sjöstedt, and I. William Zartman, "Economic and Political Models of Negotiations," in Kremenyuk and Sjöstedt, eds., *International Economic Negotiations* (London: Edward Elgar, 2000); and I. William Zartman, Daniel Druckman, Lloyd Jensen, Dean G. Pruitt, and H. Peyton Young, "Negotiation as a Search for Justice," *International Negotiation* 1 (1996): 79–98.

ent dynamic is to spin out of control, destroying the vast plain of the center where politics is played. Thus, if the parties are not able to come to an early understanding over the rules of the game governing their politics, they are in for a long struggle, even when they are headed for a negotiated outcome.

The negotiated outcome is based on two trade-offs, one diachronic and the other synchronic. One, as noted, is the trade-off of a painful present for a more advantageous future;[12] it is necessarily positive sum, or negotiations would not take place. The elements of the trade-off are a perception by both sides that each is making the present painful for the other (although not necessarily equally so), that the full realization of each side's aims is therefore not attainable (under present or foreseeable conditions, at bearable price, etc.), and that while the "whole loaf" is unattainable, "half a loaf" is available from each side for the other (in exchange for its own half a loaf and an end to the pain).

The other trade-off is that of the future, between the half loafs. The future trade-off is more difficult. The half loafs conceivable for the two sides concern—in order of decreasing immediacy and increasing difficulty—shares in future power allocations, participation in future elections, and a role in shaping the future political system. The first item concerns ministries and national executive council seats—assuring participation in the executive, but not the legislative, the judiciary, or the military. While executive council seats imply a share in general leadership responsibilities, ministries carry specific responsibilities running a gamut of implications for the nature of the system from religion to education and culture to interior.

The second item returns to the nub of the problem, for it poses a number of serious preconditions. What should be the criteria for participation in future elections? Can openly religious parties, which claim to monopolize universal religious principles, participate? Can the frequent prohibition against religious, regional, or ethnic parties stand? Is single-member, proportional list, or one of the many variants, the appropriate electoral system? What is the appropriate districting? These many technical questions, and others, are all crucial ingredients in determining a single final outcome of electoral victory or defeat. Although there is a large literature on all these matters, there is no ideal system in general, nor even an ideal system for any particular circumstances, so that the

12 See I. William Zartman and Maureen Berman, *The Practical Negotiator* (New Haven: Yale University Press, 1981).

sides in the negotiations cannot be certain that their favorite system will indeed favor them.[13]

The third item is the end itself. Studies indicate that negotiations to end protracted internal conflicts cannot usually simply resolve specific grievances and fold the rebellion back into the existing political system; they have to create a new political system in which there is room for the rebellious group and assurance of its participation in politics.[14] Political religious movements in the Muslim world today represent an important part of the population who see themselves excluded from or unrepresented in the current political system. Negotiations offer a chance to broaden the base of the state, restore its legitimacy, and at the same time open a contest for leadership of the new system.

Colombia since the 1980s is a particularly striking example of negotiations where the political system was redefined to bring in rebel-represented segments of society excluded in the political pact of the previous three decades, yet where the same leadership as before retained control of the enlarged system, in part through garnering credit for having opened it.[15] At the same time, the government maintained tough military pressure against that part of the rebellion that refused to join the newly enlarged political system its own military pressure had gained. The fact that the rebellion was not religious is only incidental in this case; the lessons of the internal negotiations are important for religious challenges to the state as well. On the other hand, the fact that not all the rebel groups were brought into the political system through this device and that much of the rebellion continues only underscores the difficulty of defining a mutually acceptable half loaf in secular, let alone religious, rebellions.

How these three items in the future trade-off are established depends in part on the ability of the two sides to formulate an agreement, that is, on the way in which each side reads the technical advantages and con-

[13] Concerning such uncertainties and debates with respect to the recent negotiations on the electoral system in Namibia, see I. William Zartman, *Ripe for Resolution* (New York: Oxford University Press, 1989), chap. 5; for Algeria, see Jean Leca et al., "L'Algérie: politique et société," *Maghreb-Machrek* 133 (July 1991): 89–139; Mohammed Harbi and Jacques Fontaine, "Algérie: constitution et élections," *Maghreb-Machrek* 135 (January 1992): 145–66; Hubert Gourdon, "La constitution algérienne du 28 novembre 1996," *Maghreb-Machrek* 156 (April 1997): 36–48; and Daho Djerbal and Jacques Fontaine, "Algérie: les élections législatives du 5 juin 1997," *Maghreb-Machrek* 157 (July 1997): 149–80.

[14] See I. William Zartman, ed., *Elusive Peace: Negotiating an End to Civil Wars* (Washington, D.C.: Brookings Institution Press, 1995).

[15] See Todd Eisenstadt and Daniel Garcia, "Colombia: Negotiating an End to a Shifting Insurgency," in I. William Zartman, ed., *Elusive Peace.*

structs a formula that is of benefit both to all and to itself. But it is also determined by the ability of each side to hold out and pursue conflict—that is, on its power to resist the other side and make life unpleasant for it—and on the strength of its commitment to particular outcomes as part of its sense of a just outcome for it. The conflict goes on as negotiations do, to make the other aware of each party's power and ability to achieve alternative outcomes (security point). The religious nature of one of the sides may not make its behavior in conflict any more humane, but it does enable it to hold out, even beyond the degree of its power, in expectation of an outcome that it can find just.

In sum, negotiations can lead to a whole spectrum of outcomes, from the integration of the Islamists into politics under democratic rules to the collapse of democracy into an Islamist system, with the mid-range being a new political system that changes some of the rules in order to let the Islamists in. Standard trade-offs include amnesty in exchange for peaceful entry (the unsuccessful Algerian solution), power-sharing in exchange for support (for a while, the Turkish solution), and electoral access in exchange for neutral control of the state (the Jordanian solution), among others. The fact that there are so few solid, successful examples testifies to the difficulty in finding a negotiated solution. The power of the parties, including their fatigue in the conflict, determines the result.

## CONCLUSION

I have attempted here to wrestle intellectually with the problem of reconciling political religion and secular democracy and have found such reconciliation impossible. Each seeks a different sort of validation that excludes the other. To the political religionist, religion includes politics; those who do not acknowledge that fact or interpretation should be excluded from politics. "We will have free electoral competition among all those who subscribe to the Way," said Abassi al-Medani during the 1991 Algerian election campaign. To the secular democrat, politics excludes religion as a political principle (although not necessarily as an individual belief); yet, troublingly, the principles of democracy may be used by political religionists to win democratically and end democracy. It would have been agreeable to find an effective overlap in these two beliefs, but they are playing a game in which each side has a different suit that it trumps.

Instead, it must be recognized that the problem is one of conflict and the solution one of negotiation, so that each side must give up something of its position if it is to come to any agreement with the other. What and how much is to be given up will be determined by the power of the two sides in the conflict and their commitment to specific notions of justice. Power takes the determination of the outcome out of the realm of philosophy, but justice brings it back—back to the incompatibility that the two domains have posed all along. Since negotiation is an indeterminate process, there is no telling where the compromise will lie—other than to say that it will lie at different points for different countries, where the relations of power are locally determined. This, at least, is a comforting conclusion insofar as it recognizes the strength of different national traditions and histories. The Islamist movement, and politics in general, are not the same in Algeria as in Tunisia, Morocco as in Egypt, Jordan as in Iran, or anywhere else.

One final thing should be acknowledged as beyond debate, however, and that is that the conflict cannot be reconciled by redefining its elements. Specifically, democracy is democracy, a particular system of politics that comprises repeated competitive elections, the chance for the voter to choose, and the chance to repent. Democracy does not hang on geographic points; there is no Western, Eastern, Northern, or Southern democracy. At most, these qualificatives may be used to designate cultural variations on the basically defined system of government, just as one may speak of different monarchical practices within the commonly defined system of single, hereditary rule. Democracy should be no more culturally loaded in the Arab world than petroleum, neither of which is an Arabic word; nor algebra more culturally loaded than admiral in the West, both of which are Arabic words. Democracy is a universal form of activity that exists here and there around the globe, and it is under consideration because many Muslims aspire to it.[16]

[16] See Ali E. Dessouki, ed., *Democracy in the Arab World*, *Cairo Papers* (Cairo: American University of Cairo Press, 1981).

# Contributors

As'ad AbuKhalil is associate professor of political science at California State University, Stanislaus, and research fellow at the Center for Middle Eastern Studies at the University of California, Berkeley. He is the author of *Historical Dictionary of Lebanon*. His articles on Middle East politics and society have appeared in a number of publications in English, Arabic, German, and Spanish.

Said Bensaid Alaoui, professor in the Department of Philosophy at Mohamed V University in Rabat, Morocco, has also served as dean of the Faculty of Letters there since 1995. He is the author of *The Political Thought of Mawardi; Ideology and Modernity*; and *Jurisprudence and Modernization: Introduction to Moroccan Salafi Thought* (in Arabic) and co-author of *Le Maroc et l'Europe: Pensée et histoire*.

Mounia Bennani-Chraibi is the author of *Soumis et rebelles*, published by CNRS Editions in 1994. The author of several articles on Moroccan youth, the processes of socialization, and the role of the media, Bennani-Chraibi is professor of development studies in the Department of Political Science at the University of Lausanne, Switzerland.

Charles E. Butterworth is professor of government and politics at the University of Maryland. His publications include critical editions of most of the Middle Commentaries written by Averroes on Aristotle's logic; translations of books and treatises by Averroes, Alfarabi, and Alrazi, as well as Maimonides; and studies of different aspects of the political teaching of these and other thinkers in the ancient, medieval, and modern tradition of philosophy. In addition, he has written monograph analyses of the political thought of Frantz Fanon and Jean-Jacques Rousseau and is the editor and co-author, with I. William Zartman, of *Political Islam*. He is a member of several learned organizations, a former vice-president and board member of the American Research Center in Egypt, past-president of the American Council for the Study of Islamic Societies (ACSIS), and president of the Société Internationale pour l'Étude de l'Histoire de la Philosophie et la Science Arabe et Islamique.

Iliya Harik is professor emeritus of political science at Indiana University, where he taught from 1964 until 1998. He is the author of numerous works on Middle East politics and economic policy written in English and Arabic, including *Privatization and Liberalization in the Middle East*; and *al-Turāth al-ʿArabī wa al-Dīmūqirāṭiyya*; and *Subsidization Policies in Egypt: Neither Distribution nor Equity*. He has been a member of the advisory board of the *Middle East Journal*, a board member of the research council of the International Forum for Democratic Studies, and a member of the board of directors of the American Research Center in Egypt.

Ibrahim A. Karawan is the associate director of the Middle East Center and associate professor of political science at the University of Utah. From 1995 to 1997, he was the head of the Middle East Program at the International Institute for Strategic Studies (IISS) in London. Karawan's research focuses on the politics of Islamic resurgence, Arab military establishments, inter-Arab relations, nuclear weapons and Middle Eastern conflicts, and Egypt's foreign and defense policies. His recent publications include *The Islamist Impasse*, and "The Case for a Nuclear-Weapon-Free Zone in the Middle East" in *Nuclear Weapons-Free Zones*, ed. Ramesh Thakur.

Jean Leca, professor of political science and director of Ph.D. studies in political science at the Paris Institute of Political Studies, was director of the Institute of Political Science in independent Algeria from 1962–7. In 1975, he co-authored *L'Algérie politique* with Jean-Claude Vatin and has since written several articles on North Africa, Middle Eastern politics, and social theory. With Madeleine Grawitz, Leca edited *Le traité de sciences politiques* and is currently completing a book on political philosophy and political sociology. From 1994 to 1997, he was president of the International Political Science Association. He has traveled extensively in Algeria, Tunisia, Morocco, Jordan, Egypt, and Lebanon.

Şerif Mardin, now dean of the faulty at Sabanci University in Turkey, was Chair Professor of Islamic Studies at the School of International Service, American University, from 1988 until 1999. In addition to having been a faculty member in the Faculty of Political Science of Ankara University, Turkey, for several years, he has also been a fellow at St. Antony's College, Oxford University, and a visiting professor at Columbia University, Princeton University, and the University of California, Los Angeles. Among Mardin's publications are *The Genesis of Young Ottoman Thought: A Study in the Modernization of Turkish Political Ideas; Historical Determinants of Stratification: Social Class and Class Consciousness in Turkey*; and *Religion and Social Change in Modern Turkey: The Case of Bediüzzaman Said Nursi*; as well as *Din ve Ideoloji: Türkiye'de Halk Katindaki Dinsel Inançlarin Siyasal Eyleme Etkilendirmesine Iliski*; and *Cultural Transitions in the Middle East*, of which he is the editor and a coauthor.

Timothy J. Piro is the author of *The Political Economy of Market Reform in Jordan*. He was the recipient of a Fulbright Research Grant to the University of Jordan in 1989–90 and a Center for Arabic Studies Abroad fellowship to the American University in Cairo in 1988–9. He is the author of several articles and conference papers on Middle East politics and history and has traveled extensively throughout Jordan, Egypt, Israel, and Lebanon.

Meriem Vergès is completing a book on Algerian political culture, with special emphasis on urban youth. Vergès studied at the Paris Institute of Political Studies. She has contributed several articles and conference papers on Algerian politics in French and also in English (published by the Presses of Political Science in Paris and the Center of International Studies in Princeton), in 1994–5.

Antoine B. Zahlan is an international science policy consultant. Formerly he was a professor of physics at the American University of Beirut. Zahlan is a founding member and the first director of the Royal Scientific Society (Jordan), in addition to being a member of other Arab scientific institutions. He has published extensively in the fields of molecular spectroscopy, science policy, institution building, labor planning, brain drain, international relations in science and technology, and the history of technology change in the Arab world. His publications include *Science and Higher Education in Israel; Science and Science Policy in the Arab World; The Arab Construction Industry*; and *Acquiring Technological Capacity: A Study of Arab Consulting and Contracting Firms*. His most recent book is *Science and Technology in the Arab World: Progress without Change*, published in Arabic.

I. William Zartman is Jacob Blaustein Professor of International Organization and Conflict Resolution at the Nitze School of Advanced International Studies of the Johns Hopkins University. He is the author, as well as editor and coauthor, of a number of works on North Africa, the Middle East, and negotiation analysis, including *Elites in the Middle East; Beyond Coercion: The Durability of the Arab State*; and *Political*

*Islam*. Founding executive secretary of the Middle East Studies Association and its president in 1981–2, founding president of the American Institute of Maghrib Studies, and president of the Tangier American Legation Museum Society, he has also been Elie Halévy Professor at the Institute of Political Studies at the University of Paris, Olin Professor at the U.S. Naval Academy, Distinguished Fellow of the United States Institute of Peace, and visiting professor at the American University in Cairo. He has served as chair of the Near East committee of the Council for the International Exchange of Scholars (the Fulbright Council), and member of the Joint Committee on the Near and Middle East of the Social Science Research Council.

# Index

Other books in the series (*continued from page iii*)

Theodore Taranovski, editor, *Reform in Modern Russian History: Progress or Cycle?*

Deborah S. Davis, Richard Kraus, Barry Naughton, Elizabeth J. Perry, editors, *Urban Spaces in Contemporary China: The Potential for Autonomy and Community in Post-Mao China*

William M. Shea and Peter A. Huff, editors, *Knowledge and Belief in America: Enlightenment Traditions and Modern Religious Thought*

W. Elliott Brownlee, editor, *Funding the American State, 1941–1995: The Rise and Fall of the Era of Easy Finance*

W. Elliott Brownlee, *Federal Taxation in America: A Short History*

R. H. Taylor, editor, *The Politics of Elections in Southeast Asia*

Sumit Ganguly, *The Crisis in Kashmir: Portents of War, Hopes of Peace*

James W. Muller, editor, *Churchill as Peacemaker*

Donald R. Kelley and David Harris Sacks, editors, *The Historical Imagination in Early Modern Britain: History, Rhetoric, and Fiction, 1500–1800*

Richard Wightman Fox and Robert B. Westbrook, editors, *In Face of the Facts: Moral Inquiry in American Scholarship*

Morton Keller and R. Shep Melnick, editors, *Taking Stock: American Government in the Twentieth Century*

Richard Grassby, *Kinship and Capitalism: Marriage, Family, and Business in the English-Speaking World, 1580–1720*